Microsoft® Official Academic Course: Microsoft Office Excel 2003 Expert Skills

Microsoft Corporation

PUBLISHED BY
Microsoft Press
A Division of Microsoft Corporation
One Microsoft Way
Redmond, Washington 98052-6399

Library of Congress Cataloging-in-Publication Data
Microsoft Official Academic Course: Microsoft Office Excel 2003 Expert Skills / Microsoft Corporation.
     p. cm.
   Includes index.
   ISBN 0-7356-2093-8 (Microsoft Press)
   ISBN 0-07-225608-7 (McGraw-Hill)
   1. Microsoft Excel (Computer file) 2. Business--Computer programs. 3. Electronic spreadsheets. I. Microsoft Corporation.

HF5548.4.M523M5438   2004
005.54--dc22   2004049991

Printed and bound in the United States of America.

1 2 3 4 5 6 7 8 9   QWT   9 8 7 6 5 4

Distributed in Canada by H.B. Fenn and Company Ltd.

A CIP catalogue record for this book is available from the British Library.

Microsoft Press books are available through booksellers and distributors worldwide. For further information about international editions, contact your local Microsoft Corporation office or contact Microsoft Press International directly at fax (425) 936-7329. Visit our Web site at www.microsoft.com/learning/. Send comments to *mspinput@microsoft.com*.

Acquisitions Editor: Linda Engelman
Project Editors: Dick Brown, Valerie Woolley
Production Services: Custom Editorial Productions, Inc.

Body Part No. X10-43197

Excel

Contents

Course Overview

Welcome to the *Microsoft Official Academic Course* series for Microsoft Office System 2003 Edition. This series facilitates classroom learning, enabling you to develop competence and confidence in using Office applications. In completing courses taught with the *Microsoft Official Academic Course* series, you learn to use the software productively and discover how to make the software work for you. This series addresses core-level and expert-level skills in Microsoft Office Word 2003, Microsoft Office Excel 2003, Microsoft Office Access 2003, Microsoft Office PowerPoint 2003, Microsoft Office Outlook 2003, Microsoft FrontPage 2002/2003, and Microsoft Project 2002/2003.

The *Microsoft Official Academic Course* series provides:

- A time-tested, integrated approach to learning.
- Task-based, results-oriented learning strategies.
- Exercises based on realistic business scenarios.
- Complete preparation for Microsoft Office Specialist (MOS) certification.
- Attractive student guides with full-featured lessons.
- Lessons with accurate, logical, and sequential instructions.
- Comprehensive coverage of skills from the basic to the expert level.
- Review of core-level skills provided in expert-level guides.
- A CD-ROM with Microsoft's e-learning tool as well as practice files.

A Task-Based Approach Using Business Scenarios

The *Microsoft Official Academic Course* uses the time-tested approach of learning by doing. By studying with a task-based approach, you learn more than just the features of the software. You learn how to accomplish real-world tasks so that you can immediately increase your productivity using the software application.

The lessons are based on tasks that you might encounter in the everyday work world. This approach allows you to quickly see the relevance of the training beyond just the classroom. The business focus is woven throughout the series, from business examples within procedures, to scenarios chosen for practice files, to examples shown in the e-learning tool.

An Integrated Approach to Training

The *Microsoft Official Academic Course* series distinguishes itself from other series on the market with its consistent delivery and completely integrated approach to learning across print and online training media.

The textbook component of the *Microsoft Official Academic Course* series uses easily digested units of learning so that you can stop and restart lessons easily.

For those who prefer online training, this series includes an e-learning tool, the Microsoft e-Learning Library Version 2 (MELL 2). MELL 2 offers highly interactive online training in a simulated work environment, complete with graphics, sound, video, and animation. Icons in the margin of the textbook direct you to related topics within the e-learning tool so that you can choose to reinforce your learning more visually. MELL 2 also includes an assessment feature that students and teachers can use to gauge preliminary knowledge about the application.

Preparation for Microsoft Office Specialist (MOS) Certification

This series has been certified as approved courseware for the Microsoft Office Specialist certification program. Students who have completed this training are prepared to take the related MOS exam. By passing the exam for a particular Office application, students demonstrate proficiency in that application to their employers or prospective employers. Exams are offered at participating test centers. For more information, see *www.microsoft.com/traincert/mcp/officespecialist/requirements.asp.*

Designed for Optimal Learning

Lessons in the *Microsoft Official Academic Course* series are presented in a logical, easy-to-follow format, helping you find information quickly and learn as efficiently as possible. The colorful and highly visual series design makes it easy for you to see what to read and what to do when practicing new skills.

Lessons break training into easily assimilated sessions. Each lesson is self-contained, and lessons can be completed in sequences other than the one presented in the table of contents. Sample files for the lessons don't depend on completion of other lessons. Sample files within a lesson assume only that you are working sequentially through a complete lesson.

Each book within the *Microsoft Official Academic Course* series features:

- **Lesson objectives.** Objectives clearly state the instructional goals for the lesson so that you understand what skills you will master. Each lesson objective is covered in its own section, and each section or topic in the lesson is covered in a consistent way. Lesson objectives preview the lesson structure, helping you grasp key information and prepare for learning skills.

- **Key terms.** Terms with which you might not be familiar are listed at the beginning of the lesson. When these terms are used later in the lesson, they appear in boldface type and are defined. The Glossary contains all of the key terms and their definitions.

- **Informational text for each topic.** For each objective, the lesson provides easy-to-read, technique-focused information.

- **The Bottom Line.** Each main topic within the lesson has a summary of what makes the topic relevant to you.

- **Hands-on practice.** Numbered steps give detailed, step-by-step instructions to help you learn skills. The steps also show results and screen images to match what you should see on your computer screen. The accompanying CD contains the sample files needed for each lesson.

Excel

- **Full-color illustrations.** Illustrated screen images give visual feedback as you work through exercises. The images reinforce key concepts, provide visual clues about the steps, and give you something to check your progress against.

- **MOS icon.** Each section or sidebar that covers a MOS certification objective has a MOS icon in the margin at the beginning of the section. The complete list of MOS objectives and the location in the text where they are covered can be found in the MOS Objectives section of this book.

- **Reader aids.** Helpful hints and alternate ways to accomplish tasks are located throughout the lesson text. Reader aids provide additional related or background information that adds value to the lesson. These also include things to watch out for or things to avoid.

- **Check This Out.** These sidebars contain parenthetical topics or additional information that you might find interesting.

- **Button images in the margin.** When the text instructs you to click a particular button, an image of the button is shown in the margin.

- **Quick Reference.** Each main section contains a condensed version of the steps used in its procedures. This section is helpful if you want only a fast reminder of how to complete a certain task.

- **Quick Check.** These questions and answers provide a chance to review material covered in that section of the lesson.

- **Quick Quiz.** You can use the true/false, multiple choice, or short-answer Quick Quiz questions to test or reinforce your understanding of key topics within each lesson.

- **On Your Own exercises.** These exercises give you another opportunity to practice skills that you learned in the lesson. Completing these exercises helps you to verify whether you understand the lesson and to reinforce your learning.

- **One Step Further exercises.** These exercises give you an opportunity to build upon what you have learned by applying that knowledge in a different way. These might also require researching on the Internet.

- **Glossary.** Terms with which you might not be familiar are defined in the glossary. Terms in the glossary appear in boldface type within the lessons and are also defined within the lessons.

- **Index.** Student guides are completely indexed. All glossary terms and application features appear in the index.

- **MELL icons in the margin.** These icons direct you to related topics within the Microsoft e-Learning Library. For more information on MELL, please see the Microsoft e-Learning Library section later in this book.

Lesson Features

Excel

Lesson Objectives

Key Terms

Quick Reference

Quick Check

New for 2003

Quick Check

Q. What does placeholder text do in a template?

A. Placeholder text is text that you will either delete or replace with your own text. It usually indicates what information should replace it.

LESSON 1

Getting Started with Word

1

After completing this lesson, you will be able to:
✓ Start Word.
✓ Explore the Word window.
✓ Use menus.
✓ Use personalized menus.
✓ Enter text in a document.
✓ Insert text by using Click And Type.
✓ Save a document.
✓ Close a document and quit Word.
✓ Get help with Word.

KEY TERMS
- Ask A Question box
- button
- cascading menu
- character
- Close button
- dialog box
- document
- file
- folder
- Formatting toolbar
- icon
- insertion point
- Maximize/Restore Down button
- menu
- menu bar
- minimize
- Minimize button
- mouse pointer
- navigation buttons
- Office Assistant
- ruler
- ScreenTip
- scroll bars
- selection area
- Standard toolbar
- status bar
- taskbar
- task pane
- template
- title bar
- toggle
- toolbar
- window
- word wrap

Not too many years ago, correspondence was created with paper and pencils, pens, or typewriters. Gone are the days, however, of correction fluid, crossed-out words, and wads of crumpled papers scattered around your trash can. Today, most personal and professional correspondence is created using computers. And, in most cases, those computers are running a word-processing program to make the creation of documents easier and more accurate.

Microsoft Office Word 2003 is one such word-processing program. With the help of Microsoft Word, you can quickly and easily create memos, faxes, reports, letters, charts, and newsletters. You can also, among other

---

Lesson 3 Using Templates and Wizards 61

QUICK REFERENCE ▼
Create a template from a template

1. On the File menu, click New to display the New Document task pane.
2. Click On My Computer in the Templates section.
3. Click the desired category tab (or search for the desired template).
4. Double-click the template icon on which you want to base the new template.
5. Update the current template with changes that you want for the new template, and click the Save button.
6. In the File Name box, type the name of the new template.
7. Click the Save As Type down arrow, and click Document Template.
8. Click the Save button.

Using a Wizard

THE BOTTOM LINE

A wizard is a Word tool that automatically creates a document for you after you answer a series of questions. This can save a great deal of time in creating some commonly used document types.

You can automate the creation of a document by using one of Word's wizards. You can use wizards to create memos, letters, faxes, and many other business documents. The major difference between a wizard and a template is that a wizard walks you through text entry for many parts of a document, whereas a template simply displays placeholder text that you replace on your own. After you create a document by using a wizard, you will still need to replace some placeholder text. However, you'll notice less placeholder text than if you had created the same document by using a template.

You could also use a wizard to create a document that you would like to save as a template. For example, if you often create memos, you could use the memo wizard to enter personal information that never changes in the memos that you create. You could then save that memo as a template and simply fill in the information that varies each time you create a memo.

Create a document using a Wizard

In this exercise, you first create a document using the Memo Wizard, then modify and save the memo created by the wizard.

1. On the File menu, click New.
   The New Document task pane appears.

TROUBLESHOOTING
Clicking New Blank Document on the Standard too... same as choosing New on the File menu. It will not... Document task pane.

The Bottom Line

MELL Correlation

---

100 **Lesson 4** Formatting Text

Previewing a Document

THE BOTTOM LINE
As is the case in many situations, it is very important to check your work before sending it. In the case of a document, one of the easiest ways to do this is to look at the document in Print Preview. This allows you to take an overview of the document and to verify that it is going to print the way that you expected. You can then catch any obvious errors, thereby saving time and paper.

Previewing Documents for Printing

To see exactly how your document will look after it is printed, you can use Print Preview. The **Print Preview** window shows you exactly how the lines on the page will appear when they're printed and where page breaks will occur. If you don't like the layout, you can make adjustments before you print. Using Print Preview can help you identify desired formatting changes without wasting paper.

TIP
In Print Layout view, you can show or hide the white space between the pages. Position the pointer between the pages until the Show White Space pointer or Hide White Space pointer appears, and then click the page.

Preview a document before printing

We've made many edits to our brochure, changing the format and style as well as adding borders and shading. We are getting nearer to being ready to print the brochure. But first we must view it in Print Preview to be sure it looks the way we want it to before printing it.

1. On the Standard toolbar, click the Print Preview button.
   The Print Preview screen appears with the Contoso brochure displayed.

2. If the ruler isn't visible, click the View Ruler button.

TROUBLESHOOTING
The number of pages displayed in the Print Preview depends upon the last way it was used. You may see more than one page.

3. If necessary, on the Print Preview toolbar, click the Multiple Pages button, and click the second button in the top row to view two pages at a time.

MOS Icon

Hands-on Practice

Buttons

Excel

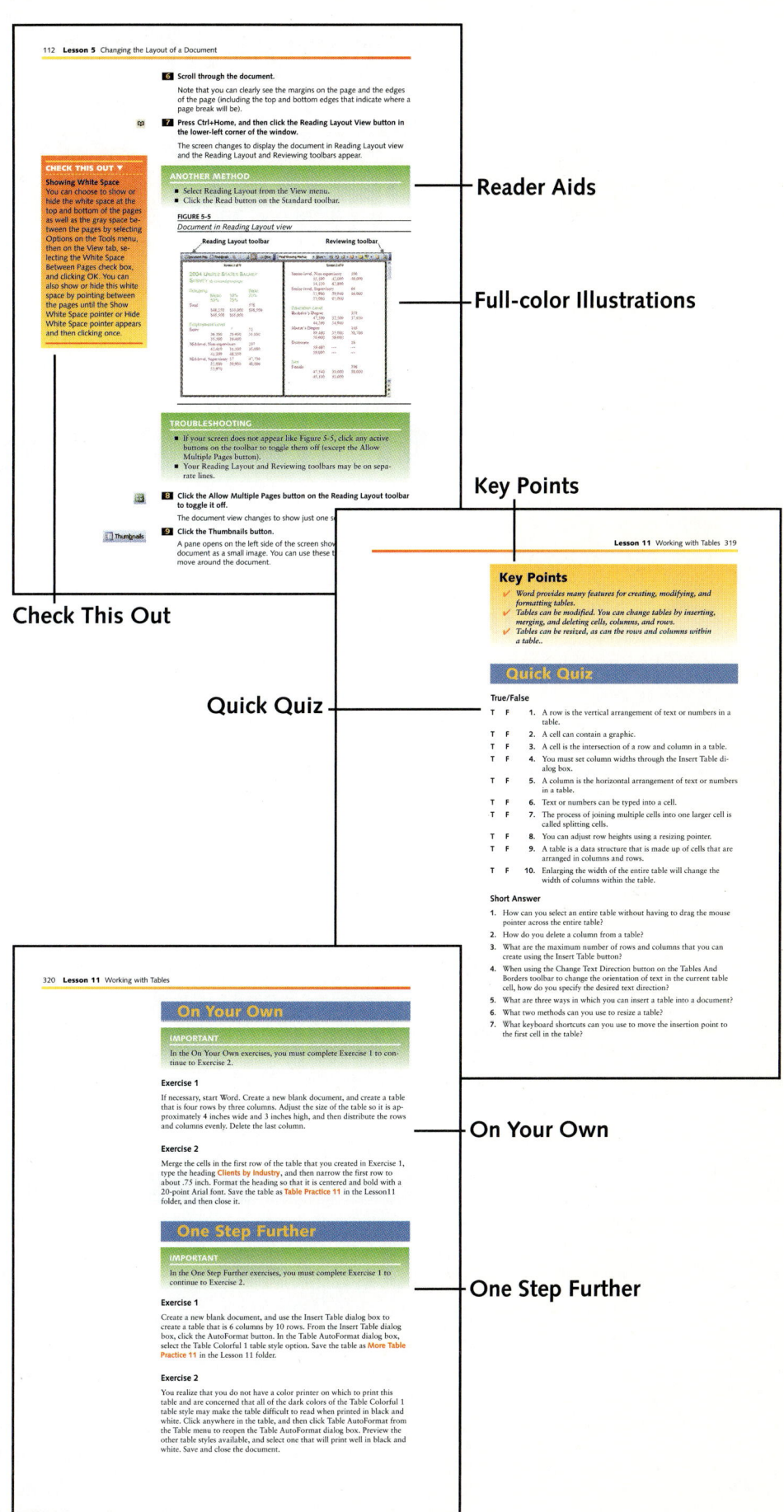

Reader Aids

Full-color Illustrations

Key Points

Check This Out

Quick Quiz

On Your Own

One Step Further

Conventions and Features Used in This Book

This book uses special fonts, symbols, and heading conventions to highlight important information or to call your attention to special steps. For more information about the features available in each lesson, refer to the "Course Overview" section.

Convention	Meaning
NEW FOR 2003	This icon in the margin indicates a new or greatly improved feature in this version of the software.
MICROSOFT OFFICE SPECIALIST	This icon indicates that the section where it appears covers a Microsoft Office Specialist (MOS) exam objective. For a complete list of the MOS objectives, see the "MOS Objectives" section.
THE BOTTOM LINE	These paragraphs provide a brief summary of the material to be covered in the section that follows.
◆ **Close the file.**	Words preceded by a yellow diamond in a black box give instructions for opening, saving, or closing files or programs. They also point out items you should check or actions you should carry out.
QUICK REFERENCE ▼	These provide an "at-a-glance" summary of the steps involved to complete a given task. These differ from procedures because they're generic, not scenario-driven, and they're brief.
QUICK CHECK	This is a quick question and answer that serves to reinforce critical points and provides a chance to review the material covered.
TIP	Reader aids appear in green boxes. *Another Method* provides alternative procedures related to particular tasks, *Tip* provides helpful hints related to particular tasks or topics, and *Troubleshooting* covers common mistakes or areas in which you may have trouble. *Important* highlights warnings or cautions that are critical to performing exercises.

Excel

Convention	Meaning
CHECK THIS OUT ▼	These notes in the margin area provide pointers to information elsewhere in the book (or another book) or describe interesting features of the program that are not directly discussed in the current topic or used in the exercise.
🖫	When a toolbar button is referenced in the lesson, the button's picture is shown in the margin.
Alt+Tab	A plus sign (+) between two key names means that you must press those keys at the same time. For example, "Press Alt+Tab" means that you hold down the Alt key while you press Tab.
Boldface type	Indicates a key term entry that is defined in the Glossary at the end of the book.
Type **Yes**.	Anything you are supposed to type appears in red bold characters.
✐▷	This icon alongside a paragraph indicates reated coverage within the Microsoft e-Learning Library, (MELL)the e-learning tool. Find more information on MELL later in this book.

Using the CD-ROMs

There are two CD-ROMs included with this student guide. One contains the practice files that you'll use as you perform the exercises in the book. You can use the other CD-ROM, described below, to install a 180-day trial edition of Microsoft Office Professional Edition 2003. By using the practice files, you won't waste time creating the samples used in the lessons, and you can concentrate on learning how to use Microsoft Office Excel 2003. With the files and the step-by-step instructions in the lessons, you'll learn by doing, which is an easy and effective way to acquire and remember new skills.

System Requirements

Your computer system must meet the following minimum requirements for you to install the practice files from the CD-ROM and to run Microsoft Excel 2003.

> **IMPORTANT**
>
> This course assumes that Excel 2003 has already been installed on the PC you are using. Microsoft Office Professional Edition 2003—180-Day Trial, which includes Excel, is on the second CD-ROM included with this book. Microsoft Product Support does not support these trial editions.
>
> For information on how to install the trial edition, see "Installing or Uninstalling Microsoft Office Professional Edition 2003—180-Day Trial" later in this part of the book.

- A personal computer running Microsoft Excel 2003 on a Pentium 233-megahertz (MHz) or higher processor.
- Microsoft Windows® 2000 with Service Pack 3 (SP3), Windows XP, or later.
- 128 MB of RAM or greater.
- At least 2 MB of available disk space (after installing Excel 2003 or Microsoft Office).
- A CD-ROM or DVD drive.
- A monitor with Super VGA (800 X 600) or higher resolution with 256 colors.
- A Microsoft mouse, a Microsoft IntelliMouse, or other compatible pointing device.

Excel

If You Need to Install or Uninstall the Practice Files

Your instructor might already have installed the practice files before you arrive in class. However, your instructor might ask you to install the practice files on your own at the start of class. Also, if you want to work through any of the exercises in this book on your own at home or at your place of business after class, you will need to first install the practice files.

Install the practice files

1 **Insert the CD-ROM in the CD-ROM drive of your computer.**

A menu screen appears.

IMPORTANT

If the menu screen does not appear, start Windows Explorer. In the left pane, locate the icon for your CD-ROM, and click this icon. In the right pane, double-click the file StartCD.

2 **Click Install Practice Files, and follow the instructions on the screen.**

The recommended options are preselected for you.

3 **After the files have been installed, click Exit.**

A folder called Excel Expert Practice has been created on your hard disk; the practice files have been placed in that folder.

4 **Remove the CD-ROM from the CD-ROM drive.**

Use the following steps when you want to delete the lesson practice files from your hard disk. Your instructor might ask you to perform these steps at the end of class. Also, you should perform these steps if you have worked through the exercises at home or at your place of business and want to work through the exercises again. Deleting the practice files and then reinstalling them ensures that all files and folders are in their original condition if you decide to work through the exercises again.

Unistall the practice files from the Windows XP or later operating system

1 **On the Windows taskbar, click the Start button and then click Control Panel.**

2 **If you are in Classic View, double-click the Add Or Remove Programs icon. If you are in Category View, single-click the Add Or Remove Programs link.**

3 **In the Add Or Remove Programs dialog box, scroll down and select Excel Expert Practice in the list. Click the Change/Remove button.**

4 **Click Yes when the confirmation dialog box appears.**

Uninstall the practice files from the Windows 2000 operating system

1 On the Windows taskbar, click the Start button, point to Settings, and then click Control Panel.

2 Double-click the Add/Remove icon.

3 Click Excel Expert Practice in the list, and click the Remove or the Change/Remove button.

4 Click Yes when the confirmation dialog box appears.

Using the Practice Files

Each lesson in this book explains when and how to use any practice files for that lesson. The lessons are built around scenarios that simulate a real work environment, so you can easily apply the skills you learn to your own work. The scenarios in the lessons use the context of the fictitious Contoso, Ltd, a public relations firm, and its client, Adventure Works, a resort located in the mountains of California.

By default, Excel 2003 places the Standard and Formatting toolbars on the same row below the menu bar to save space. To match the lessons and exercises in this book, the Standard and Formatting toolbars should be separated onto two rows before the start of this course. To separate the Standard and Formatting toolbars:

■ Position the mouse pointer over the move handle at the beginning of the Formatting toolbar until it turns into the move pointer (a four-headed arrow), and drag the toolbar down until it appears on its own row.

The following is a list of all files and folders used in the lessons.

File Name	Description
Lesson01-folder	Folder used in Lesson 1
AW Departmental Expenses.xls	File used in Lesson 1
BudgetAW.xls	File used in On Your Own
BudgetEast.xls	File used in Lesson 1
BudgetSum.xls	File used in Lesson 1
BudgetWest.xls	File used in Lesson 1
Employee History Bonus.xls	File used in Lesson 1 and in On Your Own
Pledges.xls	File used in On Your Own
Restaurant Conference.xls	File used in One Step Further
Sales2wk.xls	File used in Lesson 1
SalesSummer.xls	File used in Lesson 1 and in On Your Own
Summer Sales Comparing Performers.xls	File used in Lesson 1 and in On Your Own

Excel

File Name	Description
Lesson02-folder	Folder used in Lesson 2
AdventureWorks.bmp	Graphic used in Lesson 2
Bonus.txt	File used in Lesson 2
Current_Exchange_Rates.htm	File used in Lesson 2
Exchange Rates.xls	File used in Lesson 2
Guests.doc	File used in Lesson 2
Guests.mdb	File used in Lesson 2
Orders.dbf	File used in Lesson 2
Reservations.xls	File used in Lesson 2
Lesson03-folder	Folder used in Lesson 3
Employees.xls	File used in Lesson 3
Orders.xls	File used in On Your Own
Lesson04-folder	Folder used in Lesson 4
Human Resources.xls	File used in On Your Own
Personnel.xls	File used in Lesson 4
Restaurant Staff.xls	File used in Lesson 4
Sales Summer 2005.xls	File used in Lesson 4
Lesson05-folder	Folder used in Lesson 5
AW Marketing.xls	File used in Lesson 5 and in One Step Further
AW Reservation Stats	File used in On Your Own
Lesson06-folder	Folder used in Lesson 6
AW Guests Supplies.xls	File used in Lesson 6 and in One Step Further
AW Personnel.xls	File used in On Your Own
AW Reservation Stats.xls	File used in On Your Own
Quarterly Quota.xls	File used in Lesson 6
Sales Averages.xls	File used in On Your Own
Lesson07-folder	Folder used in Lesson 7
AW Budget Final.xls	File used in Lesson 7
AW Budget Tracking.xls	File used in Lesson 7
AW Budget.xls	File used in Lesson 7 and in On Your Own
AW Departmental Expenses.xls	File used in On Your Own
AW Marketing TC.xls	File used in On Your Own
Employees.xls	File used in Lesson 7
SalesSummer	File used in Lesson 7
Lesson08-folder	Folder used in Lesson 8
Financial.htm	File used in Lesson 8
Pivot.xls	File used in Lesson 8 and in On Your Own
PivotXML.xml	File used in Lesson 8
Publish.xls	File used in Lesson 8 and in One Step Further
Smart.xls	File used in Lesson 8
Structured.xls	File used in Lesson 8
WebData.xls	File used in Lesson 8

File Name	Description
Lesson09-folder	Folder used in Lesson 9
2005 Timesheet.xls	File used in Lesson 9
AW Logo.tif	Graphic used in Lesson 9
Purchase Order 185.xls	File used in On Your Own
Lesson10-folder	Folder used in Lesson 10
Figures.xls	File used in On Your Own and One Step Further
SG&A Budget.xls	File used in Lesson 10
Lesson11-folder-	Folder used in Lesson 11
AW Marketing.xls	File used in On Your Own
AW Personnel.xls	File used in Lesson 11
Quarterly Quota.xls	File used in Lesson 11
SG&A Budget.xls	File used in Lesson 11

Replying to Install Messages

When you work through some lessons, you might see a message indicating that the feature that you are trying to use is not installed. If you see this message, insert the Microsoft Office Excel 2003 CD or Microsoft Office CD 1 in your CD-ROM drive, and click Yes to install the feature.

Locating and Opening Files

After you (or your instructor) have installed the practice files, all the files you need for this course will be stored in a folder named Excel Expert Practice located on your hard disk.

Navigate to the Excel Expert Practice folder from within Excel and open a file

1 On the Standard toolbar, click the Open button.

2 In the Open dialog box, click the Look In down arrow, and click the icon for your hard disk.

3 Double-click the Excel Expert Practice folder.

4 Double-click the file that you want to open.

All the files for the lessons appear within the Excel Expert Practice folder.

Excel

If You Need Help with the Practice Files

If you have any problems regarding the use of this book's CD-ROM, you should first consult your instructor. If you are using the CD-ROM at home or at your place of business and need additional help with the practice files, contact McGraw-Hill for support:

E-mail: techsup@mcgraw-hill.com

Phone: (800) 331-5094

Post: McGraw-Hill Companies

          1333 Burr Ridge Parkway

          Burr Ridge, IL 60521

IMPORTANT

For help using Excel 2003, rather than this book, you can visit support.microsoft.com or call Microsoft Product Support at (425) 635-7070 on weekdays between 5 A.M. and 9 P.M. Pacific Standard Time or on Saturdays and Sundays between 6 A.M. and 3 P.M. Pacific Standard Time. Microsoft Product Support does not provide support for this course. Also please note that Microsoft Product Support does not support trial editions of Office.

Installing or Uninstalling Microsoft Office Professional Edition 2003—180-Day Trial

An installation CD-ROM for Microsoft Office Professional Edition 2003—180-Day Trial is included with this book. Before you install your trial version, please read this entire section for important information on setting up and uninstalling your trial software.

Excel

CAUTION

For the best performance, the default selection during Setup is to uninstall previous versions of Office. There is also an option not to remove previous versions of Office. With all trial software, Microsoft recommends that you have your original CDs available to reinstall if necessary. If you want to return to your previous version of Office, you need to uninstall the trial software. This should be done through the Add or Remove Programs icon in Microsoft Windows Control Panel.

Installation of Microsoft Office Professional Edition 2003—180-Day Trial software will remove your existing version of Microsoft Outlook. However, your contacts, calendar, and other personal information will not be deleted. At the end of the trial, if you choose to upgrade or to reinstall your previous version of Outlook, your personal settings and information will be retained.

Setup Instructions

1 Insert the trial software CD into the CD drive on your computer. The CD will be detected, and the Setup.exe file should automatically begin to run on your computer.

2 When prompted for the Office Product Key, enter the Product Key provided with the software, and then click Next.

3 Enter your name and organization user name, and then click Next.

4 Read the End-User License Agreement, select the I Accept The Terms In The License Agreement check box, and then click Next.

NOTE

Copies of the product License Agreements are also available for review at http://www.microsoft.com/office/eula.

5 Select the install option, verify the installation location or click Browse to change the installation location, and then click Next.

The default setting is Upgrade. You will have the opportunity to specify not to remove previous versions of Office from your computer later in the installation wizard.

6 Verify the program installation preferences, and then click Next.

Excel

CAUTION

For best performance, the default selection during setup is to uninstall (remove) previous versions of Office. There is also the option not to remove previous versions of Office. With all trial software, Microsoft recommends that you have your original CDs available to reinstall if necessary.

7 To finish Setup, select the check boxes you want so that you can receive the online updates and downloads or to delete the installation files, then click Finish.

Upgrading Microsoft Office Professional Edition 2003—180-Day Trial Software to the Full Product

You can convert the software into full use without removing or reinstalling software on your computer. When you complete your trial, you can purchase a product license from any Microsoft reseller and enter a valid Product Key when prompted during Setup.

Uninstalling the Trial Software and Returning to Your Previous Office Version

If you want to return to your previous version of Office, you need to uninstall the trial software. This should be done through the Add or Remove Programs icon in Control Panel.

1 Quit any programs that are running, such as Microsoft Excel or Outlook.

2 In control Panel, click Add or Remove Programs.

3 Click Microsoft Office Professional Edition 2003, and then click Remove.

NOTE

If you selected the option to remove a previous version of Office during installation of the trial software, you need to reinstall your previous version of Office. If you did not remove your previous version of Office, you can start each of your Office programs either through the Start menu or by opening files for each program, such as Excel, Microsoft Word, and Microsoft PowerPoint files. In some cases, you may have to recreate some of your shortcuts and default settings.

MOS Objectives
Expert Skills

Objective	Activity	Page
XL03E-1	**Organizing and Analyzing Data**	
XL03E-1-1	Use subtotals	82
XL03E-1-2	Define and apply advanced filters	65
XL03E-1-3	Group and outline data	83, 87
XL03E-1-4	Use data validation	94, 96
XL03E-1-5	Create and modify list ranges	52, 54
XL03E-1-6	Add, show, close, edit, merge, and summarize scenarios	132
XL03E-1-7	Perform data analysis using automated tools	114, 129, 132, 136
XL03E-1-8	Create PivotTable and PivotChart reports	114, 115, 126
XL03E-1-9	Use lookup and reference functions	15
XL03E-1-10	Use database functions	68
XL03E-1-11	Trace formula precedents, dependents, and errors	102, 104, 105
XL03E-1-12	Locate invalid data and formulas	101
XL03E-1-13	Watch and evaluate formulas	107
XL03E-1-14	Define, modify, and use named ranges	12
XL03E-1-15	Structure workbooks using XML	188
XL03E-2	**Formatting Data and Content**	
XL03E-2-1	Create and modify custom data formats	77
XL03E-2-2	Use conditional formatting	80
XL03E-2-3	Format and resize graphics	35, 200
XL03E-2-4	Format charts and diagrams	129
XL03E-3	**Collaborating**	
XL03E-3-1	Protect cells, worksheets, and workbooks	166, 167
XL03E-3-2	Apply workbook security settings	163
XL03E-3-3	Share workbooks	153
XL03E-3-4	Merge workbooks	155
XL03E-3-5	Track, accept, and reject changes to workbooks	146, 150

Excel

Taking a Microsoft Office Specialist Certification Test

The Microsoft Office Specialist (MOS) program is the only Microsoft-approved certification program designed to measure and validate your skills with the Microsoft Office suite of desktop productivity applications: Microsoft Word, Microsoft Excel, Microsoft PowerPoint, Microsoft Access, and Microsoft Outlook.

By becoming certified, you demonstrate to employers that you have achieved a predictable level of skill in the use of a particular Office application. Employers often require certification either as a condition of employment or as a condition of advancement within the company or other organization. The certification examinations are sponsored by Microsoft but administered through Nivo International.

The MOS program typically offers certification exams at the "core" and "expert" levels. For a core-level test, you demonstrate your ability to use an application knowledgeably and without assistance in a day-to-day work environment. For an expert-level test, you demonstrate that you have a thorough knowledge of the application and can effectively apply all or most of the features of the application to solve problems and complete tasks found in business.

Preparing to Take an Exam

Unless you're a very experienced user, you'll need to use a test preparation course to prepare to complete the test correctly and within the time allowed. The *Microsoft Official Academic Course* series is designed to prepare you for either core-level or expert-level knowledge of a particular Microsoft Office application. By the end of this course, you should have a strong knowledge of all exam topics, and with some additional review and practice on your own, you should feel confident in your ability to pass the appropriate exam.

After you decide which exam to take, review the list of objectives for the exam. This list can be found in the "MOS Objectives" section at the front of the appropriate *Microsoft Official Academic Course* student guide. You can also easily identify tasks that are included in the objective list by locating the MOS symbol in the margin of the lessons in this book.

For an expert-level test, you'll need to be able to demonstrate any of the skills from the core-level objective list, too. Expect some of these core-level tasks to appear on the expert-level test.

You can also familiarize yourself with a live MOS certification test by downloading and installing a practice MOS certification test from www.microsoft.com/traincert/mcp/officespecialist/requirements.asp.

Excel

To take the MOS test, first see www.microsoft.com/traincert/mcp/office-specialist/requirements.asp to locate your nearest testing center. Then call the testing center directly to schedule your test. The amount of advance notice you should provide will vary for different testing centers, and it typically depends on the number of computers available at the testing center, the number of other testers who have already been scheduled for the day on which you want to take the test, and the number of times per week that the testing center offers MOS testing. In general, you should call to schedule your test at least two weeks prior to the date on which you want to take the test.

When you arrive at the testing center, you might be asked for proof of identity. A driver's license or passport is an acceptable form of identification. If you do not have either of these items of documentation, call your testing center and ask what alternative forms of identification will be accepted. If you are retaking a test, bring your MOS identification number, which will have been given to you when you previously took the test. If you have not prepaid or if your organization has not already arranged to make payment for you, you will need to pay the test-taking fee when you arrive. The current test-taking fee is $75 (U.S.). Prices are subject to change and may vary depending on the testing center.

Test Format

All MOS certification tests are live, performance-based tests. There are no multiple-choice, true/false, or short-answer questions. Instructions are general: you are told the basic tasks to perform on the computer, but you aren't given any help in figuring out how to perform them. You are not permitted to use reference material other than the application's Help system.

As you complete the tasks stated in a particular test question, the testing software monitors your actions. An example question might be:

> Open the file named AW Guests and select the word Welcome in the first paragraph. Change the font to 12 point, and apply bold formatting. Select the words at your convenience in the second paragraph, move them to the end of the first paragraph using drag and drop, and then center the first paragraph.

The sample tests available from www.microsoft.com/traincert/mcp/office-specialist/requirements.asp give you a clear idea of the type of questions that you will be asked on the actual test.

When the test administrator seats you at a computer, you'll see an online form that you use to enter information about yourself (name, address, and other information required to process your exam results). While you complete the form, the software will generate the test from a master test bank and then prompt you to continue. The first test question will appear in a window. Read the question carefully, and then perform all the tasks stated in the test question. When you have finished completing all tasks for a question, click the Next Question button.

You have 45 to 60 minutes to complete all questions, depending on the test that you are taking. The testing software assesses your results as soon as you complete the test, and the test administrator can print the results of the test so that you will have a record of any tasks that you performed incorrectly. A passing grade is 75 percent or higher. If you pass, you will receive a certificate in the mail within two to four weeks. If you do not pass, you can study and practice the skills that you missed and then schedule to retake the test at a later date.

Tips for Successfully Completing the Test

The following tips and suggestions are the result of feedback received from many individuals who have taken one or more MOS tests:

- Make sure that you are thoroughly prepared. If you have extensively used the application for which you are being tested, you might feel confident that you are prepared for the test. However, the test might include questions that involve tasks that you rarely or never perform when you use the application at your place of business, at school, or at home. You must be knowledgeable in all the MOS objectives for the test that you will take.

- Read each exam question carefully. An exam question might include several tasks that you are to perform. A partially correct response to a test question is counted as an incorrect response. In the example question on the previous page, you might apply bold formatting and move the words at your convenience to the correct location, but forget to center the first paragraph. This would count as an incorrect response and would result in a lower test score.

- You are allowed to use the application's Help system, but relying on the Help system too much will slow you down and possibly prevent you from completing the test within the allotted time. Use the Help system only when necessary.

- Keep track of your time. The test does not display the amount of time that you have left, so you need to keep track of the time yourself by monitoring your start time and the required end time on your watch or a clock in the testing center (if there is one). The test program displays the number of items that you have completed along with the total number of test items (for example, "35 of 40 items have been completed"). Use this information to gauge your pace.

- If you skip a question, you cannot return to it later. You should skip a question only if you are certain that you cannot complete the tasks correctly.

Excel

- Don't worry if the testing software crashes while you are taking the exam. The test software is set up to handle this situation. Find your test administrator and tell him or her what happened. The administrator will work through the steps required to restart the test. When the test restarts, it will allow you to continue where you left off. You will have the same amount of time remaining to complete the test as you did when the software crashed.

- As soon as you are finished reading a question and you click in the application window, a condensed version of the instruction is displayed in a corner of the screen. If you are unsure whether you have completed all tasks stated in the test question, click the Instructions button on the test information bar at the bottom of the screen and then reread the question. Close the instruction window when you are finished. Do this as often as necessary to ensure you have read the question correctly and that you have completed all the tasks stated in the question.

If You Do Not Pass the Test

If you do not pass, you can use the assessment printout as a guide to practice the items that you missed. There is no limit to the number of times that you can retake a test; however, you must pay the fee each time that you take the test. When you retake the test, expect to see some of the same test items on the subsequent test; the test software randomly generates the test items from a master test bank before you begin the test. Also expect to see several questions that did not appear on the previous test.

Microsoft e-Learning Library

Microsoft Learning is pleased to offer, in combination with our new *Microsoft Official Academic Course* for *Microsoft Office System 2003 Edition*, in-depth access to our powerful e-Learning tool, the Microsoft® e-Learning Library Version 2 (MELL 2) Desktop Edition for Office System 2003. The MELL Version 2 Desktop Edition for Office System 2003 will help instructors and students alike increase their skill and comfort level with Microsoft software and technologies—as well as help students develop the skills they need to succeed in today's competitive job market.

MELL Features

The MELL Version 2 Desktop Edition for Office System 2003 product included with this *Microsoft Official Academic Course* features:

- Fully customizable learning environments that help instructors pre-assess student's skill levels and direct them to the tasks that are appropriate to their needs.
- High-quality, browser-based training and reinforcement that offers students a familiar environment in which to acquire new skills.
- A powerful search tool that quickly scans a full library of learning materials and provides snappy answers to specific questions.
- Interactive exercises and focused lessons on specific subjects to help instructors direct their students quickly to exactly the content they need to know.
- Reliable, in-depth content, engaging simulations, automated support tools, and memorable on-screen demonstrations.
- An after hours and after class reference and reinforcement tool that students can take with them and use in their working lives.

Additionally, MELL Version 2 Desktop Edition for Office System 2003 fits easily into an existing lab and includes:

- Training solutions that are compatible with all existing software and hardware infrastructures.
- An enhanced learning environment that works without a separate learning management system (LMS) and runs in any SCORM-compliant LMS.
- The ability to send and receive shortcut links via e-mail to relevant help topics, which facilitates the learning experience in a classroom setting and encourages peer-to-peer learning.

Instructors who are preparing students for the MCSE/MCSA or MCAD credential can also use MELL 2 IT Professional Edition and MELL 2 Developer Edition to help students develop the skills they need to succeed in today's competitive job market. Both editions provide outstanding training and reference materials designed to help users achieve professional certification while learning real-world skills. Check out www.microsoft.com/mspress/business for more information on these additional MELL products.

Excel

Focused Students, Mastering Tasks

The MELL Version 2 Desktop Edition for Office System 2003 helps focus students on the tasks they need to know and helps them master those tasks through a combination of the following:

- Assessments that help determine the lessons that will require focus in the classroom or lab.
- Realistic simulations that mirror the actual software without requiring that it already be installed—making it ideal for students who may not have access to the latest Microsoft products outside of the classroom and labs.
- Within the simulation, the ability for a student to follow each step on his or her own, have the computer perform the step, or any combination of the two.

The MELL Version 2 Desktop Edition for Office System 2003 provides deep premium content that allows and encourages students to go beyond basic tasks and achieve proficiency and effectiveness—in class and eventually in the workplace. This depth is reflected in the fact that our desktop training titles are certified by the Microsoft Office Specialist Program.

The MELL Assessment Feature

MELL Version 2 Desktop Edition for Office System 2003 includes a skill assessment designed to help instructors identify topics and features that might warrant coverage during lecture or lab meetings. The skill assessment gives instructors an opportunity to see how much students already know about the topics covered in this course, which in turn allows instructors to devote meeting time to topics with which students are unfamiliar.

To use the assessment feature, follow these steps (note that the illustrations are specific to the Excel Core course, but the steps apply to all of the courses):

1 **Insert the Microsoft Official Academic Course companion CD that accompanies this textbook into your CD drive.**

2 From the menu, select "View e-Learning Course."

3 Click on the training course you are interested in via the left navigation pane.

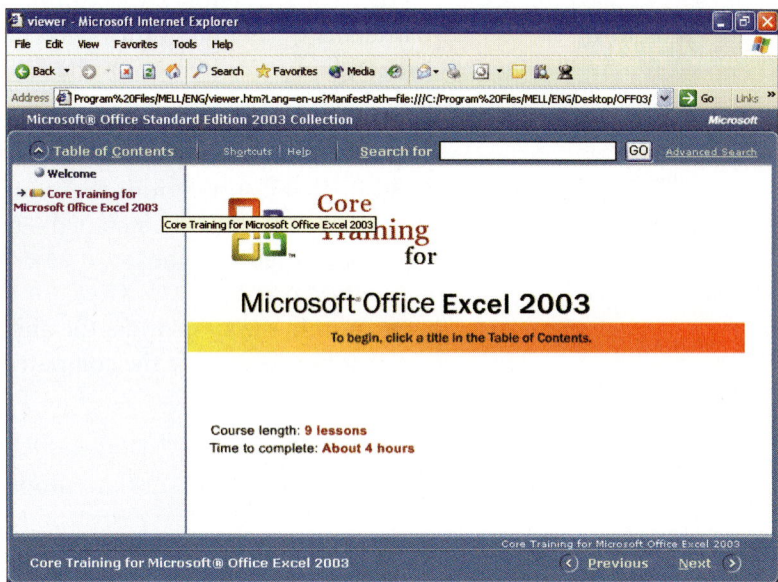

4 Click on "Pre-Assessment" within any core training topic on the accompanying MELL Version 2 Desktop Edition for Office System 2003 CD-ROM.

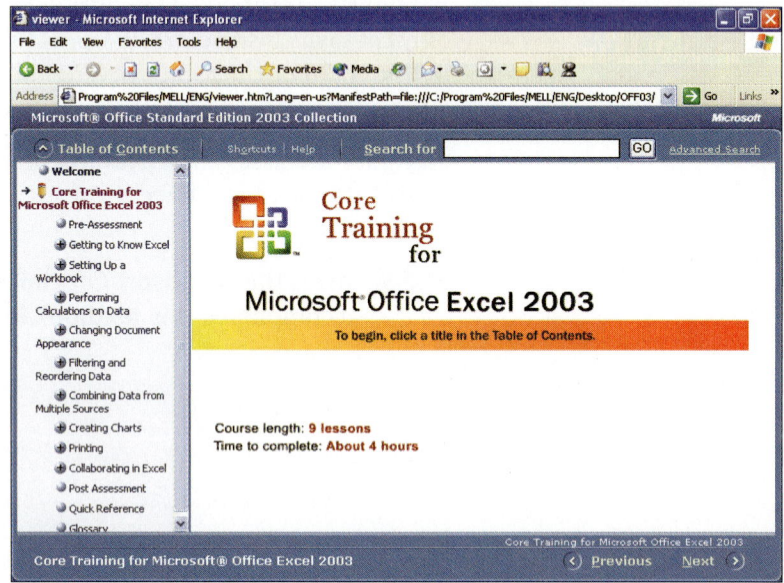

5 **Click on "Take the Pre-Assessment."**

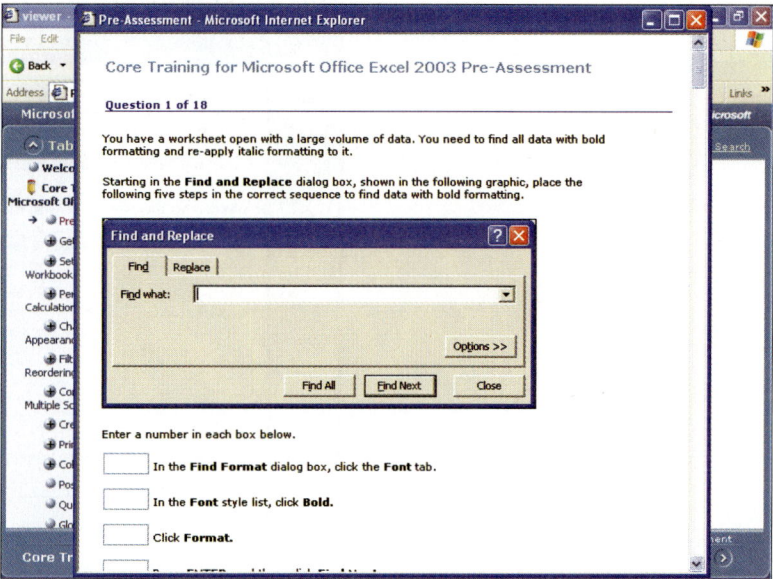

6 **Input some correct answers and, if you choose, some incorrect answers as you move through the Pre-Assessment.**

7 **Click on "Show My Score" at the bottom of the Skills Assessment.**

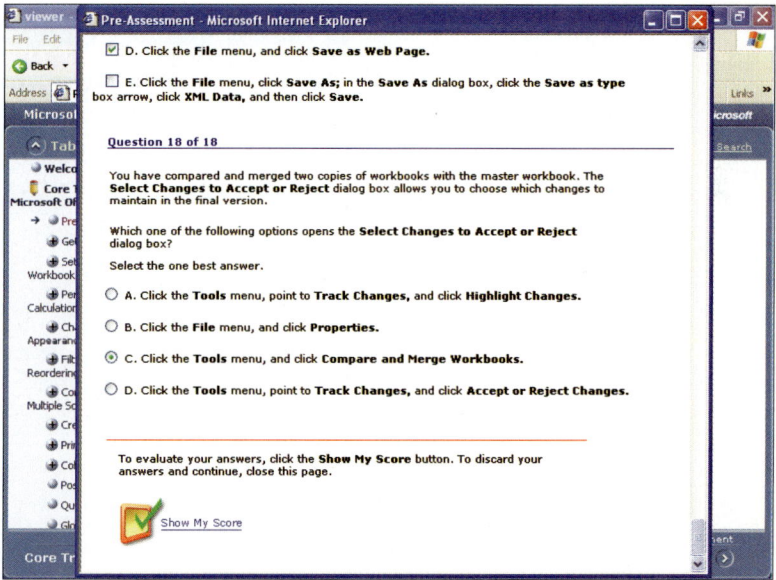

8 The "Show My Score" box details all the correct and incorrect answers and also provides correct answers for all the incorrect responses.

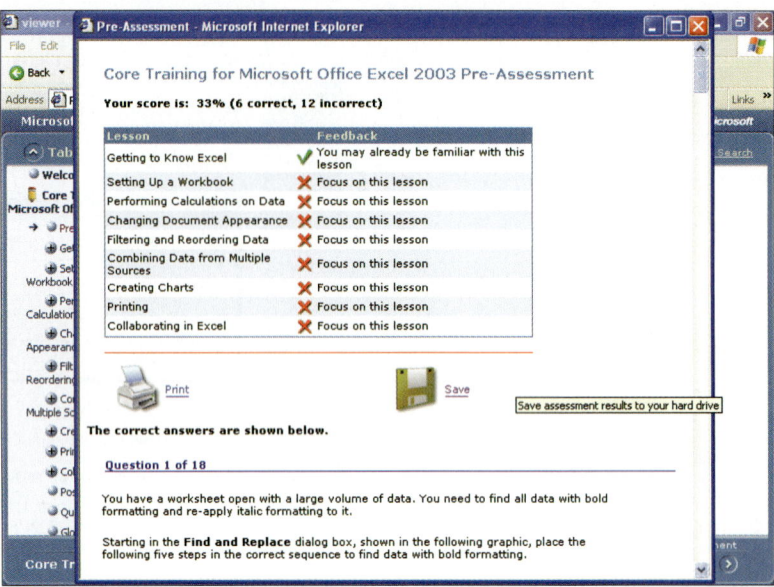

9 Additionally, the resultant table also provides a basic learning plan, directing you to areas you need to master while acknowledging the skills you already possess.

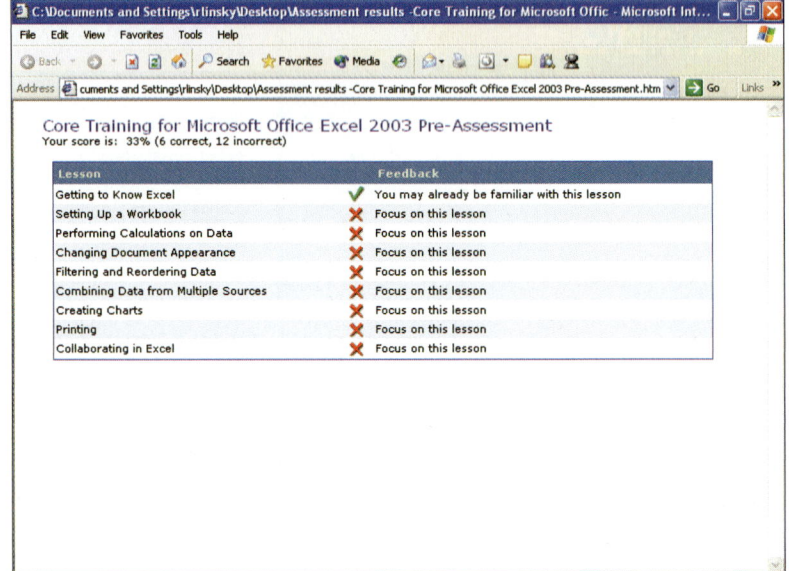

10 Click on either the "Print" or "Save" button to print or save to disk your Pre-Assessment results for future reference.

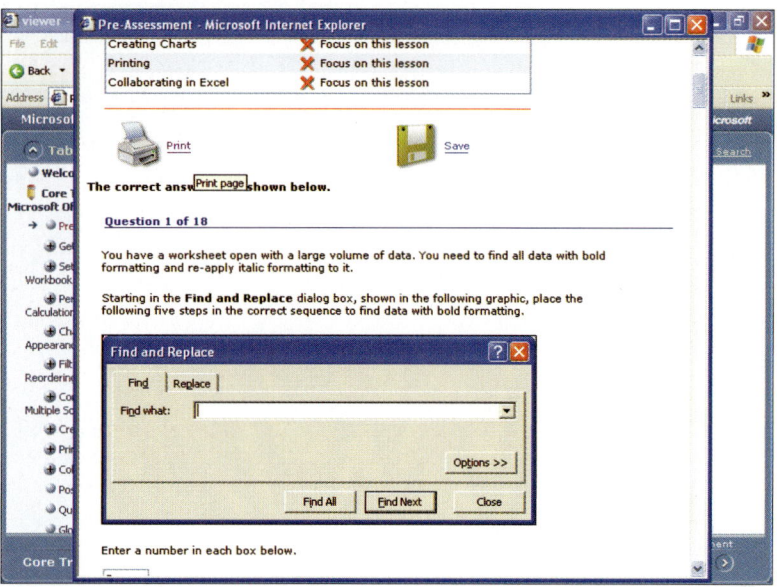

11 You are now ready to begin your interactive learning experience with MELL Version 2 Desktop Edition for Office System 2003!

Working with Workbooks

After completing this lesson, you will be able to:

✔ *Use multiple workbooks.*
✔ *Use a workspace.*
✔ *Link workbooks.*
✔ *Work with named ranges.*
✔ *Use HLOOKUP and VLOOKUP functions.*
✔ *Preview and print a workbook.*
✔ *Consolidate data.*

KEY TERMS

- absolute references
- arguments
- data consolidation
- dependent workbook
- external reference
- lookup functions
- relative references
- source workbook
- table
- three-dimensional formula
- workspace

While working in Microsoft Excel, you may find that you need to have multiple workbooks open at the same time. Suppose that you want to create budget information for the next quarter. You will create a workbook and begin entering current budget information. But you discover that many of the budget amounts can be calculated more quickly by applying a formula to the amounts from the previous quarter's budget, which is stored in a separate workbook file. Using Excel features, you will link these workbooks and share data between them.

You also will learn how to create a name for a range of cells so that you can use the name in a formula, rather than specifying a cell range. In addition, you will explore functions that allow you to retrieve information stored in another location in the same workbook or in a different workbook. Finally, you learn how to consolidate data from different locations in a worksheet or in different worksheets in order to generate summaries.

IMPORTANT

Before you can use the practice files in this lesson, you must install them from the book's companion CD to their default location. For additional information on how to find and open files used in this book, see the "Using the CD-ROM" section at the beginning of this book.

Using Multiple Workbooks

THE BOTTOM LINE

You can easily analyze and keep track of large amounts of data stored in more than one workbook by managing the display of workbooks and worksheets on the screen.

Excel makes using multiple workbooks easy. By default, each workbook opens in a separate window. But if you need more than one workbook open at a time because you refer to them all, you can easily review and compare data by arranging the individual windows so that you can see all of them at the same time. For example, you might want to have the workbooks for the previous quarter's budget and the current quarter's budget open side by side so that you can compare income and expenses. You can arrange multiple worksheets in the same way. You can cascade the windows, or align them horizontally or vertically.

◆ **To complete the procedures in this lesson, you must use the files AW Departmental Expenses, BudgetAW, BudgetEast, BudgetSum, BudgetWest, Employee History Bonus, Pledges, Restaurant Conference, Sales2wk, SalesSummer, and Summer Sales Comparing Performers in the Lesson01 folder in the Excel Expert Practice folder located on your hard disk. These workbooks have been created for a company named Adventure Works—an outdoor adventure resort. Throughout this course, Adventure Works is used to provide business case studies to help you think about course topics and Excel features in a realistic business context. Most of the Excel files that you create or open during this course are based on business practices and requirements at Adventure Works.**

Open and arrange workbooks

In this exercise, you open several Excel workbook files and manipulate the display of the files.

1 Start Excel.

2 If necessary, display the Getting Started task pane, and click More in the Open section of the task pane.

ANOTHER METHOD

- Click the Open button on the Standard toolbar.
- Press Ctrl+O.

3 In the Open dialog box, navigate to the Lesson01 folder of the Excel Expert Practice folder located on your hard disk. Open Sales2wk, SalesSummer, and BudgetSum.

The three workbooks open in the Excel window, although only one workbook is visible.

4 **On the Window menu, click Arrange.**

The Arrange Windows dialog box appears, as shown in Figure 1-1.

FIGURE 1-1

Arrange Windows dialog box

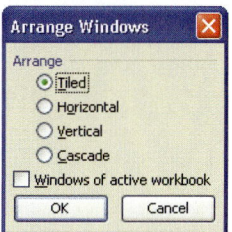

5 **Make sure that the Tiled option is selected, and click OK.**

The workbooks appear in a tiled arrangement within the Excel window.

FIGURE 1-2

Tiling the three workbook windows

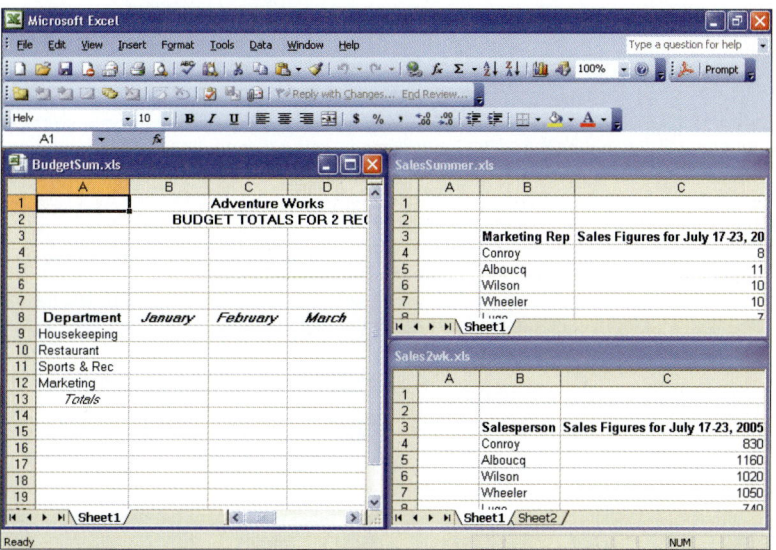

6 **Close the SalesSummer and BudgetSum workbooks, and click the Maximize button in the top right corner of the Sales2wk workbook window.**

7 **On the Window menu, click New Window.**

A copy of the Sales2wk workbook opens and is automatically named Sales2wk:2. The original is designated as Sales2wk:1.

IMPORTANT

Depending on how your preferences are set, your file names may appear with extensions; for example, Sales2wk.xls:1.

8 **On the Window menu, click Arrange.**

The Arrange Windows dialog box appears.

9 **Click the Horizontal option in the Arrange dialog box, and click OK.**

The two sheets of the workbook appear one on top of the other.

10 **Click in the Sales2wk:1 window, and then click the Sheet2 tab.**

Now you can compare the sales figures for two different weeks in July.

FIGURE 1-3

Comparing data from two worksheets

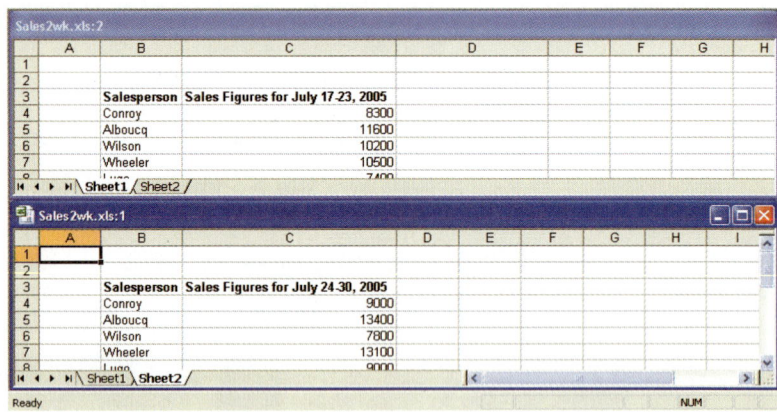

◆ **Close both copies of Sales2wk.**

QUICK REFERENCE ▼

Arrange Excel workbooks

1 On the Window menu, click Arrange.

2 Click one of the options in the Arrange dialog box to select the way you want to arrange the workbooks, and click OK.

Arrange two worksheets in one workbook

1 Open a workbook.

2 On the Window menu, click New Window.

3 Click the second sheet tab at the bottom of the worksheet to display the second worksheet.

4 On the Window menu, click Arrange.

5 Click one of the options in the Arrange dialog box to select the way you want to arrange the worksheets, and click OK.

Using a Workspace

Summarizing and Grouping Multiple
Sets of Data

THE BOTTOM LINE

A workspace is a timesaving feature that allows you to group workbooks so that you can open and save them with only a single set of commands.

If you're like many Excel users, you find yourself working with the same workbooks most of the time. Although the workbooks might not be related to each other, you have them open while you're working and frequently switch between them. If the workbooks are related to each other, you might find yourself sharing data between them and creating formulas that combine data from two or more of the workbooks.

To facilitate this kind of data sharing, Excel gives you the ability to create a **workspace,** a group of workbooks that can be saved and opened as a single file. Excel saves workspaces with an .xlw extension, and they can be saved to any folder on your local hard disk or on a network. When you open the workspace, it appears on the screen just as you saved it—with the same workbook and worksheet active or with two or more of the workbooks arranged on the screen. The workspace file also saves information on window sizes and arrangements.

Workspaces are especially useful for workbooks that are often used together. For instance, the marketing coordinator at Adventure Works uses separate workbooks to keep track of print and television advertising expenses, and she frequently works with these workbooks at the same time. By saving these workbooks as a workspace, she can access both of them quickly.

◆ **Open BudgetSum and SalesSummer from the Excel Expert Practice/Lesson01 folder.**

Create and save a workspace

In this exercise, you create a workspace consisting of two workbooks, and then you close and reopen it.

1 **On the Window menu, click Arrange.**

The Arrange Windows dialog box appears.

2 **Click the Tiled option, and click OK.**

The two workbooks appear side by side.

CHECK THIS OUT ▼

Workspace Options
If you want a group of workbooks to open when you start Excel, you must save the workspace containing these workbooks in the XLStart folder, which is located in the C:\Program Files\Microsoft Office\ Office11 folder. The files that are part of the workspace can be saved anywhere you need them; the workspace must be saved in the XLStart folder.

3 **On the File menu, click Save Workspace to display the Save Workspace dialog box.**

By default, the Save Workspace dialog box displays the name of the previously saved workspace in case you want to add the current workbooks to an existing workspace. In Figure 1-4, notice that one of the open workbooks was saved to a workspace named *financials*, so this workspace name appears in the dialog box.

FIGURE 1-4

Save Workspace dialog box

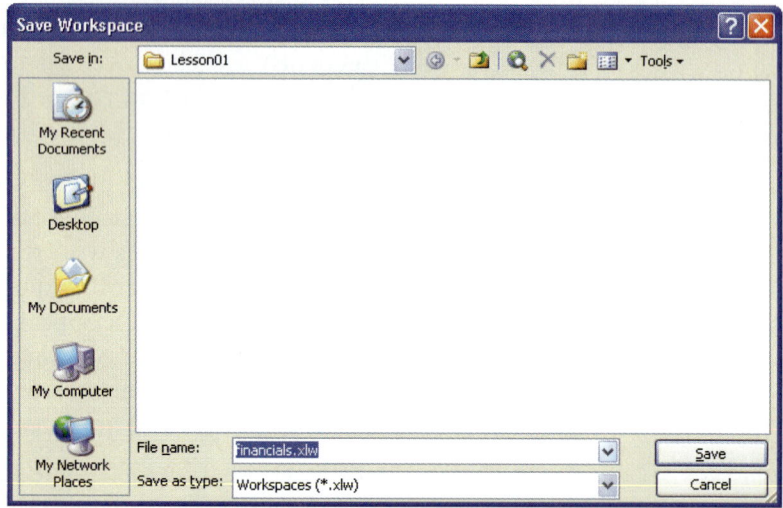

TROUBLESHOOTING

The workspace name that appears in your Save Workspace dialog box might not be the same as that shown in Figure 1-4.

4 **In the File Name box, type Sales Workspace, and click Save.**

Excel saves the workspace.

 5 **Close both workbooks by clicking their Close Window buttons.**

ANOTHER METHOD

Press the Shift key, click the File menu, and click Close All.

 6 **Click the Open button on the Standard toolbar.**

The Open dialog box appears.

ANOTHER METHOD

- On the File menu, select Open.
- Press Ctrl+O.

7 Navigate to the Lesson01 folder in the Excel Expert Practice folder, and double-click Sales Workspace.xlw.

The BudgetSum and SalesSummer workbooks open.

◆ Close the open workbooks.

QUICK REFERENCE ▼

Create a workspace

1 Open all of the workbooks that you want to be part of the workspace.

2 Arrange the workbooks in the way you want them to appear when the workspace is opened in the future—the arrangement will be part of the saved workspace.

3 On the File menu, click Save Workspace.

4 Type a name for the workspace in the File Name box of the Save Workspace dialog box.

5 Click Save.

Linking Workbooks

Summarizing and Grouping Multiple Sets of Data

THE BOTTOM LINE

Excel's linking feature gives you the flexibility of using existing data from other workbooks, saving you the time of retyping data and reconstructing formulas. Also, the data that links two workbooks is dynamic, so when data is updated in its original workbook location, it's automatically updated in any linked workbooks.

Another powerful feature in Excel is the ability to link data in two or more workbooks. This is useful when it is impractical to combine large, complex worksheets in one workbook. To create a link between workbooks, you enter a formula in one workbook that references one or more cells in another workbook. The workbook that contains the formula is called the **dependent workbook,** and the workbook that contains the referenced information is called the **source workbook.**

For example, at Adventure Works, the chief financial officer (CFO) is preparing a budget for the upcoming fiscal year. For many of the budget items, she wants to multiply the budget amount from the previous year's workbook by a specified percentage and apply that formula to the same budget lines in the budget workbook for the upcoming year. She estimates that guest occupancy for the upcoming year will increase by 20 percent, so she wants to increase the budget item for housekeeping supplies by 20 percent. She creates a formula in the current workbook (the dependent workbook) that multiplies the amount of housekeeping supplies in the previous year's workbook (the source workbook) by 20 percent.

You can specify an **external reference** in the dependent workbook by selecting the appropriate cell or range of cells in the source workbook or by typing the reference for the appropriate cell or range of cells. You also can create an external reference when you give a formula in one workbook a name that refers to a cell in a different workbook. The references in the formula, however, must begin with the name of the source workbook to which the formula is linking, enclosed in square brackets, and the worksheet name followed by an exclamation point. This type of formula, with external links, is called a **three-dimensional formula.**

TIP

For more information on three-dimensional references, see Lesson 7, "Performing Basic Calculations," of the *Microsoft Official Academic Course Excel 2003 Core Skills* book.

When a workbook containing an external reference formula is saved, the name of the source workbook also is saved. You should save all source workbook files before saving the dependent workbook.

TIP

There are two kinds of references: absolute and relative. **Absolute references** are cell references that refer to cells in a specific location. **Relative references** are cell references that are relative to the position of the formula. If you have a formula in cell B6 that contains a relative reference to cell A5 and you copy that formula to cell B7, the new formula will reference cell A6 because cell A6 is in the same position relative to cell B7 that cell A5 is to cell B6. An absolute reference would lead to cell A5 in both formulas. An absolute reference in a formula is designated by a dollar sign that precedes any part of the cell reference, such as A1, $A1, or A$1. The dollar sign designates the parts of the reference that do not change.

Creating Formulas to Calculate Values

◆ **Open BudgetSum, BudgetEast, and BudgetWest from the Excel Expert Practice/Lesson01 folder.**

Link workbooks

In this exercise, you display two workbooks that contain related budget information, as well as a third workbook in which you summarize the budget information. Adventure Works East and Adventure Works West are two resorts run by Adventure Works. You create a formula that links the BudgetEast and BudgetWest workbooks with the BudgetSum workbook.

1 **On the Window menu, click Arrange.**

The Arrange Windows dialog box appears.

2 **Make sure the Tiled option is selected, and click OK.**

The workbook windows appear in a tiled arrangement.

3 Click the BudgetSum window to activate it, click cell B9, and type an equal sign (=).

The Formula bar is activated.

4 Click in the BudgetEast window, and then click cell B9.

BudgetEast becomes the active workbook, and the cell reference appears in the Formula bar as well as in cell B9 of the BudgetSum workbook. The reference is absolute, however; it must be a relative reference to calculate properly.

TROUBLESHOOTING

You must click in the BudgetEast window twice: the first time to activate the window and the second time to select cell B9.

FIGURE 1-5

Adding a workbook reference

Cell reference from BudgetEast workbook

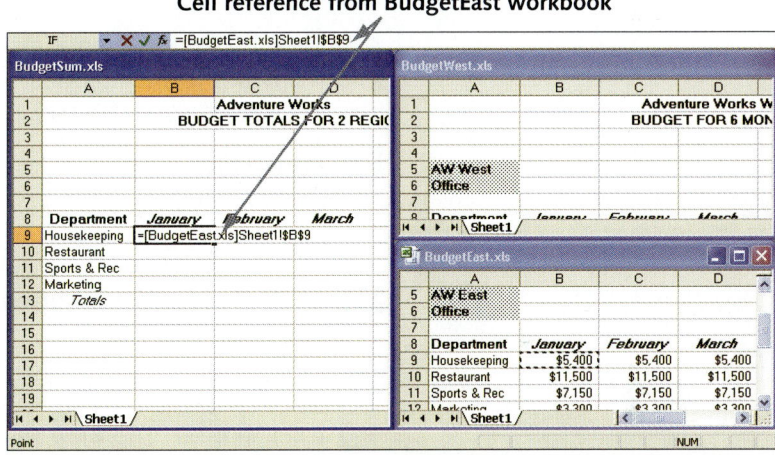

TIP

As you press F4, notice how the dollar sign, which designates the static parts of the cell reference, moves through each absolute reference possible (B9, B$9, $B9) before disappearing.

5 Press F4 three times.

The absolute reference changes to a relative reference.

6 Type a plus sign (+), click in the BudgetWest window to make it active, and click cell B9.

BudgetWest becomes the active window, and the operator and cell reference appear in the Formula bar and in the BudgetSum window, as shown in Figure 1-6.

FIGURE 1-6

Adding a second workbook reference

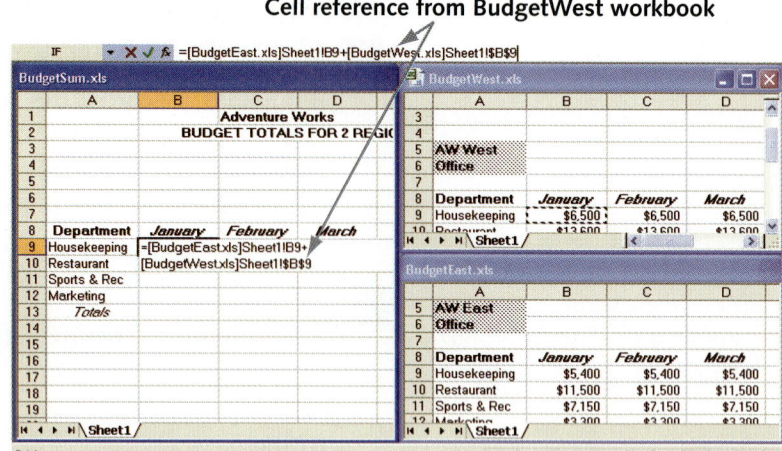

Cell reference from BudgetWest workbook

7 **Press F4 three times.**

The absolute reference changes to a relative reference, and the following formula appears in the Formula bar:
=[BudgetEast.xls]Sheet1!B9+[BudgetWest.xls]Sheet1!B9

8 **Press Enter.**

The result of the formula ($11,900) appears in cell B9 of the BudgetSum workbook.

9 **Click the Maximize button in the top right corner of the BudgetSum window.**

The window maximizes to fill the Excel window.

10 **Click cell B9, and drag the Fill handle at the bottom right corner of the cell to cell B13.**

The formula in cell B9 is copied into the other cells, with the appropriate references.

FIGURE 1-7

Copying a three-dimensional formula

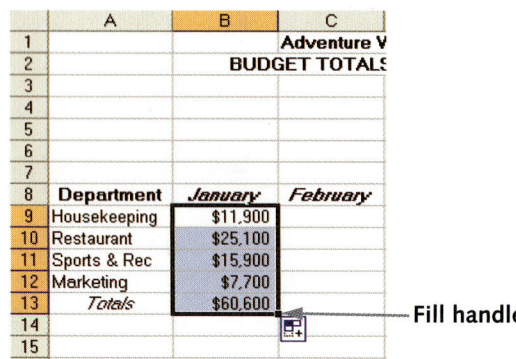

Fill handle

11 **Drag the Fill handle of the selected range to cell G13.**

The formula is copied to the range C9:G13.

12 **Click any cell outside of the selected range.**

The range is deselected, and the worksheet should look similar to Figure 1-8.

FIGURE 1-8

Worksheet with data from two other workbooks

	A	B	C	D	E	F	G
1			Adventure Works				
2			BUDGET TOTALS FOR 2 REGIONAL OFFICES				
3							
4							
5							
6							
7							
8	Department	January	February	March	April	May	June
9	Housekeeping	$11,900	$11,900	$11,900	$13,100	$13,100	$13,100
10	Restaurant	$25,100	$25,100	$25,100	$26,300	$26,300	$26,300
11	Sports & Rec	$15,900	$15,900	$15,900	$17,100	$17,100	$17,100
12	Marketing	$7,700	$7,700	$7,700	$8,900	$8,900	$8,900
13	Totals	$60,600	$60,600	$60,600	$65,400	$65,400	$65,400

13 **Click the Restore Window button in the top right corner of the worksheet window.**

The window returns to its original size.

14 **Click the BudgetEast window to activate it, click cell B9, type 7500, and press Enter.**

The formula referencing cell B9 in the BudgetSum worksheet now contains the updated data, as do the cells containing the totals.

◆ **Save and close BudgetSum, BudgetEast, and BudgetWest.**

QUICK REFERENCE ▼

Create a formula that links workbooks

1 With all necessary workbooks open, click the cell in the worksheet where you want the formula to be placed.

2 Type the formula you want to use.

3 Cycle through the open workbooks, and click the cell in a different workbook that includes a value or another entry that you want to include in the formula.

4 In the formula, click to the right of the values, and type a closing parenthesis.

5 Press Enter.

QUICK CHECK

Q. In a formula, what distinguishes an absolute cell reference from a relative cell reference?

A: **An absolute reference is designated by a dollar sign ($).**

Working with Named Ranges

Naming Cell Ranges

THE BOTTOM LINE

You can name ranges of data so that you can easily identify their content and specify them when making selections or building formulas.

In Excel, you might have workbooks with worksheets that contain information in hundreds, or even thousands, of cells. You can more easily identify and categorize worksheet contents by naming ranges according to the data they contain. Once you name a range, you can select it from the Name Box list and then perform a variety of functions on it, such as cutting and pasting it to a different worksheet or workbook or creating a formula that uses the range name instead of referencing the range address.

For example, in a budgeting worksheet, you can build a formula that subtracts expenses from income using named ranges for cells containing expenses and for cells containing income sources. The formula would simply be =*Expenses-Income*; you do not need to reference the individual ranges as you enter the formula.

You also might want to assign a name to an individual cell. For instance, the budgeting worksheet can get quite lengthy, containing hundreds of rows and dozens of columns. To find the total expenses value, you might give the cell a name, such as *GrandTotal*. Then you can locate this cell quickly by clicking the Name Box down arrow and clicking *GrandTotal* on the list of names.

If you want to change the parameters of the named range, you can easily redefine the cells to be included in the range by using the Define Name dialog box. You also can delete a range name through this dialog box.

TROUBLESHOOTING

You can't include any spaces in a range name. For example, if you try to use the name *Grand Total* as a name for a range of cells, a message box will open, telling you that this is an invalid name. However, you could use *GrandTotal* or *Grand_Total* as the name for a range of cells.

◆ **Open Summer Sales Comparing Performers from the Excel Expert Practice/Lesson01 folder.**

Work with a named range

In this exercise, you name a range, copy and paste a named range to a different worksheet, insert a named range in a formula, and modify the named range.

1 Select the range C6:E12.

2 On the Insert menu, point to Name, and click Define.

The Define Name dialog box appears.

FIGURE 1-9

Define Name dialog box

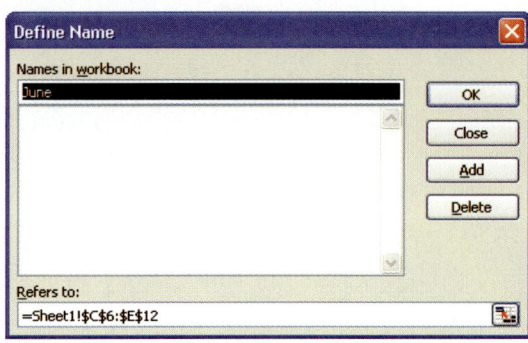

3 Type SummerSales, click Add, and click OK.

The range is named, and the name now appears in the Name Box to the left of the Formula bar, as shown in Figure 1-10.

FIGURE 1-10

Name Box displays range name

Range name

SummerSales		fx 12000				
	A	B	C	D	E	F	G
1							
2							
3							
4							
5			June	July	August		
6		Conroy	$12,000	$11,500	$13,000		
7		Alboucq	$9,000	$11,000	$8,500		
8		Wilson	$11,200	$11,300	$11,400		
9		Wheeler	$10,100	$15,000	$8,300		
10		Lugo	$7,500	$6,000	$9,000		
11		Penn	$4,000	$5,000	$5,500		
12		Nagata	$6,000	$6,200	$7,000		Named range
13							
14			Total Summer Sales				
15							
16							
17			Top Performer Sales				

Sheet1 / Sheet2 / Sheet3 /

4 Click outside of the selected range, click the Name Box down arrow, and click SummerSales.

All of the cells in the named range are selected.

  5 On the Standard toolbar, click the Copy button, click the Sheet2 tab, click cell C6, and click the Paste button.

Excel copies the selected range to the Sheet2 worksheet.

ANOTHER METHOD

- On the Edit menu, select Copy, click the location where you want to paste the selection, and select Paste on the Edit menu.
- Press Ctrl+C, click the location where you want to paste the selection, and press Ctrl+V.

6 **Click the Sheet1 tab.**

Excel returns to the Sheet1 worksheet.

7 **Click cell D15, which will contain the sales total, type =SUM(SummerSales), and press Enter.**

The sales total, 188500, appears in cell D15.

FIGURE 1-11

Using a named range in a formula

	D15		▼		f_x =SUM(SummerSales) ◄		── Range name used in formula
		A	B	C	D	E	
4							
5				June	July	August	
6			Conroy	$12,000	$11,500	$13,000	
7			Alboucq	$9,000	$11,000	$8,500	
8			Wilson	$11,200	$11,300	$11,400	
9			Wheeler	$10,100	$15,000	$8,300	
10			Lugo	$7,500	$6,000	$9,000	
11			Penn	$4,000	$5,000	$5,500	
12			Nagata	$6,000	$6,200	$7,000	
13							
14					Total Summer Sales		
15					188500		
16							
17					Top Performer Sales		

8 **Select the range C6:E10.**

This range excludes the sales figures for the lowest-performing salespeople.

9 **On the Insert menu, point to Name, and click Define.**

The Define Name dialog box appears.

10 **In the Names In Workbook box, type TopPerformers, click Add, and click OK.**

The range is named.

11 **Click cell D18, type =SUM(TopPerformers), and press Enter.**

The sales for the top performers (154,800) appears in cell D18.

12 **On the Insert menu, point to Name, and click Define.**

The Define Name dialog box appears.

13 **Click TopPerformers in the Names In Workbook box, click the Collapse Dialog button on the Refers To box, click cell E6, press the Ctrl key, and click cell E8 and cell E10.**

The three cells are selected to be part of the modified named range.

14 **Click the Expand dialog button, and click OK in the Define Name dialog box.**

The sales for the top performers changes to 33400 to reflect the change to the cells included in the named range.

◆ **Save and close Summer Sales Comparing Performers.**

QUICK REFERENCE ▼

Create a named range

1 Select the range you want to name.

2 On the Insert menu, point to Name, and click Define.

3 Type the name of the range in the Names In Workbook box.

4 Click Add and then click OK.

Delete a range name

1 On the Insert menu, point to Name, and click Define.

2 Select the name of the range you want to delete.

3 Click Delete, and click OK.

Using HLOOKUP and VLOOKUP Functions

Locating and Retrieving Data from a Database

THE BOTTOM LINE

Lookup functions are an efficient way to search for and insert a value in a cell when the desired value is stored elsewhere in the workbook or even in a different workbook.

Excel provides two **lookup functions** that can be used to retrieve information stored in a specified range on the same worksheet, a different worksheet, or a different workbook. The VLOOKUP and HLOOKUP functions search rows or columns in a specified range (called a lookup **table** in Excel) to locate a certain value. The functions are designed to retrieve corresponding information from the table that relates to this value and place the data in the active cell.

For example, the recreation director at Adventure Works keeps a table of names, room numbers, and birthdays for the children of guests at the resort. Each day she uses the VLOOKUP function to search for that day's date in the table and to display the name and room number of each child whose birthday is on that day. She uses this information to send birthday gifts to the appropriate rooms.

The HLOOKUP function looks in rows (a horizontal lookup), and the VLOOKUP function looks in columns (a vertical lookup). Each function can use up to four arguments (all of which are required except for *range_lookup*). **Arguments** are the values that a function uses to perform operations or calculations.

HLOOKUP(lookup_value,table_array,row_index_num,range_lookup)

VLOOKUP(lookup_value,table_array,col_index_num,range_lookup)

Argument	Description
lookup_value	The value to be found in the row or the column; the lookup value can be a constant value, a text contact enclosed in quotation marks, or the address or name of a cell that contains a numeric or text constant
table_array	The table of information in which data is looked up; this can be the row-and-column coordinates of the table or the name of a range
row_index_num	The numeric position of the row that is to be searched (used only for HLOOKUP)
col_index_num	The numeric position of the column that is to be searched (used only for VLOOKUP)
range_lookup	If the function is to return the nearest value, even when there is no match, this value should be set to TRUE; if an exact match is required, this value should be set to FALSE; if this argument is not included, the function assumes the value to be TRUE

To better understand the use of VLOOKUP and HLOOKUP, briefly review the following lookup table (named "BonusTable) that the sales manager of Adventure Works created to formulate end-of-year bonuses for the sales staff. Years is column 1 in the lookup table, Standard Bonus is column 2 in the lookup table, and Excellence Award is column 3. "Years, Standard Bonus, Excellence Award" is row 1 of the lookup table.

	Column 1	Column 2	Column 3
Row 1	Years	Standard Bonus	Excellence Award
Row 2	1	$50.00	$200.00
Row 3	3	$75.00	$300.00
Row 4	5	$100.00	$400.00
Row 5	7	$250.00	$1,000.00
Row 6	9	$500.00	$2,000.00
Row 7	11	$750.00	$3,000.00
Row 8	13	$1,000.00	$4,000.00
Row 9	15	$1,500.00	$6,000.00

Now review the following lookups and their results:

- =VLOOKUP(D7,BonusTable,2) **Result:** $1,000
  VLOOKUP looks in cell D7 (Row 8 at Column 1 in the BonusTable shown above) of the worksheet and finds the value 13 stored there. The function then looks in the BonusTable range for a matching value and finds it in the second-to-last row. The function retrieves the value ($1,000.00) in column 2 of the same row and places the value in the active cell.
- =VLOOKUP(12,BonusTable,2,TRUE) **Result:** $750.00
  VLOOKUP looks for the value 12 in the BonusTable range but does not find it. However, because the Range_lookup argument is set to TRUE, the function finds the closest (next lower) value, 11 in this case. The function returns the value ($750.00) in column 2 of the same row and places the value in the active cell.

- =VLOOKUP(14,BonusTable,2,FALSE) **Result:** #N/A
  VLOOKUP looks for the value 14 in the BonusTable range but does not find it. Because the Range_lookup argument is set to FALSE (which means an exact match is required), the function places the #N/A error value in the active cell to indicate that no match existed.
- =HLOOKUP("StandardBonus",BonusTable,4,FALSE) **Result:** $100.00
  HLOOKUP looks for the value "Standard Bonus" in the BonusTable range, finds the value in column 2, and returns the value ($100.00) in row 4 of the column.

◆ **Open Employee History Bonus from the Excel Expert Practice/Lesson01 folder.**

Apply the VLOOKUP and HLOOKUP functions

In this exercise, you use the VLOOKUP function to calculate the yearly bonus, based on years of service, for an Adventure Works employee named Benson. Then you use the fill handle to copy the VLOOKUP function to cells for other employees. You also use the HLOOKUP function to return the "Excellence Award" value in a specified row of a lookup table.

1 **Click cell E7, and type** =vlookup(d7,bonustable,2).

Cell D7 contains the number of years worked, which is the lookup value. VLOOKUP looks for the closest match to the D7 value in the BonusTable range (A20:C28), and it retrieves the corresponding value in the second column.

TROUBLESHOOTING

Be careful not to insert any spaces when you type this formula.

TIP

BonusTable has already been defined as a range name for cells A20:C28. You can verify this by clicking the Name Box down arrow and clicking BonusTable. Arguments used in a VLOOKUP or HLOOKUP function are not case-sensitive, so you can type them in uppercase, lowercase, or any combination of uppercase and lowercase characters. Also, the VLOOKUP and HLOOKUP function names are not case-sensitive.

2 **Press Enter.**

The result of the function ($1000.00) appears in cell E7.

ANOTHER METHOD

You also can access the VLOOKUP and HLOOKUP functions from the Function Arguments dialog box, which you open by clicking Function on the Insert menu or by clicking the Insert Function button on the Standard toolbar or on the Formula bar.

3 **Click cell E7, and drag the fill handle down to cell E15.**

The bonuses for the other employees are calculated.

FIGURE 1-12

Copying a VLOOKUP function

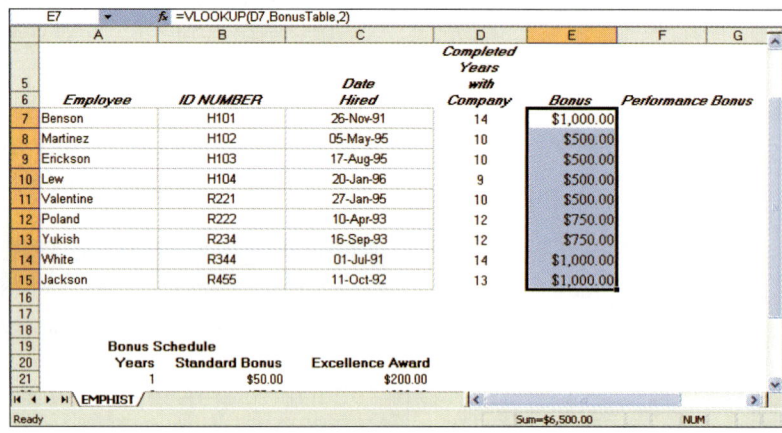

4 **Click cell F7.**

5 **Type =hlookup("excellence award",bonustable,8,false), and press Enter.**

Excel searches for the text string "excellence award" in the first row of the BonusTable range and locates it in column C. Then Excel retrieves the value ($4,000.00) in cell C27 (row 8 in the table) and places it in cell F7.

FIGURE 1-13

Applying the HLOOKUP function

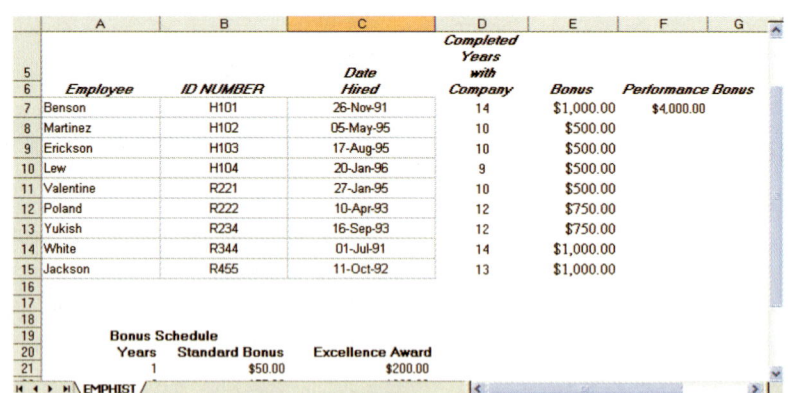

◆ **Save and close Employee History Bonus.**

TIP

If you have trouble remembering the syntax for an HLOOKUP or VLOOKUP function, you can use the Function Arguments dialog box to help you enter the lookup information. To display a list of categories and function names, on the Insert menu, click Function, or click the Insert Function button on the Standard toolbar or on the Formula bar. In the categories list, click Lookup & Reference. In the function list, click VLOOKUP or HLOOKUP, and click OK. Excel will prompt you for the information required to perform the lookup.

QUICK REFERENCE ▼

Use the HLOOKUP and VLOOKUP functions

1 Click the cell that you want to contain the value obtained from the lookup.

2 Type the syntax for the lookup you want to perform, and press Enter.
Or

1 Click the cell that you want to contain the value obtained from the lookup.

2 Click the Insert Function button, or on the Insert menu, click Function.

3 Click Lookup & Reference in the categories list.

4 Click HLOOKUP (or VLOOKUP) on the function list, and click OK.

5 Enter the values in the HLOOKUP (or VLOOKUP) Function Arguments dialog box, and click OK.

QUICK CHECK

Q. What's the main difference between the HLOOKUP and VLOOKUP functions?

A: The HLOOKUP function looks in rows, and the VLOOKUP function looks in columns.

Previewing and Printing Workbooks

THE BOTTOM LINE

You can see how the data and sheets in a workbook look before printing them by displaying the workbook in the Print Preview window. Previewing can help you spot formatting inconsistencies and irregular page breaks, which you can then correct before printing. Having a printout of workbook data also can help you identify errors or formatting problems, but it's also useful when you want to distribute copies to people who don't have access to the electronic file.

Using Excel, you can print an entire workbook, a single sheet in a workbook, or a selected range of data. For example, at Adventure Works, the CFO sometimes wants to print all four quarters of sales information to compare the sales amounts. Because sales information for each quarter is on a separate worksheet, she needs to print the entire workbook so that she can review the information on all four worksheets.

At other times, she wants to print the sales information only for the current quarter so that she can distribute the printed document to managers. In this case, she wants to print only the worksheet for the current quarter.

In another situation, she wants to print and send sales totals only for a particular department so that she can review the amounts with the appropriate department manager. In this situation, she selects the range of cells that contains the amounts for a particular department; then she prints only that range of cells. When you want to print a range of cells, you can select the range of cells you want to print prior to displaying the Print dialog box or you can specify the range you want to print in the Print dialog box.

Before printing a file, you should preview the active worksheet. The Print Preview window displays a full-page view of the file as it will be printed so that you can check the format and overall layout before actually printing. The Print Preview window is shown in Figure 1-14.

FIGURE 1-14

Print Preview window

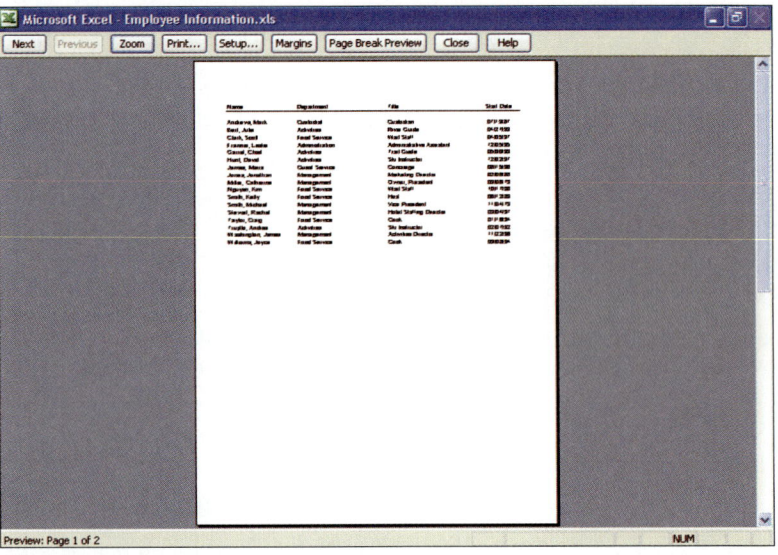

Commands available in the Print Preview window appear as buttons across the top of the window. The current page number and total number of pages in the worksheet appear in the bottom left corner of the window.

A final feature that comes in handy when you print Excel worksheets is Intelliprint, which prevents any blank pages at the end of a document from being printed. For example, if you have a 15-page worksheet and you set your print area to include all of those pages, Excel will print them. If, however, you delete enough data to reduce the worksheet's size to ten pages but don't resize the print area, the print area will have five pages of blank cells at the end. Rather than print those blank pages, Intelliprint recognizes that the pages are blank and stops printing after the last page with data in the body of the worksheet.

◆ **Open Sales2wk from the Excel Expert Practice/Lesson01 folder.**

Preview and print parts of a workbook

In this exercise, you preview and print the first page of a worksheet and a selected range in a worksheet.

1 **On the File menu, click Print.**

The Print dialog box appears. The name of your default printer appears in the Name box. The printer name that you see will probably differ from the name shown in the following illustration.

FIGURE 1-15

Print dialog box

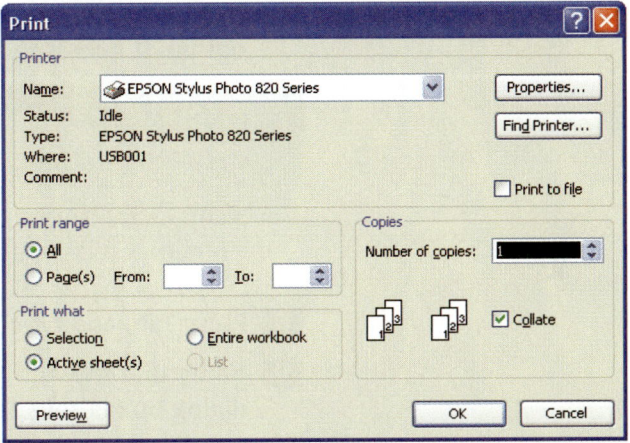

ANOTHER METHOD

Press Ctrl+P.

2 **In the Print What area of the Print dialog box, click the Entire Workbook option, and click the Preview button.**

The workbook appears in the Print Preview window.

3 **Click any area of the document to zoom in, and click again to zoom out.**

4 On the Print Preview toolbar, click Next to move from page 1 to page 2.

When you have moved through one page in a workbook, clicking Next displays the next worksheet. Clicking Previous displays the previous worksheet.

5 On the Print Preview toolbar, click the Close button.

The Print Preview window closes, and the worksheet reappears.

6 On the File menu, click Print.

The Print dialog box appears.

7 In the Print Range area of the Print dialog box, click the Pages option. If necessary, click in the From box, and type 1.

8 Press Tab, and type 1 in the To box.

9 Verify that the Active Sheet(s) option in the Print What area of the dialog box is selected, and click OK.

Only the first page of the active worksheet prints.

10 Select the range C3:C8.

11 On the File menu, point to Print Area, and click Set Print Area.

12 On the File menu, click Print.

The Print dialog box appears.

13 In the Print dialog box, click OK.

Only the selected area prints.

14 On the File menu, point to Print Area, and click Clear Print Area.

◆ Close Sales2wk.

QUICK REFERENCE ▼

Preview the worksheets in a workbook

1 On the File menu, click Print.

2 In the Print What area of the Print dialog box, select Entire Workbook.

3 Click the Preview button.

4 Click anywhere in the worksheet to zoom in, or click the Zoom button on the Print Preview toolbar to zoom in or zoom out.

5 To move from one page to the next, click Previous or Next.

6 Click the Close button on the Print Preview toolbar to close Print Preview.

Print a selected area

2 Select the range you want to print.

2 On the File menu, point to Print Area, and click Set Print Area.

3 On the File menu, click Print.

4 In the Print dialog box, click OK.

Consolidating Worksheet Data

Summarizing and Grouping Multiple Sets of Data

THE BOTTOM LINE

Data consolidation is a quick and easy method for generating summaries of data stored in various worksheets within a single workbook or in multiple workbooks.

You've learned how Excel's linking feature and various window display options let you manipulate and review the data in multiple workbooks. Excel's **data consolidation** feature provides another option for bringing existing data from other locations together in a summary worksheet. For example, the sales manager at Adventure Works tracks sales by month in different worksheets, one worksheet per month. He also summarizes the monthly sales in a single worksheet that represents the entire year.

It's easiest to consolidate data when all of the worksheets involved are designed the same way. In other words, the categories of data should be stored in the same rows and columns in each worksheet. For example, if the Division 1 sales data is stored in column C of Sheet2, then the Division 1 sales data should be stored in column C of Sheet3, Sheet4, Sheet5, and so on. This way, when you're ready to consolidate the data, you can easily indicate the sheets and cell references that you want to include in the consolidation formula.

If data is not stored in this manner, you can still consolidate it, but you must select each cell in each worksheet that you want to include in the summary. This approach is still effective, but it takes more time.

In the summary worksheet, you add all of the heading information, and then you create the consolidation formulas. A consolidation formula starts with an equal sign (=) and, if necessary, a function name. You build the formula using the Consolidate dialog box.

◆ **Open AW Departmental Expenses from the Excel Expert Practice/Lesson01 folder.**

Consolidate data

In this exercise, you consolidate three worksheets that contain operating expenses for three departments in the Adventure Works organization.

1 On the Insert menu, click Worksheet.

A new worksheet appears.

ANOTHER METHOD

Right-click a sheet tab, click Insert on the shortcut menu, click Worksheet in the Insert dialog box, and click OK.

2 Double-click the Sheet1 tab, type Expense Summary, and then press Enter.

The new worksheet is named.

ANOTHER METHOD

Right-click the sheet tab, click Rename, type the new name, and press Enter.

3 Drag the Expense Summary sheet tab to the right of the existing sheet tabs.

4 Click cell A5 on the Expense Summary worksheet.

5 Type Total Departmental Expense, and press Enter. Widen column A to fit the text.

6 Click cell B5 and on the Data menu, click Consolidate.

The Consolidate dialog box appears, as shown in Figure 1-16.

FIGURE 1-16

Consolidate dialog box

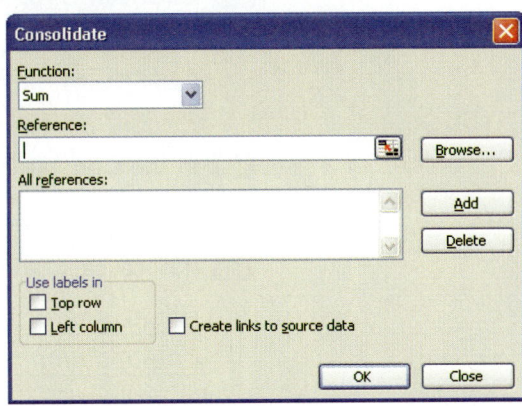

7 In the Consolidate dialog box, click in the Reference box.

8 Click the Guest Services sheet tab. (If necessary, click the sheet tab scrolling buttons to the left of the sheet tabs to bring the Guest Services sheet tab into view.)

9 Click cell G10.

10 In the Consolidate dialog box, click the Add button.

Cell G10 of the Guest Services worksheet is added to the All References list.

TIP

You probably won't have to click cell G10 in the Operations or Marketing worksheets. Cell G10 should already be the active cell; this is indicated by the moving marquee around the cell.

11 Click the Operations sheet tab.

12 Click cell G10, if necessary, and in the Consolidate dialog box, click the Add button.

Cell G10 of the Operations worksheet is added to the All References list.

FIGURE 1-17

Adding references for the consolidation

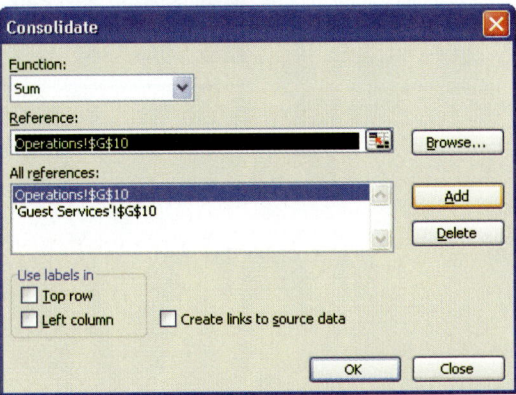

13 Click the Marketing sheet tab.

14 Click cell G10, if necessary, and in the Consolidate dialog box, click the Add button.

Cell G10 of the Marketing worksheet is added to the All References list.

15 In the Consolidate dialog box, click OK.

The consolidated data appears in cell B5.

16 If necessary, widen column B so all the data is displayed.

FIGURE 1-18

Consolidation result

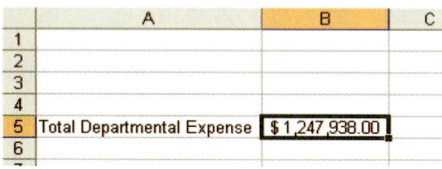

◆ Save the workbook and then close it. If you are continuing to other lessons, leave Excel open. If you are not continuing to other lessons, save and close all open workbooks. Click the Close button in the top right corner of the Excel window.

QUICK REFERENCE ▼

Consolidate data from worksheets

1 Click the cell where you want the top-left portion of the data to appear.

2 On the Data menu, click Consolidate.

3 In the Function box, enter the function you want to use, or select it from the list.

4 Click the sheet tab and the cell you want to include in the consolidation.

5 Click Add.

6 Repeat the selection and addition of more references, as necessary.

7 Click OK.

QUICK CHECK

Q. What does a consolidation formula start with?

A: A consolidation formula always starts with an equal (=) sign.

Key Points

✔ *Excel offers a number of options for how you can arrange open worksheet and workbook windows. Managing the display of workbooks and worksheets helps you to more easily analyze and keep track of large amounts of data stored in them.*

✔ *A workspace is a timesaving feature that allows you to group workbooks so that you can open and save them with only a single set of commands.*

✔ *Excel's linking feature gives you the flexibility of using existing data from other workbooks, saving you the time of retyping data and reconstructing formulas.*

✔ *You can name ranges of data so that you can easily identify their content and specify them when making selections or building formulas.*

✔ *Lookup functions are an efficient way to search for and insert a value in a cell when the desired value is stored elsewhere in the worksheet. Excel provides two lookup functions: HLOOKUP and VLOOKUP.*

✔ *Through the Print dialog box, you can specify what parts of a workbook to print. You can see how the sheets in a workbook look before printing them by displaying the workbook in the Print Preview window.*

✔ *Data consolidation is a quick and easy method for generating summaries of data stored in various worksheets within a single workbook or in multiple workbooks.*

Quick Quiz

True/False

T   F   1. You can open multiple workbooks at the same time through the Open dialog box by pressing Ctrl, clicking each workbook name to select it, and clicking the Open button.

T   F   2. A workspace can include a maximum of three workbooks.

T   F   3. A workspace must be saved to the Program Files folder on your hard disk.

T   F   4. In linked workbooks, the dependent workbook contains the formula that references cells in another workbook.

T   F   5. A range name can contain the underscore (_) character.

T   F   6. In the Print dialog box, you can choose to print a selected range on a worksheet, a single worksheet, or all of the worksheets in the workbook.

Multiple Choice

1. Which of the following is *not* an option in the Arrange Windows dialog box?
   a. Scaled
   b. Horizontal
   c. Vertical
   d. Tiled

2. What file extension does a workspace have?
   a. xls
   b. xlt
   c. xlw
   d. wsp

3. What character identifies a cell reference as being absolute?
   a. !
   b. #
   c. $
   d. &

4. Which of the following is *not* an acceptable range name?
   a. 1st Qtr
   b. 1stQtr
   c. 1st_Qtr
   d. 1stQtr.

Short Answer

1. How do you print a selected area of a worksheet in Excel?

2. If you had two workbooks open in separate windows, how could you tile them in the same window?

3. How do you print an entire workbook in Excel?

4. How do you link two workbooks?

5. How do you create a workspace?

6. How would you create a named range called WinterTime for the range C8:G12?

On Your Own

◆ **Open Pledges from the Excel Expert Practice/Lesson01 folder.**

Exercise 1

Create a new window, and display the windows in the tiled arrangement. In one window, display the sheet named Worksheet; in the other window, display the worksheet named Chart.

◆ **Close Pledges.**

◆ **Open Summer Sales Comparing Performers and Employee History Bonus from the Excel Expert Practice/Lesson01 folder.**

Exercise 2

Create a workspace for these two workbooks, and name it **Performance Review**. Arrange the workbook windows so that you can see both at the same time. Close the workbooks, and then open the workspace.

◆ **Close Summer Sales Comparing Performers and Employee History Bonus.**

◆ **Open BudgetAW and SalesSummer from the Excel Expert Practice/Lesson01 folder.**

Exercise 3

You need to determine whether your sales are keeping pace with the normal budget for a month—whether you are making a profit or losing money. Arrange the BudgetAW and SalesSummer workbooks so that you can see the data in both of them. In the SalesSummer workbook, create a formula in cell C12 to determine the total sales. In the BudgetAW workbook create a formula that takes the total budgeted expenses for the month of June, divides it by four (approximately four weeks in a month), and subtracts that amount from the total sales calculated in the SalesSummer workbook.

◆ **Close BudgetAW and SalesSummer.**

One Step Further

Exercise 1

Is it possible to use a named range in a three-dimensional reference? If so, how would this appear in a formula?

◆ **Open Restaurant Conference from the Excel Expert Practice/Lesson01 folder.**

Exercise 2

Using the data provided in the worksheet, devise a lookup function to determine whether the restaurant employees listed can attend the conference.

◆ **Close Restaurant Conference.**

LESSON 2

Importing and Exporting Data

After completing this lesson, you will be able to:

✔ *Import data from text files.*
✔ *Import data from other programs.*
✔ *Import a table from an HTML file.*
✔ *Export Excel data to other programs.*

KEY TERMS

- export
- Hypertext Markup Language (HTML)
- import
- import filters
- object
- tab-delimited

Sharing Data Between Excel and Other Office Programs

Microsoft Excel is a versatile program, enabling you to import data from another program so that you can format and manipulate it just like you do the raw data you enter directly in a workbook. To **import** data means to bring data from another program, such as Microsoft Word, into an Excel workbook. For example, the sales manager at Adventure Works created a Word table that contains sales data in row-and-column format. Because several of the sales manager's coworkers do not use Excel, it made sense to create the sales table in Word—a program more familiar to his coworkers. However, he now wants to add formulas so that he can forecast sales. He knows that adding formulas is easier to do in Excel, so he imports the Word table into an Excel worksheet.

You also may need to **export** Excel data, which means to save Excel data in another format—such as a Word table or an Access database table. Suppose the sales manager at Adventure Works added formulas to his sales worksheet in Excel to provide the forecasting data that he wanted to view. Now he wants to return the sales data to its original Word table format so that his coworkers can read the data more easily. In Excel, performing importing and exporting operations is easy to do.

IMPORTANT

Before you can use the practice files in this lesson, you must install them from the book's companion CD to their default location. For additional information on how to find and open files used in this book, see the "Using the CD-ROM" section at the beginning of this book.

Importing Data

THE BOTTOM LINE

Importing data gives you the flexibility to incorporate existing data in a workbook, thus eliminating the time and effort needed to create the data or object from scratch.

When you want to use data created in other programs in an Excel worksheet, you can copy and paste the data into your worksheet or you can import the data as a file. For example, you might want a logo created in a graphics program to appear in the header of all of the worksheets in your workbooks, or you might want to pull a table from a database file so that you can use Excel's advanced calculation and data analysis tools on it.

Excel includes several **import filters** that can be used to open files created in other programs so that you can view the file content in Excel. You can import text files, including Word documents and other word processor and text formats, or files created in Lotus 1-2-3, Microsoft Works, Quattro Pro, dBASE, and several other programs. When you import a file created in another program, you may lose some of the formatting that was provided in the originating program; however, you can easily reformat the data in Excel.

When you import a file created by a different program, Excel displays the data in a worksheet, but it does not convert the file to Excel format. After you import a file, you can save it as an Excel worksheet or you can make changes and save it using the original format.

Importing Data from Text Files

When you import data from a text file, you get the best results if the data is already in a row-and-column format. For example, if the text to be imported is in a Word file, it is easiest to import the text when it is formatted as a table or with tabs that separate the text into columns. However, if you import text that is not already in row-and-column format, you can still format the data in Excel after the text has been imported.

When you use Excel to open a text file, Excel detects that the file is not in worksheet format and starts the Text Import Wizard. The wizard walks you through the steps required to import the file. Often the wizard will detect the current format of the text automatically, in which case you need only click the Next button to let the wizard proceed on its own. If the wizard cannot detect the current format of the text, you will need to specify the format and other options as you work through the wizard.

◆ **To complete the procedures in this lesson, you must use the files Bonus.txt, AdventureWorks.bmp, Guests.doc, Guests.mdb, Orders.dbf, Exchange Rates.xls, Current_Exchange_Rates.htm, and Reservations.xls in the Lesson02 folder in the Excel Expert Practice folder located on your hard disk.**

◆ **Start Excel.**

Import a text file

In this exercise, you import a text file containing information about bonuses into an Excel worksheet.

1 **Click cell C4.**

2 **On the Data menu, point to Import External Data, and click Import Data.**

The Select Data Source dialog box appears.

TIP

The Bonus file is a tab-delimited text file. You can accept all of the defaults in the first dialog box of the Text Import Wizard.

3 **Navigate to the Lesson02 folder in the Excel Expert Practice folder on your hard disk, and double-click Bonus.txt.**

The Text Import Wizard appears.

FIGURE 2-1

Text Import Wizard – Step 1 of 3 dialog box

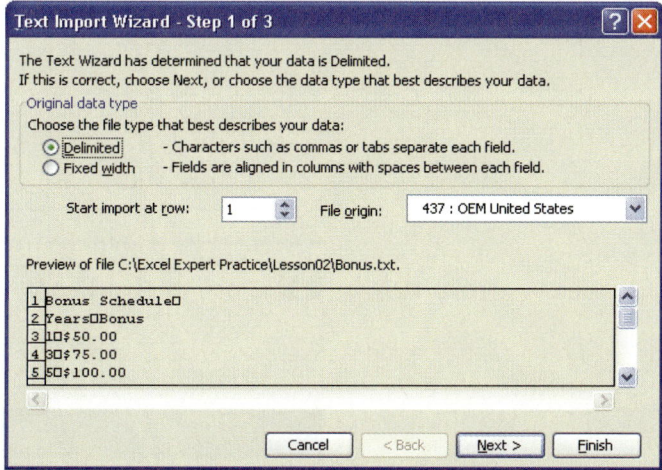

IMPORTANT

If a text file you want to import is not a **tab-delimited** file—that is, it was not prepared using tabs to separate data into rows and columns—you must select other options in the Text Import Wizard. If you want a different cell than the one you initially selected to be the location of the top left corner of your data, the wizard gives you an opportunity to change the starting cell.

4 **Click Next two times, and click the Finish button to complete the wizard.**

The Import Data dialog box appears.

FIGURE 2-2

Import Data dialog box

5 **Click OK to accept the defaults.**

The text file is placed on the worksheet and the External Data toolbar opens, as shown in Figure 2-3.

FIGURE 2-3

Imported data

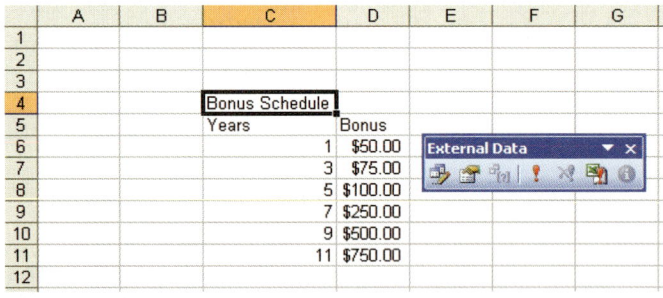

◆ **Close the workbook without saving it.**

QUICK REFERENCE ▼

Import text files to Excel

1 Click the cell where you want the top left corner of the data to be.

2 On the Data menu, point to Import External Data, and click Import Data.

3 Type the file name; or navigate to find the text file, and click it.

4 Click Import.

5 In the Original Data Type section, click either the Delimited or Fixed Width option.

6 Accept the default in the Start Import At Row box, which is 1, unless you want to change this to another row number. Look in the Preview pane at the bottom of the Text Import Wizard dialog box to ensure that the import looks correct.

7 Click Next.

8 In the Delimiters section, select the check boxes you want to apply to the data you are importing, click Next, and click Finish.

QUICK CHECK

Q. In a text file, what characters typically serve as delimiters?

A: **Characters such as commas or tabs typically serve as delimiters.**

Inserting Graphics

You can insert in a worksheet pictures that were created or saved in just about any graphics program. A picture is any drawing, photograph, or other artwork saved in an electronic format. Excel provides graphics filters that allow you to insert pictures by using the Insert menu. You can't format an object the way you format text and values in cells. However, you do have some formatting options available in Excel; you can move and resize an object as well.

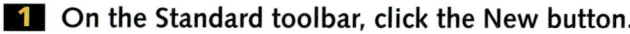

Insert a graphic

In this exercise, you insert a graphic to serve as the title logo for your worksheet and format and resize it.

1 On the Standard toolbar, click the New button.

Excel displays a blank worksheet.

ANOTHER METHOD

- On the File menu, select New, and click Blank Workbook.
- Press Ctrl+N.

2 On the Insert menu, point to Picture, and click From File.

The Insert Picture dialog box appears.

3 Navigate to the Lesson02 folder in the Excel Expert Practice folder, select the AdventureWorks.bmp file, and click Insert.

The logo is inserted in the worksheet and the Picture toolbar opens, as shown in Figure 2-4.

FIGURE 2-4

Importing a graphics file

Formatting and Resizing Graphics

4 Drag the object to a location in the approximate range C1:H11.

5 Resize the graphic by dragging its sizing handles so that it fits in the approximate range C1:F8.

CHECK THIS OUT ▼

Adding Objects to a Worksheet
You can insert an object created in many different types of programs by using the Object command on Excel's Insert menu. For example, you can insert an entire document created in Microsoft Word or slides from a Microsoft PowerPoint presentation. You can even insert sound and video clips. When you insert an **object**, it becomes embedded in the Excel file. To edit the object, you double-click it to open it in the program in which it was created.

6 On the Picture toolbar, click the Line Style button, and select 1 pt.

A border appears around the logo, as shown in Figure 2-5.

FIGURE 2-5

Formatting a graphic

7 Save the workbook as AW Guest List.

◆ Leave the workbook open for the next exercise.

QUICK REFERENCE ▼

Insert a picture

1 On the Insert menu, point to Picture, and click From File.
2 In the Insert Picture dialog box, select the file you want, and then click Insert.

Edit a picture

1 Move the picture by dragging it.
2 Resize the picture by dragging one of its handles.
3 Format a picture by using options on the Picture toolbar.

Copying Content from Word Documents

If you work regularly in Microsoft Word or another word-processing program, you might find it easier to copy and paste data from the program to Excel rather than import a text file. For example, if you have a Word document and an Excel workbook open at the same time, you can simply copy and paste from one window to the other without having to go through the steps of the Text Import Wizard.

As with the Text Import Wizard, though, the data you copy from a Word document looks best pasted in the worksheet when it's already set up in a row-and-column format. The Copy and Paste features work the same in Word as they do in Excel.

Copy data from a Word document

In this exercise, you copy and paste text from a Microsoft Word document.

1 Open Windows Explorer.

IMPORTANT

You must open Windows Explorer, My Computer, or Microsoft Word to access the Guests.doc file—you can't access it from Excel.

2 In Windows Explorer, navigate to the Excel Expert Practice folder. In the Lesson02 folder, double-click Guests.doc.

3 On the Table menu in Word, point to Select, and click Table. On the Edit menu, click Copy.

ANOTHER METHOD

- Click the Copy button on the Standard toolbar.
- Press Ctrl+C.

4 Close Microsoft Word.

5 On the taskbar, click the Microsoft Excel button to make Excel the active window, and click cell D11.

6 On the Edit menu, click Paste.

The table you copied from Word appears, with the top left corner in cell D11.

ANOTHER METHOD

- Click the Paste button on the Standard toolbar.
- Press Ctrl+V.

7 If necessary, select the range D11:E17 (the table). On the Format menu, point to Column, and click AutoFit Selection.

The columns are widened so that each column can display its longest entry.

FIGURE 2-6

Data copied from Word

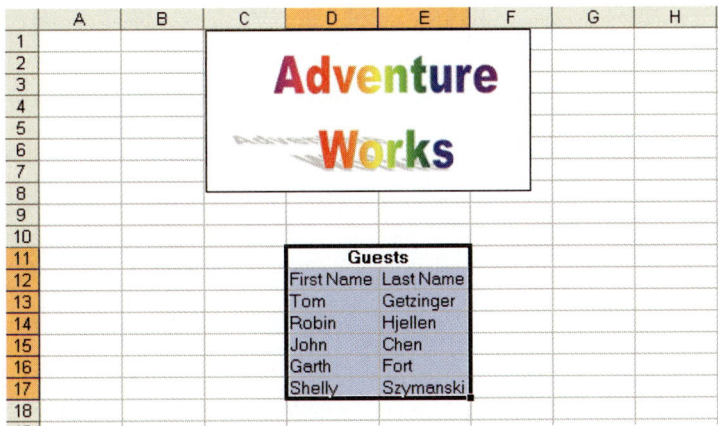

QUICK CHECK

Q. How do you copy data to a Word document?

A: **Select the data you want to copy, and click the Copy button on Word's Standard toolbar; or click Copy on Word's Edit menu.**

Locating and Retrieving Data from a Database

QUICK REFERENCE ▼

Copy data from other programs into Excel

1 In the other program, select and copy the data.

2 Display the Excel workbook window, and click the cell where you want the top left corner of the data to appear.

3 On the Edit menu, click Paste, or click the Paste button on the Standard toolbar.

Importing Data from a Database

Databases are designed to store information, and they often contain numerous tables, which, in turn, contain many records. The structure of a database table is very similar to the row-and-column format of an Excel worksheet, making it conducive to importing to a workbook file. Once the table data is imported, you can use Excel's powerful calculating and data analysis tools to manipulate and interpret it in different ways.

Import database data

In this exercise, you import data from an Access database table and you open a dBASE file in Excel that contains an inventory of items for Adventure Works guest rooms.

1 Click cell D20.

2 On the Data menu, point to Import External Data, and click New Database Query.

The Choose Data Source dialog box opens.

IMPORTANT

You may need to install Microsoft Query if this was not included in the original installation. If you are unable to install Microsoft Query, you can achieve the same results by opening the Guest table in the database, selecting all of the records, and copying and pasting them into the worksheet.

3 Select MS Access Database, and click OK.

The Select Database dialog box opens.

4 Use the Directories list, if necessary, to navigate to the Lesson02 folder in the Excel Expert Practice Folder. Select the Access database Guests.mdb in the left pane, and then click OK.

The Query Wizard-Choose Columns dialog box opens.

FIGURE 2-7

Query Wizard – Choose Columns dialog box

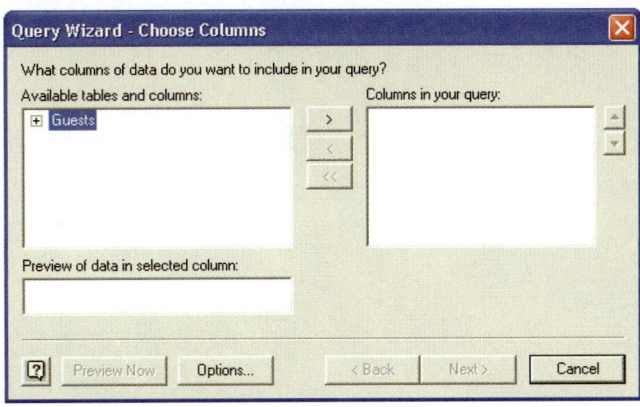

5 **Click the right-pointing select arrow to move all of the database columns into your query. Then click Next.**

The Query Wizard-Filter Data dialog box opens.

6 **In this case, you want to import all of the columns, so click Next to avoid any filtering of the data.**

The Query Wizard-Sort Order dialog box opens.

7 **You want to leave the data in the same order that it appears in the database, so click Next to avoid sorting the data.**

The Query Wizard-Finish dialog box opens.

8 **Select Return Data To Microsoft Excel, if necessary, and click Finish.**

The Import Data dialog box opens.

9 **Verify that Existing Worksheet is selected. The cell you selected before you began the import process is entered automatically. Click OK.**

The table you imported from Access appears, with the top left corner in cell D20, as shown in Figure 2-8.

FIGURE 2-8

Database table records imported to worksheet

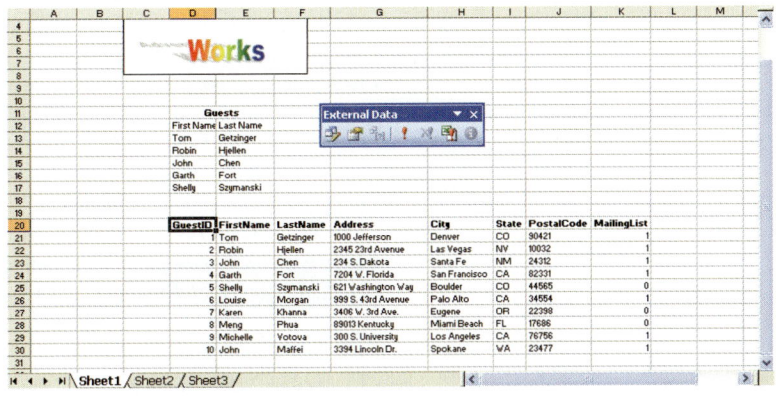

10 Resize the columns as necessary.

◆ Save AW Guest List, and then close it.

11 On the File menu, click Open.

Excel displays the Open dialog box.

12 Click the Files Of Type down arrow, scroll down, and click dBASE files (*.dbf).

The Open dialog box displays a list of dBASE files stored in the Lesson02 folder. In this case, only one file appears.

TIP

You also can import a dBASE file into a worksheet in a manner similar to that used to import an Access database.

---

13 Double-click Orders.dbf.

The file opens as a workbook in Excel.

FIGURE 2-9

Opening a dBASE file in a workbook

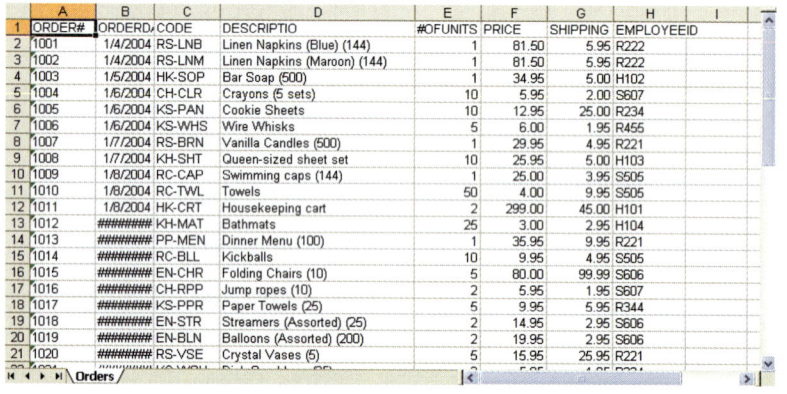

TROUBLESHOOTING

Notice that the original width of column B (ORDERDATE) is not fully displayed. You can easily correct this by widening the column.

◆ Save the workbook and then close it.

QUICK REFERENCE ▼

Import data from an Access table

1 On the Data menu, point to Import External Data, and click New Database Query.

2 In the Choose Data Source dialog box, select MS Access Database, and click OK.

3 In the Select Database dialog box, select the database file you want to import, and click OK.

4 Select the columns to include, determine if you want to filter and sort the data, and select the option to return the data to Excel in the Query Wizard dialog boxes. Then click Finish.

5 In the Import Data dialog box, click Existing Worksheet, and click OK.

Open a database file in Excel

1 In Excel, access the Open dialog box.

2 In the Files Of Type list box, click the database file type you want to open.

3 Double-click the database file you want to open.

Using XML Data Capabilities and Retrieving Web Data

Importing Data from an HTML File

With so much information available on the Internet, you might locate a useful **Hypertext Markup Language (HTML)** table while you're browsing the Web. If so, you can import the HTML table into a worksheet and use Excel's formatting, editing, and calculating tools on it. For example, the travel manager at Adventure Works needs to know exchange rates for foreign currency, which can be imported from a Web page in table format. Similarly, an investment manager can import a list of stocks and their current values in table format. You also can import a table from an HTML file located on your hard disk, on a network drive, or on an intranet. In Excel, the process of importing an entire Web page is similar to the process of importing a file from another program.

> **IMPORTANT**
>
> You will learn more about importing and exporting HTML and other Web files in Lesson 8, "Publishing Information on the Web," of this course.

◆ Open **Exchange Rates** from the Excel Expert Practice/Lesson02 folder.

Import data from a Web page

In this exercise, you import a table from a Web page to get exchange rate information.

1 Click cell C5.

2 On the Data menu, point to Import External Data, and click New Web Query.

The New Web Query dialog box appears.

TROUBLESHOOTING

If your hard disk drive letter is not C, replace the C in the file path with the appropriate letter.

3 In the Address box, type C:\Excel Expert Practice\Lesson02\ Current_Exchange_Rates.htm, and click the Go button.

The file appears in the New Web Query dialog box.

TIP

For the purposes of this exercise, an HTML file has been provided. To import a table from the Web, you simply type the URL in the Address box or click the list arrow next to the Address box, which will list the Web sites you have visited recently.

4 Click the yellow arrow box next to the table to select it.

The table is selected.

FIGURE 2-10

Selecting the table data

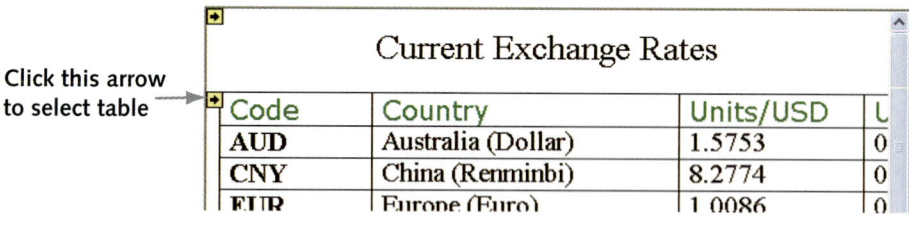

5 Click the Options button on the New Web Query toolbar.

The Web Query Options dialog box opens.

6 Select the Rich Text Formatting Only option, and click OK.

The New Web Query dialog box should look similar to that shown in Figure 2-11.

TIP

Use Rich Text Formatting when you want to maintain the formatting, but not the hyperlinks and merged cells. Click the None option when you don't want the data to be formatted, or click the Full HTML Formatting option when you want the HTML formatting to be preserved as much as possible.

FIGURE 2-11

New Web Query dialog box

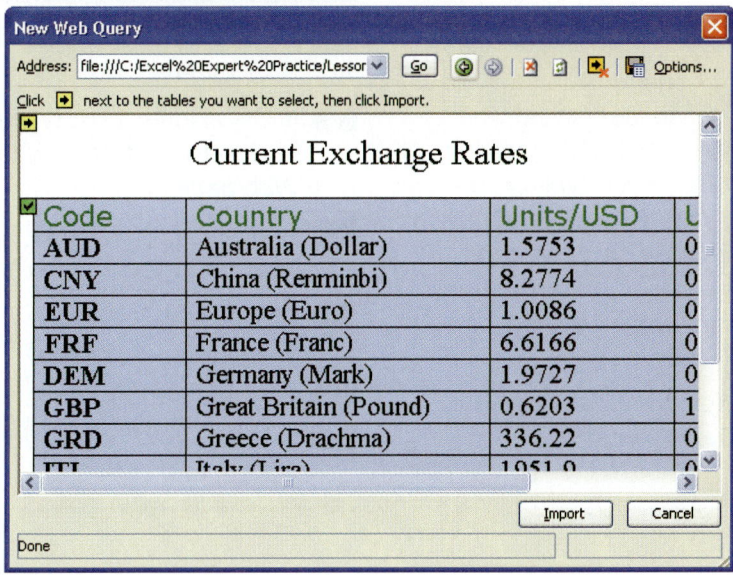

7 **Click Import.**

The Import Data dialog box appears, asking where you want to put the data, with the default being the cell you selected before you began the import process.

8 **Click the Existing Worksheet option, if necessary, and click OK.**

Excel retrieves the data from the HTML file and places it in the worksheet, following the instructions you provided. You can edit this data as you would any other data.

FIGURE 2-12

Data imported from an HTML file

◆ **Save and close Exchange Rates.**

QUICK REFERENCE ▼

Import HTML tables

1 On the Data menu, point to Import External Data, and click New Web Query.

2 In the Address box, type the name of the file, or click the Browse Web button to start your Web browser. Then, navigate to the desired Web page.

3 Click the yellow arrow to select the part of the Web page you want inserted into the worksheet.

4 Click the Options button to alter any formatting of the Web page data. Click OK to close the Web Query Options dialog box.

5 Click Import.

6 In the Import Data dialog box, select where you want the data to be placed, and click OK.

Exporting Excel Data to Other Programs

THE BOTTOM LINE

You can easily export worksheet data and charts to files created in other programs. This is an effective way to enhance a document or table with supporting data from Excel.

You can export data and charts from an Excel workbook to files in a variety of formats, including text, earlier versions of Excel, other spreadsheet formats, presentations, and database tables.

For example, the reservations manager at Adventure Works wants to keep a running list of room reservations in an Access database. The data already exists in Excel, so the Access database can be created by exporting the Excel data to an Access database table.

Export worksheet data

In this exercise, you export data from an Excel worksheet to an Access database table.

1 **Start Access, click Create A New File in the Open section of the Getting Started task pane, and click Blank Database in the New section of the New File task pane.**

The File New Database dialog box opens.

2 Click the Save In list arrow, and select the Excel Expert Practice/Lesson02 folder. Name the database **Reservations**, and click **Create**.

The Database window opens with the Tables object selected.

3 On the File menu, point to Get External Data, and click Import.

The Import dialog box opens.

4 Click the list arrow next to the Files Of Type text box, and select Microsoft Excel from the list.

5 If necessary, browse to the Lesson02 folder in the Excel Expert Practice folder, and select the Reservations workbook. Click Import.

The Import Spreadsheet Wizard opens with a sample of how the data will be imported.

FIGURE 2-13

Import Spreadsheet Wizard dialog box

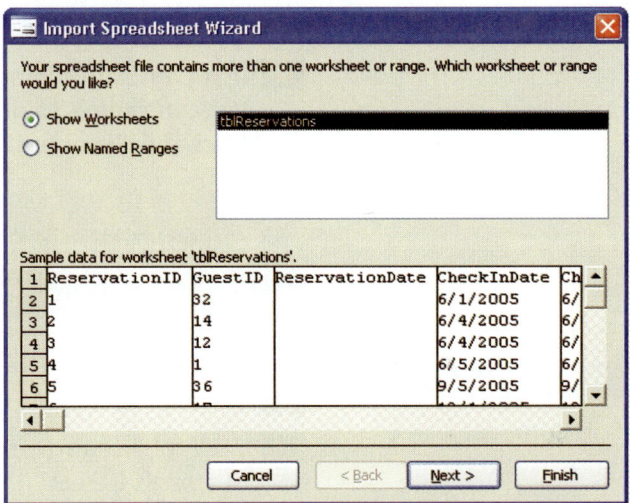

6 Click Next to accept the default configuration of the data.

7 Select the First Row Contains Column Headings check box, if necessary, and click Next.

8 Click the In A New Table option, if necessary, click Next three times to accept all of the default configurations, and then click the Finish button.

An information box appears when the wizard has finished the file.

9 In the Import Spreadsheet Wizard information box, click OK.

The data in the Excel worksheet is now a table in an Access database.

10 Double-click tblReservations to open the Access table containing the Excel data, as shown in Figure 2-14.

FIGURE 2-14

Excel data in a database table

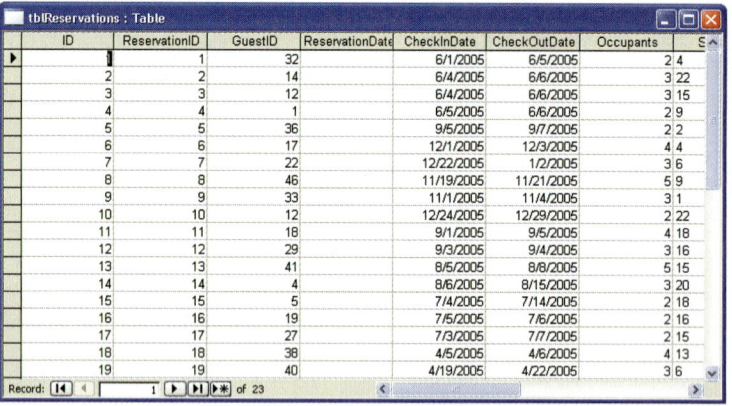

 11 Click the Close button in the top right corner of the Access window to close the database and the Access program.

◆ If you are continuing to other lessons, leave Excel open. If you are not continuing to other lessons, save and close all open workbooks. Click the Close button in the top right corner of the Excel window.

QUICK REFERENCE ▼

Export Excel data to an Access table

1 Open an Access database file.

2 On the File menu, point to Get External Data, and click Import.

3 Click the list arrow next to the Files Of Type text box, and select Microsoft Excel.

4 Browse to the folder that contains the Excel file to be imported, select the file, and click Import.

5 Make selections as appropriate in the Import Spreadsheet Wizard dialog boxes, and then click Finish.

6 Click OK in the Import Spreadsheet Wizard information box.

QUICK CHECK

Q. When you import a workbook file to an Access table, can you import column headings along with the raw data?

A: **Yes, you can import column headings along with the raw data.**

Key Points

✔ *Importing data gives you the flexibility to incorporate existing data in a workbook, thus eliminating the time and effort needed to create the data or object from scratch.*

✔ *You can import data from a text file using the Text Import Wizard. The wizard walks you through the steps required to import the file.*

✔ *You can insert in a worksheet pictures that were created or saved in a graphics program. A picture is any drawing, photograph, or other artwork saved in an electronic format.*

✔ *The structure of a database table is very similar to the row-and-column format of an Excel worksheet, making it conducive to importing to a workbook file, where you can apply Excel's advanced calculating and data analysis tools to the data.*

✔ *You can import a table from a Web page to a worksheet and then use Excel's formatting, editing, and calculating tools on it.*

✔ *You can easily export worksheet data and charts to files created in other programs. This is an effective way to enhance a document or table with supporting data from Excel.*

Quick Quiz

True/False

T F   1. To import data to a workbook means that you need to save Excel data in another format so that it can be used in a program other than Excel.

T F   2. Text files that you want to bring into Excel should be in a paragraph format with subheadings.

T F   3. You cannot resize or format graphics that you insert in a worksheet if they were created in a program other than Excel.

T F   4. You can easily copy a table in a Word document to an Excel worksheet.

T F   5. Database tables are set up in the row-and-column format that's similar to an Excel worksheet.

T F   6. You cannot calculate data you bring into Excel from a Web page.

T F   7. When you bring a table from an Access database into an Excel worksheet using the Query Wizard, you must import all of the table's columns and maintain the current sort order.

Multiple Choice

1. If you want to bring data from another program into an Excel workbook, which of the following would you do?
   a. import
   b. export
   c. report
   d. all of the above

2. A text file in which tabs are used to separate data into rows and columns is referred to as which of the following?
   a. tab-delimited
   b. tab-separated
   c. tab-aligned
   d. fixed-width

3. Which feature enables you to open files created in other programs so that you can view the file content in Excel?
   a. import screen
   b. import filter
   c. External Data Monitor
   d. AutoFilter

Short Answer

1. Why would you want to import data in another format into Excel?

2. How do you copy data from a Word document into Excel?

3. How do you import an Access database table to Excel using the Query Wizard?

4. What's the difference between importing and exporting data?

5. How do you import table data from a Web page to an Excel worksheet?

On Your Own

Exercise 1

Use the New Web Query feature to import the Dow Jones Industrial Average Index table on the following Web page:

http://moneycentral.msn.com/scripts/webquote.dll?iPage=qd&Symbol=%24INDU

Import the table using the Rich Text Formatting option, and name the workbook **DowJonesQuotes**.

Exercise 2

Open a blank workbook and name it **Bonuses**. Click cell A1, and use the Text Import Wizard to import Bonus.txt from the Excel Expert Practice/Lesson02 folder. Delete row 1. Start Access, and create a new database file named **Personnel**. Use Access's Import Spreadsheet Wizard to import the Bonuses workbook as a database table. Accept the default selections in the Wizard, and name the new table **Bonuses**.

Exercise 3

Open a blank workbook. Insert a picture from Clip Art that represents outdoor activities. Use the options on the Picture toolbar to edit and format the clip art as desired.

One Step Further

Exercise 1

In this lesson, you explored importing tab-delimited text into Excel. Is it possible to save data in an Excel worksheet as a tab-delimited text file? If so, how is this done?

Exercise 2

In this lesson, you opened the Orders.dbf file through Excel. If you wanted, instead, to import the Orders.dbf file into an existing worksheet, how would you perform this operation?

LESSON 3

Creating and Using Excel Lists

After completing this lesson, you will be able to:

✔ *Create and format a list.*
✔ *Modify a list using a data form.*
✔ *Search for records using a data form.*
✔ *Sort records.*
✔ *Set up a list filter.*
✔ *Use database functions on a list.*

KEY TERMS

- criteria range
- data form
- field
- filter
- headers
- list
- record

To take advantage of Excel's data manipulation features, you can structure the data in your worksheet into a list. A **list** is an organized collection of data from which you can quickly access any individual piece of information. A telephone directory is an example of a list: it contains data for a group of individuals arranged alphabetically by last name. Other examples of lists include personnel listings, customer account listings, and inventory control sheets. You can create all of these lists and more using Excel.

In this lesson, you create a list; add, update, delete, and sort records; and extract specific data from the list.

IMPORTANT

Before you can use the practice files in this lesson, you must install them from the book's companion CD to their default location. For additional information on how to find and open files used in this book, see the "Using the CD-ROM" section at the beginning of this book.

Working with Lists

Performing Calculations on Filtered Data

THE BOTTOM LINE

Setting up a range as a data list enables you to perform many useful functions on it, such as sorting entries so that they're in a more meaningful order, searching for entries that meet certain criteria, and filtering out entries so that you can focus on important data or on data that has special significance.

Lists in Excel are made up of two components: fields and records. A **field** contains one piece of information, such as a person's name or a part number, while a **record** contains all related fields for each person or item on the list.

Creating and Formatting a List

In a list, each record appears in a separate row and each field within a record appears in a separate column. In general, the **headers** of a list appear in the first row of the list, as shown in Figure 3-1.

FIGURE 3-1

Structure of a list

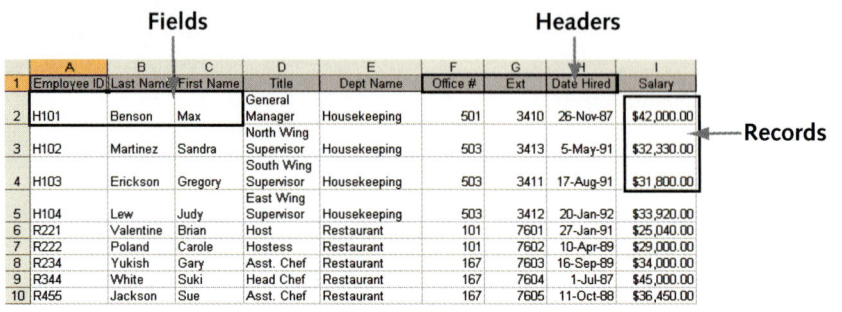

These headers should be formatted so that they stand out from the data below them. You can format headers by using different combinations of fonts, alignments, formats, patterns, borders, and capitalization styles. Avoid blank rows and columns in lists, as they can make it difficult for Excel to detect and select the list. You can use cell borders to insert lines below the headers, rather than adding blank rows. Similarly, do not type extra spaces in a cell to move the data in the cell to the right or to the left. Instead, set alignment options on the cell and indent the text.

◆ **To complete the procedures in this lesson, you must use the files Employees.xls and Orders.xls in the Lesson03 folder in the Excel Expert Practice folder located on your hard disk.**

◆ **Start Excel.**

Create and format a list

In this exercise, you create a list that holds information about newsletter subscribers.

1 **If necessary, close the Getting Started task pane. In the range A5:H5, type these headers in order:**

Last Name
First Name
Address
City
State
Zip
Sub Date
Exp Date

2 Click a cell in column A. On the Format menu, point to Column, and click Width.

3 In the Column width box, type 12, and click OK.

ANOTHER METHOD

Drag the right edge (column selector) of column A to adjust the width. Excel displays the width in a ScreenTip as you drag.

4 Repeat steps 2 and 3 for each of the other columns, using these widths:

Column B: 12
Column C: 17
Column D: 13
Column E: 5
Column F: 7
Column G: 9
Column H: 9

5 Select the range A5:H5, and click the Bold button, the Italic button, and the Center button, all on the Formatting toolbar.

The formatting is applied to the selected cells, and your worksheet should look like that shown in Figure 3-2.

FIGURE 3-2

Creating a list

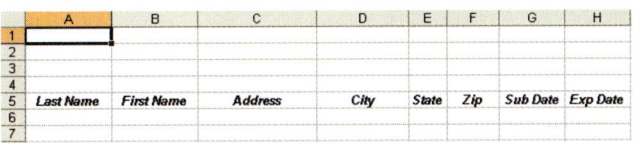

	A	B	C	D	E	F	G	H
1								
2								
3								
4								
5	Last Name	First Name	Address	City	State	Zip	Sub Date	Exp Date
6								
7								

6 Type the following records in cells A6:G8:

Jennings	Daniel	627 N. 5th Ave.	San Francisco	CA	94107	5/1/03
Da Silva	Anna	2470 1st Place	Bellevue	WA	98007	12/1/03
Fredericks	Barry	35 Mercer Way	Seattle	WA	98115	2/1/02

TIP

If necessary, change the date format in the range G6:G8 to match the format of the dates you typed in step 6.

7 Select the range A6:H8, and click the Increase Indent button on the Formatting toolbar.

8 Select the range A5:H5, click the down arrow on the Borders button, and click the Thick Box Border in the bottom right corner. Click any cell in the worksheet.

Your worksheet should look similar to Figure 3-3.

FIGURE 3-3

Formatted list

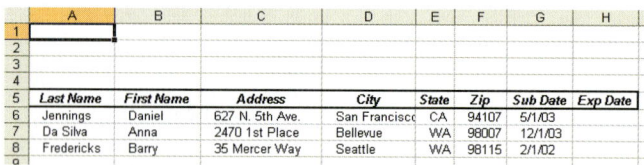

	Last Name	First Name	Address	City	State	Zip	Sub Date	Exp Date
6	Jennings	Daniel	627 N. 5th Ave.	San Francisco	CA	94107	5/1/03	
7	Da Silva	Anna	2470 1st Place	Bellevue	WA	98007	12/1/03	
8	Fredericks	Barry	35 Mercer Way	Seattle	WA	98115	2/1/02	

9 On the File menu, click Save As, and save the workbook as **Subscribers**.

ANOTHER METHOD

- Click the Save button, and enter the name for the new workbook in the Save As dialog box.
- Press Ctrl+S, and enter the name for the new workbook in the Save As dialog box.

◆ Keep the workbook open for the next exercise.

QUICK CHECK

Q. What is the difference between a field and a record?

A: A field contains one piece of information for an item or a person in a list, while a record contains all of the re-lated fields for each item or person in the list.

QUICK REFERENCE ▼

Create a list

1 Enter the field names (column labels) in adjacent columns of a worksheet.

2 Adjust the column width, as necessary, so that all text is visible.

3 Format the column labels.

4 Enter the data for a record in the row below the headers, pressing Tab to move from field to field in the record.

5 Continue to enter the records in adjacent rows below the field names.

Using a Data Form to Modify a List

You can edit list records using the same commands and toolbar buttons you use to edit other data. Some worksheet commands, such as the Fill command, are especially useful in editing lists. The Fill command allows you to quickly copy data and formulas in a list. You also can display the records on the list in a data form window. A **data form** displays the records in the list one record at a time, allowing for easy manipulation.

Use a data form

In this exercise, you display a data form, navigate using the data form, and edit records using the data form.

1 **Click cell H6, type =G6+731, and press Enter.**

The expiration date for a two-year subscription appears in cell H6.

2 **Click cell H6, click the Fill handle, and drag down to fill cells H7 and H8.**

The formula is copied to the cells.

3 **Click cell A6, and on the Data menu, click Form.**

A data form is displayed.

FIGURE 3-4

Data form

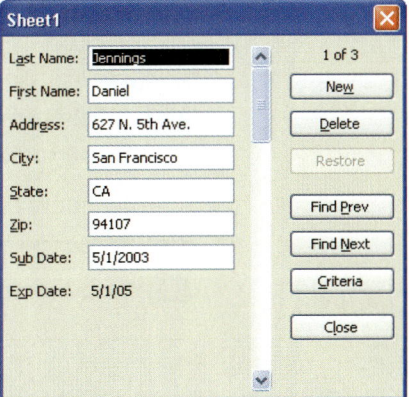

4 **Click the Find Next button to display the second record on the list. Click the down scroll arrow to display the next record, and click the up scroll arrow to display the previous record.**

5 **Click the Find Next or Find Prev button as necessary to display the record for Daniel Jennings.**

6 **Select the address in the Address field, and type 895 Market St.**

The original address is replaced with the new one.

7 **Select the current entry in the Zip field, and type 94103.**

The address and Zip Code are updated.

8 **Click the New button to add a record to the list.**

A blank form is displayed.

FIGURE 3-5

Blank data form

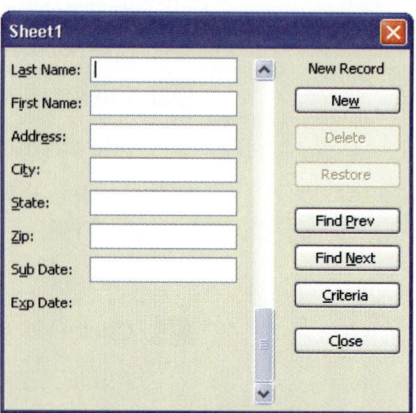

9 Type the following information in the blank form, pressing Tab to move from field to field, and then press Enter.

Smith   Jerry   1550 Park Ave.   Portland   OR   97214   5/01/02

10 Click Find Prev to display the record in the data form again. Click Close to exit the form.

The new record appears in the list.

◆ Save Subscribers, and then close the workbook.

QUICK REFERENCE ▼

Display a data form

1 Click any cell in the database.
2 On the Data menu, click Form.

Add a record to the data form

1 Click any cell in the database.
2 On the Data menu, click Form.
3 Click the New button.
4 Type information in each field. Press Tab to move from field to field.
5 Click the Close button.

Searching for Records

THE BOTTOM LINE

You can search a list of records quickly to find those that meet specified criteria by using a list's search tools.

A list can contain hundreds or even thousands of records. You can locate specific records in a list quickly by entering selection criteria in the data form. Selection criteria define the criteria for which Excel will be searching. You can enter single or multiple criteria into the search fields and then use the Find Next and Find Prev buttons in the data form window to move to records that match the specified criteria.

Use the following operators to locate exact matches or a range of values:

Operator	Indicates
=	equal to
<>	not equal to
>=	greater than or equal to
>	greater than
<=	less than or equal to
<	less than

If you choose labels as your search criteria, such as the name of a department, you can use wildcard characters (* and ?) in place of label characters to match multiple records, as shown in the following table. The * wildcard character substitutes for any number of characters, and the ? wildcard character substitutes for a single character.

Wildcard	Match
Liz	Liz, Lizzy, Lizzie, Liza, Eliza, Elizabeth
Ric?	Rick, Rich

◆ **Open Employees from the Excel Expert Practice/Lesson03 folder.**

Search a list

In this exercise, you search for a particular record.

1 On the Data menu, click Form.

The data form window opens, with the name of the current sheet (AW approved) displayed in its title bar.

2 Click the Criteria button to display the Criteria data form, as shown in Figure 3-6.

FIGURE 3-6

Criteria data form

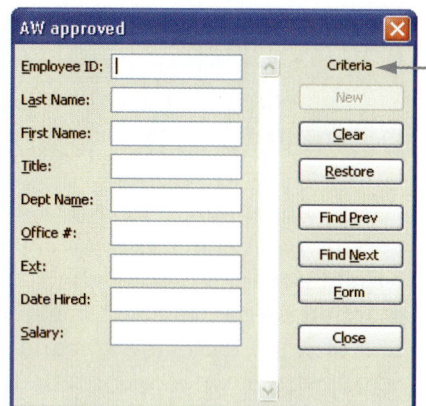

Indicates that criteria for a search will be entered in the data form

3 In the Last Name box, type Chen, and press Enter.

The record for John Chen appears in the data form window.

4 Click the Find Next button.

Excel indicates that no other records match the criteria.

5 Click the Criteria button again, and then click the Clear button.

The Criteria data form is cleared of the existing criteria.

6 In the Employee ID box, type S???, and press Enter.

The record for John Chen, whose Employee ID begins with S, appears in the data form. Notice that this record is 14 of 14.

7 Click the Find Prev button to display other records in which the Employee ID begins with S.

8 Click the Close button to close the data form.

◆ Leave the workbook open for the next exercise.

QUICK REFERENCE ▼

Search for records

1 Click any cell in the database.

2 On the Data menu, click Form.

3 Click the Criteria button.

4 Type the selection criteria.

5 Click Find Next or Find Prev.

Sorting Records

THE BOTTOM LINE

The order in which you enter data is not necessarily the most meaningful order for interpreting or analyzing it. Rearranging the order of records, or sorting them, lets you quickly and easily identify trends and generate forecasts and predictions.

After setting up a list, you might want to change the way your records are arranged. For example, you might want to view a list of employees alphabetically or according to their salaries, with the highest-paid person at the top of the list.

You use the Sort command on the Data menu to organize data in a list according to specific criteria. You can sort a list by up to three fields. When sorting records in a list, each row is considered a single entity, so the entire record moves according to where its corresponding cell in the specified sort field(s) is placed in the reordered list.

You can sort the information in a list in ascending or descending order. When the field contains numeric entries, those entries are arranged from smallest to largest in an ascending sort and from largest to smallest in a descending sort. When the field contains text entries, those entries are arranged alphabetically from A to Z in an ascending sort and from Z to A in a descending sort. Some types of data entries, such as street names, can contain numbers or text. If you sort a column such as this, numbers will precede text in an ascending sort and follow text in a descending sort. In this case, *5th Avenue* would appear above *Park Avenue* in an ascending sort. By default, Excel does not distinguish between uppercase and lowercase letters when performing a sorting operation.

TIP

After you sort a list, you can use the Undo command to return the list to its previous order.

Sort records

In this exercise, you sort the records in a list.

1 Click any cell in the list, and on the Data menu, click Sort.

The Sort dialog box appears.

2 In the Sort By box, click the down arrow, and click Last Name. Click the Ascending option, if necessary.

3 Click OK.

The list is sorted in alphabetical order by last name.

FIGURE 3-7

Sorting by the Last Name field

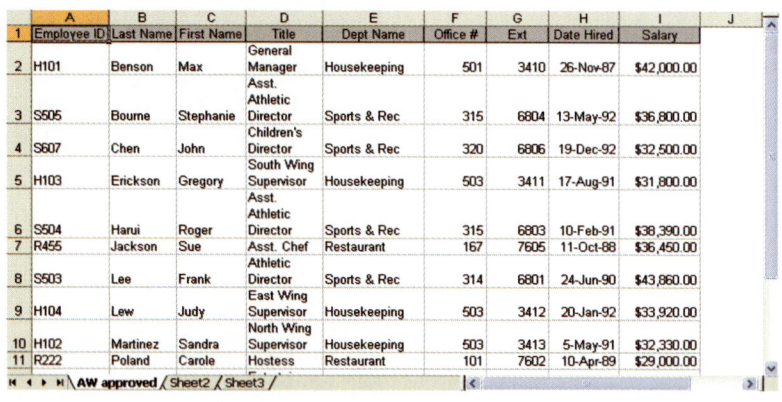

4 **On the Data menu, click Sort.**

5 **In the Sort By box, click the down arrow, click Dept Name, and click the Ascending option. Click the down arrow on the first Then By box, click Salary, and click the Descending option.**

The Sort dialog box looks like that shown in Figure 3-8.

FIGURE 3-8

Specifying two sort fields

6 **Click OK.**

The list is sorted alphabetically by department name and then according to the salary of employees, with the highest-paid person within each department listed first.

FIGURE 3-9

Sorting by two fields

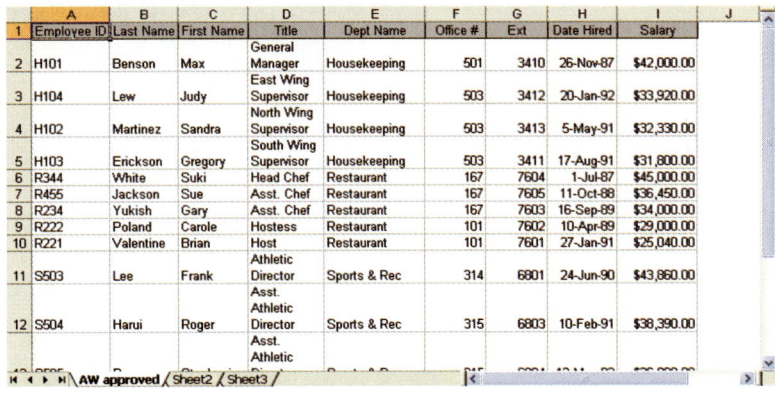

	A	B	C	D	E	F	G	H	I	J
1	Employee ID	Last Name	First Name	Title	Dept Name	Office #	Ext	Date Hired	Salary	
2	H101	Benson	Max	General Manager	Housekeeping	501	3410	26-Nov-87	$42,000.00	
3	H104	Lew	Judy	East Wing Supervisor	Housekeeping	503	3412	20-Jan-92	$33,920.00	
4	H102	Martinez	Sandra	North Wing Supervisor	Housekeeping	503	3413	5-May-91	$32,330.00	
5	H103	Erickson	Gregory	South Wing Supervisor	Housekeeping	503	3411	17-Aug-91	$31,800.00	
6	R344	White	Suki	Head Chef	Restaurant	167	7604	1-Jul-87	$45,000.00	
7	R455	Jackson	Sue	Asst. Chef	Restaurant	167	7605	11-Oct-88	$36,450.00	
8	R234	Yukish	Gary	Asst. Chef	Restaurant	167	7603	16-Sep-89	$34,000.00	
9	R222	Poland	Carole	Hostess	Restaurant	101	7602	10-Apr-89	$29,000.00	
10	R221	Valentine	Brian	Host	Restaurant	101	7601	27-Jan-91	$25,040.00	
11	S503	Lee	Frank	Athletic Director	Sports & Rec	314	6801	24-Jun-90	$43,860.00	
12	S504	Harui	Roger	Asst. Athletic Director	Sports & Rec	315	6803	10-Feb-91	$38,390.00	

AW approved / Sheet2 / Sheet3 /

7 **Click the Undo button on the Standard toolbar twice.**

The records in the list are returned to their original order.

◆ **Leave the workbook open for the next exercise.**

QUICK CHECK

Q. Are numeric entries in a field arranged in ascending order or descending order if they are ordered from smallest to largest?

A: **They are arranged in ascending order.**

QUICK REFERENCE ▼

Sort a list

1 Click any cell in the list.

2 On the Data menu, click Sort.

3 Click the Sort By down arrow.

4 Click the field and order by which to sort.

5 Specify a second and a third sort field, if desired.

6 Click OK.

Setting Up a List Filter

Limiting the Data that Appears on the Screen

THE BOTTOM LINE

You can display a subset of records that meet certain criteria by applying a filter to data. A filter temporarily hides the records that don't meet the criteria, which enables you to focus on the data that's pertinent to your review or analysis.

As described earlier in this lesson, you can locate individual records on a list using the data form window. Another method for locating information is by filtering a list. When you use a **filter** on a list, you locate and display specific data directly in the list. You can then print, format, chart, or total that data only, without having to include the other records in the list. You can define two types of filters for a list: an AutoFilter and an Advanced Filter.

Defining a List

You can further define a list using the List command on the Data menu. On the Data menu, point to List, and then click Create List. When you create a list in this manner, the list range is outlined in a dark blue border and the AutoFilter feature is automatically activated. A blank row with an asterisk appears in the list, where you can insert a new record and have it added to the list automatically. This eliminates the need to reset your list range when running filters. You can change the size of the list easily by dragging the resize handle, which is located in the bottom right corner of the blue list border. In addition, you can add a total row to your list. When you click a cell in the total row, a list arrow appears that, when clicked, displays a menu of functions (such as Sum, Average, and Count) that you can perform on the selected field.

> **TIP**
>
> Excel's filtering feature also is discussed in Lesson 5, "Organizing Worksheets and Window Display," in the *Microsoft Excel 2003 Step-by-Step Courseware Core Skills*.

Using AutoFilter

The AutoFilter feature "automates" the filtering process. You turn this feature on by selecting AutoFilter on the Data menu. A down arrow button appears in each cell in the list that Excel recognizes as a column label. Clicking the down arrow on a column label cell displays the AutoFilter menu for that column, as shown in Figure 3-10.

FIGURE 3-10

AutoFilter menu

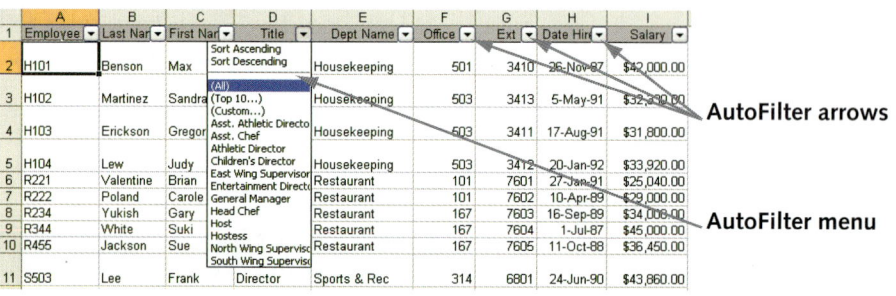

> **IMPORTANT**
>
> When you turn on filtering, Excel treats the cells in the active cell's column as a range. To ensure that the filtering works properly, you should add a label to the column you want to filter.

The AutoFilter menu contains options for sorting, for finding the top 10 values in the column, for creating a custom filter that's based on more complex criteria, and for redisplaying all values in the column (that is, removing the filter). The rest of the items on the menu are the unique values in the column—clicking one of those values displays the record or records containing that value.

The Top 10 option on the AutoFilter menu doesn't just limit the display to the top 10 values. Instead, it opens the Top 10 AutoFilter dialog box. From within this dialog box, you can choose whether to show values from the top or bottom of the list, define the number of items you want to see, or display the number of items or the percentage of items to be shown when the filter is applied. For example, you can find your top 10 salespeople or identify the top 5 percent of your customers.

With the Custom option, you can further define the criteria for which you're searching. For instance, you can define a rule that only days with total sales of less than $2,500 should be shown in your worksheet. With those results in front of you, you might be able to determine whether the weather or another factor resulted in slower business on those days.

Apply filters

In this exercise, you perform AutoFilter operations on a list.

1 On the Data menu, point to Filter, and click AutoFilter.

Down arrows appear to the right of each column label.

2 Click the Dept Name down arrow, and click Housekeeping.

The list appears filtered and displays only the records that contain *Housekeeping* in the Dept Name field.

FIGURE 3-11

Filtered list

3 Click the Dept Name down arrow, and click (All).

The hidden rows reappear.

4 Click the Dept Name down arrow, and click (Custom...).

The Custom AutoFilter dialog box appears.

5 Click the top right down arrow, and click Housekeeping; then click the Or button. Click the bottom left down arrow, and click equals; then click the bottom right down arrow, and click Restaurant.

You will search for records that contain Housekeeping *or* Restaurant in the Dept Name field, as shown in Figure 3-12.

FIGURE 3-12

Custom AutoFilter dialog box

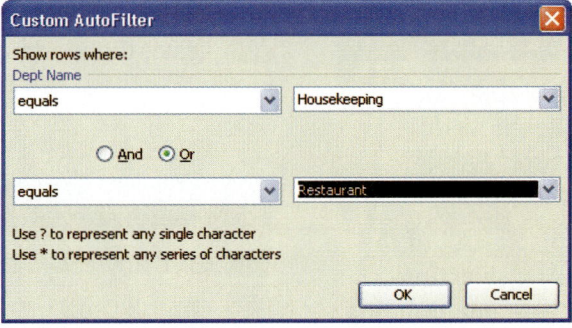

6 Click OK.

The list now displays only the records that meet the criteria specified.

FIGURE 3-13

Applying a custom filter

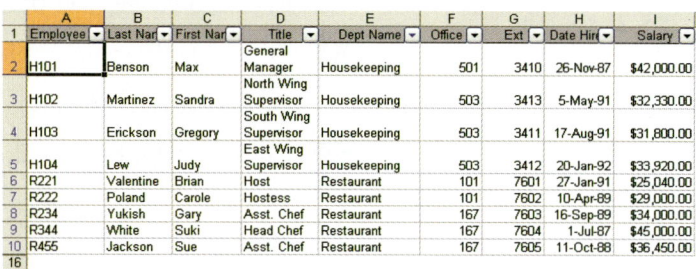

7 **Click the Salary down arrow, and click (Custom...) on the AutoFilter menu.**

The Custom AutoFilter dialog box appears.

8 **Click the top left down arrow, click "is less than," and click OK.**

9 **In the top right box, type 30000, and click OK.**

The list is filtered further and displays only those employees in the Housekeeping or Restaurant departments with salaries less than $30,000.

FIGURE 3-14

Further defining a filter

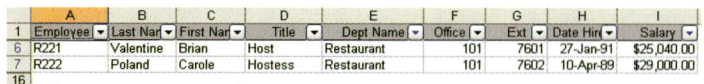

10 **On the Data menu, point to Filter, and click Show All.**

All of the records are redisplayed.

11 **On the Data menu, point to Filter, and click AutoFilter.**

AutoFilter is turned off.

◆ **Leave the workbook open for the next exercise.**

QUICK REFERENCE ▼

Use AutoFilter

1 Click any cell in the database.

2 On the Data menu, point to Filter, and click AutoFilter.

3 Click the down arrow on the desired column.

4 Click a criterion by which to filter the list.

5 To redisplay all of the records in a list, point to Filter on the Data menu, and click Show All.

6 To turn off AutoFilter, point to Filter on the Data menu, and click AutoFilter.

Customize a filter

1 Click any cell in the database.

2 On the Data menu, point to Filter, and click AutoFilter.

3 Click the down arrow on the desired column.

4 Click Custom.

5 In the Custom AutoFilter dialog box, select the operators and fields on which to perform operations or comparisons.

6 Click OK.

Defining an Advanced Filter

With an Advanced Filter, you establish a range in the worksheet—typically above the list—that includes the list headers and, in the rows below the header row, the conditions or criteria that you want records to meet. This is referred to as the **criteria range**. An Advanced Filter also gives you the option to copy the filtered list to another location on the worksheet—referred to as the copy to range—so that you can maintain various sets of filtered records and keep the original list intact.

You enter the criteria in the cell(s) directly below the list header of the column you want to search. Following are some guidelines for entering criteria in the criteria range:

- When you want to find records that meet more than one condition in the same column, enter each condition in a separate row, one beneath the other. For example, you want to find all records that have *Housekeeping* and *Restaurant* in the Dept Name column.
- When you want to find records that meet one condition in more than one column, enter the criteria in the same row under the appropriate list headers. For example, you want to find all records that have *Restaurant* in the Dept Name column and a salary greater than $30,000 (*>30,000*) in the Salary column.
- When you want to find records that meet one condition *or* another, enter the criteria in separate rows. For example, you want to find all records that have a Date Hired that's later than December 31, 1989 (*>12/31/89*) or earlier than January 1, 2000 (*<1/1/00*).

You can use the same operators and wildcard characters (* and ?) in a criteria range that you used when searching for records using the data form window. The operators are listed again in the following table:

Operator	Indicates
=	equal to
<>	not equal to
>=	greater than or equal to
>	greater than
<=	less than or equal to
<	less than

Once you've set up your criteria range, you run the Advanced Filter by selecting the Data menu, pointing to Filter, and clicking Advanced Filter. In the Advanced Filter dialog box, you specify the criteria range and, if desired, the range to which you want to copy the filtered list.

Define an Advanced Filter

In this exercise, you set up a criteria range and define an Advanced Filter.

1 **Select the range A1:A5, and on the Insert menu, click Rows.**

Five rows are inserted at the top of the worksheet. This will be the criteria range.

 2 **Select the range A6:I6, and click the Copy button on the Standard toolbar.**

 3 **Click cell A1, and click the Paste button on the Standard toolbar.**

The list headers are pasted to the criteria range.

4 **Click cell E2, type Restaurant, and press Enter.**

This is the criterion that you want records to match.

5 **On the Data menu, point to Filter, and click Advanced Filter.**

The Advanced Filter dialog box appears.

 **6** **Click the Copy To Another Location option. In the List Range box, click the Collapse Dialog button, select the range A6:I20, and click the Expand Dialog button.**

The list range is entered in the Advanced Filter dialog box.

 **7** **In the Criteria Range box, click the Collapse Dialog button, select the range A1:I2, and click the Expand Dialog button. In the Copy To box, click the Collapse Dialog button, click cell A23, and click the Expand Dialog button.**

The criteria range and the range to which the filtered list will be copied are entered in the Advanced Filter dialog box, as shown in Figure 3-15.

FIGURE 3-15

Setting up the Advanced Filter

8 **Click OK.**

The worksheet looks similar to that shown in Figure 3-16.

FIGURE 3-16

Running the Advanced Filter

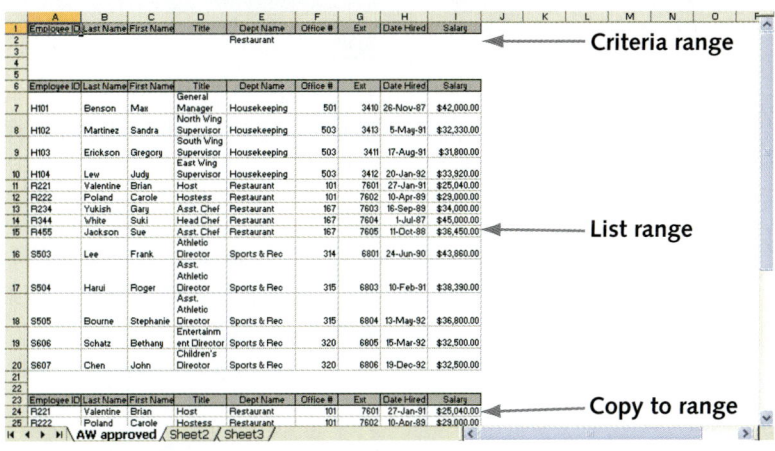

9 **Click cell E2, and press the Delete key.**

The criterion is deleted.

10 **Click cell H2, type >1/1/90; then click cell I2, and type <35000.**

11 **On the Data menu, point to Filter, and then click Advanced Filter.**

The Advanced Filter dialog box opens.

12 **Click the Copy To Another Location option.**

13 **Leave the List Range and Criteria Range selections as they are. In the Copy To box, click the Collapse Dialog button, click cell A31, and click the Expand Dialog button; in the Advanced Filter dialog box, click OK.**

The filtered list displays the records for those employees who were hired after January 1, 1990, and are making a salary of less than $35,000, as shown in Figure 3-17.

FIGURE 3-17

Advanced Filter with conditions on two columns

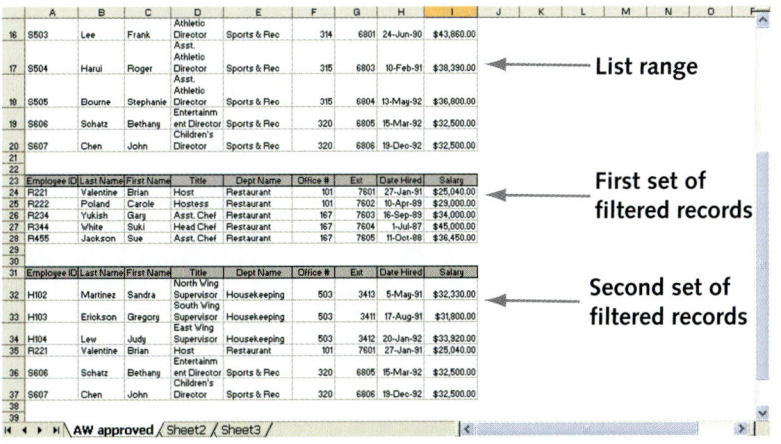

◆ **Save the workbook, and leave it open for the next exercise.**

QUICK REFERENCE ▼

Define an Advanced Filter

1 Copy the list headers to a location on the worksheet to set up a criteria range.

2 Enter the criteria in the criteria range.

3 On the Data menu, point to Filter, and then click Advanced Filter.

4 In the Advanced Filter dialog box, select to filter the list in place. Or copy the filtered list to another location, and specify the list and criteria ranges and, if necessary, the copy to range.

5 Click OK.

QUICK CHECK

Q. If you want to find records that meet one criterion or another, how do you enter the criteria in the criteria range?

A: **You enter the criteria in separate rows under the appropriate list headers.**

Using Database Functions on a List

Summarizing List Data

THE BOTTOM LINE

Excel has a number of functions designed specifically for use on a list. These functions utilize existing criteria that has been set for a list to calculate results and solutions quickly.

You are probably familiar with Excel functions such as SUM, AVERAGE, MIN, and MAX. You apply these to a range of data to produce a result quickly. Functions similar to these also are available for use on data lists. The functions, which are referred to as "Dfunctions," have three arguments: list range, the name of the field on which the function is to be performed (*not* the column letter), and the criteria range.

Using a Dfunction, you can quickly calculate a total or an average on a specific set of records in a list. For example, you've set criteria for a list to find those sales reps whose sales exceeded $3,000 for the previous week. Now you want to determine the average sales for those reps who exceeded $3,000. You can calculate this almost instantaneously by plugging the list range, criteria range, and field name into the DAVERAGE function formula.

Use a database function

In this exercise, you find the average salary for those employees hired after January 1, 1990.

1 In the criteria range, click cell I2, and press Delete.

2 Click cell J3, and then click the Insert Function button on the Standard toolbar.

The Insert Function dialog box opens.

ANOTHER METHOD

- On the Insert menu, click Function.
- Click the Insert Function button on the Formula bar.

3 Click the arrow on the Or Select A Category box, and click Database.

4 In the Select A Function box, click DAVERAGE, and click OK.

The Function Arguments dialog box opens.

5 In the Database box, click the Collapse Dialog button.

6 Select the range A6:I20, and click the Expand Dialog button.

You are returned to the Function Arguments dialog box.

7 In the Field box, type Salary, and in the Criteria box, type A1:I2.

The Function Arguments dialog box should look like that shown in Figure 3-18.

FIGURE 3-18

Arguments for the DAVERAGE function

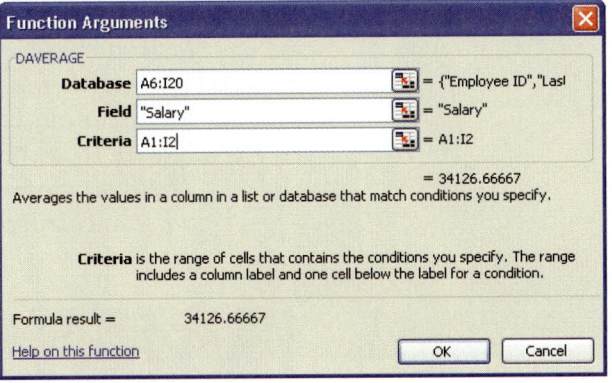

8 Click OK.

The average salary ($34,126.67) for those employees hired after January 1, 1990, is displayed in cell J3.

◆ Save Employees, and then close the workbook. If you are continuing to other lessons, save and close all open workbooks. If you are not continuing to other lessons, leave Excel open. Click the Close button in the top right corner of the Excel window.

QUICK CHECK

Q. What does the Field argument in a Dfunction represent?

A: **It represents the name of the field.**

QUICK REFERENCE ▼

Insert a Database Function

1 Click the cell to contain the function.

2 Click the Insert Function button on the Standard toolbar.

3 In the Insert Function dialog box, click the arrow on the Or Select A Category box, and click Database.

4 In the Select A Function box, click DAVERAGE, and click OK.

5 In the Function Arguments dialog box, enter the arguments for Database, Field, and Criteria.

6 Click OK.

Key Points

✔ *Setting up a range as a data list enables you to perform many useful functions on it, such as sorting entries so that they're in a more meaningful order, searching for entries that meet certain criteria, and filtering out entries so that you can focus on important data or on data that has special significance.*

✔ *You can add, edit, and review records in a list using the data form window. You also can quickly search a list of records in the data form window to find those that meet specified criteria.*

✔ *By sorting records, you can rearrange their order so that the list is more meaningful for your review and analysis, enabling you to identify trends or items of significance quickly and easily.*

✔ *You can display a subset of records that meet certain criteria by applying a filter to data. A filter temporarily hides the records that don't meet the criteria, which enables you to focus on the data that's pertinent to your review or analysis. You can define two types of filters for a list: an AutoFilter and an Advanced Filter.*

✔ *Excel's Dfunctions are designed specifically for use on a list. These functions utilize existing criteria that has been set for a list to calculate results and solutions quickly.*

Quick Quiz

True/False

T   F   **1.** In a list, a field represents a column of data.

T   F   **2.** A list should not have blank rows or columns.

T   F   **3.** You can edit records in the data form window, but you cannot add new records using a data form.

T   F   **4.** The * wildcard character can substitute for any number of characters.

T   F   **5.** Filtering a list permanently deletes records that do not meet certain conditions or criteria.

Multiple Choice

1. In a list, a row of data is referred to as which of the following?
   a. field
   b. record
   c. filter
   d. data form

2. Which of the following is *not* a guideline for structuring a list?
   a. There should be a blank row between the list headers and the records.
   b. There should be headers in the first row of the list, and they should be formatted to stand out from the rest of the data in the list.
   c. There should be no blank rows or columns in the list.
   d. There should be no extra spaces within cell entries.

3. If you entered *b?t* as search criteria, which of the following would *not* be found in the search?
   a. bat
   b. BAT
   c. BDT
   d. brat

4. Which wildcard character can substitute for any number of characters?
   a. *
   b. ?
   c. !
   d. @

5. Which of the following functions is *not* available in the data form window?
   a. entering a new record
   b. editing a record
   c. formatting a record
   d. searching for a record

Short Answer

1. How do you display a record in a data form?
2. What are the guidelines for setting up a list?
3. What's the difference between an ascending sort and a descending sort?
4. What is a criteria range?
5. How do you access AutoFilter?

On Your Own

◆ **Open Orders from the Excel Expert Practice/Lesson03 folder.**

Exercise 1

Set up the data list using the guidelines discussed in this lesson. Format the header row as desired. Open a data form and enter the following record:

1050   1/30/2005   HK-PLW   Bed Pillows (2)   20 $16.00 $7.95   H101

◆ **Save the workbook, and leave it open for the next exercise.**

Exercise 2

Sort the list by the order date in descending order. Undo the sort. Then sort the list in ascending order by the employee ID and in descending order by price. Undo the sort.

◆ **Leave the workbook open for the next exercise.**

Exercise 3

Turn on AutoFilter, and create a custom filter to display those records in which the price is greater than $100. Create an Advanced Filter that finds records with "RC" in the code *and* a price that's greater than $40. Copy the filtered list to another range on the worksheet.

◆ **Save and close Orders.**

One Step Further

Exercise 1

Open a new blank workbook, and name it **Household Inventory**. Create a list of items in your home and the estimated price you paid for them. The list should have columns for the categories of items (such as "electronics," "furniture," or "jewelry"); the name of each item; the approximate date of purchase; a brief description of each item, a serial or identification number, if applicable; and the price (estimate if you don't remember) you paid for each item. Use the List feature on the Data menu to define the list, and make sure it is set up and formatted according to the guidelines presented in this lesson.

◆ **Save Household Inventory, and leave it open for the next exercise.**

Exercise 2

Sort the items in ascending order by category name. Run a Top 10 filter to find the ten most expensive items. What kind of Advanced Filters might you define for this list? Write a short report on the filters and why these filtered lists are useful.

◆ **Close Household Inventory.**

Formatting and Organizing Data

After completing this lesson, you will be able to:

✔ *Apply number formats.*
✔ *Create custom formats.*
✔ *Use conditional formatting.*
✔ *Insert subtotals and outline data.*
✔ *Group data.*

KEY TERMS

■ conditional formats
■ grouping

Applying formats to cells can make the data more understandable to others who will view your worksheets. You have learned that Excel provides a variety of formats that you can apply to numbers, dates, and text. For instance, you can format cells so that numbers appear as currency, with dollar signs, commas, and decimal positions, or you can choose from among several date formats for cells that contain dates. For example, the date *1/01/2005* can be formatted so that it appears as *Jan 1, 2005*, *January 1, 2005*, *1/01/05*, or *1/01/2005*. You also have the option of customizing formats so that they meet special formatting needs.

You also can specify that cells will be formatted in a different manner if the values stored in the cells meet a certain condition. For instance, you can specify that values in an Inventory On Hand column in a list appear in red if they are less than 10. The red indicates those inventory items that need to be reordered. Applying different formatting to cells whose values are within a specified range can call attention to those values.

Another effective way to call out certain values is to apply Excel's grouping and subtotaling features. These features let you organize data in logical groups and calculate subtotals for the groups.

In this lesson, you learn how to create custom formats and apply conditional formatting to cells. You also learn how to group and outline a list and insert subtotals.

IMPORTANT

Before you can use the practice files in this lesson, you must install them from the book's companion CD to their default location. For additional information on how to find and open files used in this book, see the "Using the CD-ROM" section at the beginning of this book.

Applying Formats

THE BOTTOM LINE

Applying accurate formatting to data makes it more useful and easier to interpret and analyze.

You can choose to format data in cells in dozens of ways. For text entries, you can easily change the alignment, font, indentation, and so on to enhance the data's appearance. You can apply the same formats to numerical entries, in addition to other formats designed specifically for numbers.

Working with Number Formats

The format you choose will depend on the type of data and the types of values entered in the worksheet. For instance, you might want to format data in different columns in currency format, as fractions, or as percentages. You might want to include comma separators to make large numbers more readable (such as *1,003,402* instead of *1003402*). You might want to display currency rounded to the nearest dollar (such as *$1,003,402*) or with decimal places to include fractions of a dollar (such as *$1,003,402.45*). The following table describes the formats you can apply to numerical data:

Format	Result
General	Treats text and numbers the same, with characters displayed exactly as they are typed
Number	Displays numbers exactly as they are typed
Currency	Displays monetary values with currency signs and optional comma separators and decimal positions
Accounting	Lines up currency symbols and decimal points in a column
Date	Displays dates in a specified data format and allows you to use serial numbers and dates to calculate new dates; for instance, if cell G8 contains the date *1/01/03*, the formula *=G8+366* typed in a date cell will display the result as *1/02/04* (one year plus one day from the date in cell G8); or you could type *="03/01"-"02/05"* to display the difference as *1/25*
Time	Displays times in time format; for instance, if you type *3 p* in a time cell, the time will appear as *3:00 PM*
Percentage	Multiplies cell values by 100 and displays the result with a percent symbol; for instance, if you type *.0825* in a percentage cell, the value will appear as *8.25%*
Fraction	Displays decimal entries as fractions; for instance, if you type *.25* in a fraction cell, the value will appear as *1/4*
Scientific	Uses scientific or exponential notation to display large numbers that do not fit within the width of a cell; for instance, if you type *225054585* in a scientific cell that is only eight characters wide, the value will appear as *2.E+8* (eight additional digit positions); you can view the precise value in the Formula bar by clicking the cell

Format	Result
Text	Treats values as text and displays them exactly as they are entered; you can type numbers into a text cell, but you can't perform calculations on these numbers; for example, you might format cells as text and then enter inventory part numbers in the cells
Special	Displays list and database values such as Zip Codes, phone numbers, and Social Security numbers
Custom	Allows you to specify or create a format that isn't supported by any of the other formatting types

IMPORTANT

The numbers in the cells should make sense for whatever formatting option you apply. If you type the number 532 in a cell that has a Date format, it will be converted to a date. In this case, 532 is added to the date January 1, 1900, so the entry would be displayed as 06/15/01, which is probably not the value you want.

You can apply a number format to a cell or range of cells before or after data has been entered. If a cell contains any letters or numbers separated by spaces, the number formatting will not be applied to the cell. However, if the contents of a cell change so that the cell contains only numbers, the number formatting will be applied.

TIP

Use Format Painter to apply formats from one cell to another cell or range of cells. Select the cell whose format you want to copy, and click the Format Painter button. Then click the cell or select the range to which you want to apply the format.

The sales manager at Adventure Works tracks the sales performance of each member of the sales department, and he creates a bimonthly summary that lists the total sales for each salesperson. To make the sales figures easier to read, the sales manager applies currency formatting to the sales figures.

◆ **To complete the procedures in this lesson, you must use the files Sales Summer 2005, Restaurant Staff, Personnel, and Human Resources in the Lesson04 folder in the Excel Expert Practice folder located on your hard disk.**

◆ **Open Sales Summer 2005 from the Excel Expert Practice/Lesson04 folder.**

Apply number formats

In this exercise, you apply a currency number format to values in a worksheet.

1 Select the range C4:D8.

2 **On the Format menu, click Cells.**

The Format Cells dialog box appears.

3 **In the Format Cells dialog box, click the Number tab, if necessary.**

4 **In the Category list, click Number, and change the Decimal Places to 2, if necessary. Select the Use 1000 Separator (,) check box.**

FIGURE 4-1

Format Cells dialog box

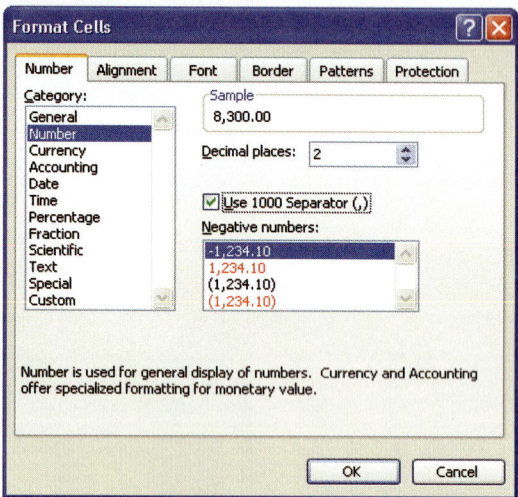

5 **Click OK.**

The selected range is formatted with two decimal places and a comma separator.

6 **On the Format menu, click Cells.**

The Format Cells dialog box appears.

7 **Click Currency in the Category list to display the available currency options.**

FIGURE 4-2

Currency format options

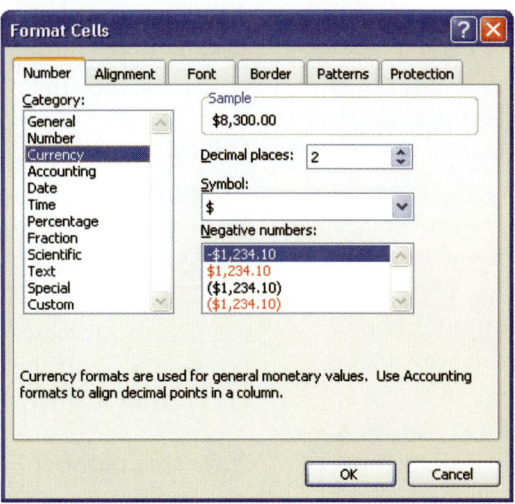

8 **Click OK to accept the defaults.**

◆ **Save the workbook, and then close it.**

QUICK REFERENCE ▼

Apply number formats

1 Select the cell or range you want to format.

2 On the Format menu, click Cells.

3 In the Format Cells dialog box, click the Number tab.

4 Select the number format from the Category list, and select other options for that category as desired.

5 Click OK.

Using Custom Date Formats

Creating Custom Formats

If none of Excel's ready-made formats seem suitable for your data, you can create your own custom formats. For example, you can create a phone number format that includes a person's phone extension (such as *800-555-1212 Ext 12*). You can create a custom format for numbers, text, dates, and times. You can choose from among Excel's ready-made custom formats, or you can create your own format using the appropriate formatting symbols.

Here are the format symbols that can be used in a custom format:

The pound sign in a custom format indicates that only a significant digit is to appear in a certain digit position. Use quotation marks to enclose text (including spaces) that you want to display in specific character positions. (See the phone number extension in the following table.)

Enter this number	Apply this format	The number appears as
0234.56	####.##	234.56
0234.56	####.#	234.6
8005551212220	(###) ###-#### "Ext" ###	(800) 555-1212 Ext 220

0   A zero indicates that insignificant zeros should appear in a certain digit position, even if the data entered has fewer digits than there are zeros in the custom format.

Enter this number	Apply this format	The number appears as
00234.56	0000.00	0234.56
234.5	0000.00	0234.50

?   Include a question mark in a custom format to add spaces for insignificant zeros on either side of the decimal point so that decimal points align. For instance, the custom format ???.??? pads the values 2.5, 102.25, and 22.435 with the appropriate number of spaces to the right and left so that all three numbers align at the decimal point. Question marks also can be used to specify digit positions and alignment for fractions.

??/??   Include a question mark in a column with fractions to align the fractions at the slash separating the numerator and denominator.

Enter this number	Apply this format	The number appears as
5.25	# ??/??	5 1/4
15.3	## ??/??	15 3/10
.003	???/????	3/1000

,   Include a comma in a custom format to scale a number in a multiple of 1,000. This format is useful when you want to representing large numbers but don't want to display the full numbers.

Enter this number	Apply this format	The number appears as
22,400,000	0.0,,	22.4
22,450,000	0.0,,	22.5
22,450,000	0.00,,	22.45

You can extend the available date formats in Excel by combining the date format codes (m, d, and y) in different ways.

Enter this number	Apply this format	The date appears as
1-7-05	m/d	1/7
1-7-05	m-dd	1-07
1-7-05	m/d/y	1/7/05
1-7-05	m-dd-y	1-07-05
1-7-05	m.dd.y	1.07.05

Enter this number	Apply this format	The date appears as
1-7-05	mmm d, yyy	Jan 7, 2005
1-7-05	mmmm, yyy	January, 2005
1-7-05	mmmm d	January 7
1-7-05	dddd, mmmm d	Friday, January 7
1-7-05	ddd, mmm. d, yyy	Fri, Jan. 7, 2005
1-7-2005	m/d/y	1/7/05
1-7-2005	m/d/yyy	1/7/2005

TIP

If you insert a date in a cell that is formatted in a nondate format, the result probably won't make sense because Excel will format the date as a number. Make sure that cells containing dates are formatted correctly. Also, if you change a cell from Date format to a different format, the result probably won't display what you want. For example, if you change a cell from Date format to General format and the cell contains *03/05/2005*, the date will be converted to its numeric equivalent, 38416, which won't be understandable to those who view or use the worksheet.

◆ **Open Restaurant Staff from the Excel Expert Practice/Lesson04 folder.**

Create a custom format

In this exercise, you modify a ready-made custom format for a telephone number to support a three-digit phone extension.

1 Select G3:G7.

2 On the Format menu, click Cells.

The Format Cells dialog box appears.

3 Click the Number tab in the Format Cells dialog box, if necessary, and click Custom on the Category list.

4 On the Type list, scroll down, and click (###)-###-#### "Ext" ##.

The custom format appears in the Type box.

5 Click at the end of the current entry in the Type box, type #, and click OK.

The cells are formatted to support a phone number with an area code in parentheses and a three-digit extension.

IMPORTANT

You should not include spaces when you type a number in a custom format.

6 Click cell G3, type 5551231234220, and press Enter.

The phone number appears in the custom format that you specified.

FIGURE 4-3

Custom format for a phone number with an extension

	A	B	C	D	E	F	G
1							
2	Employee ID	Last Name	First Name	Title	Dept Name	Office #	Phone Number
3	R221	Valentine	Brian	Host	Restaurant	101	(555) 123-1234 Ext 220
4	R222	Poland	Carole	Hostess	Restaurant	101	
5	R234	Yukish	Gary	Asst. Chef	Restaurant	167	
6	R344	White	Suki	Head Chef	Restaurant	167	
7	R455	Jackson	Sue	Asst. Chef	Restaurant	167	
8							

◆ **Save and close the workbook.**

QUICK REFERENCE ▼

Create a custom format

1 Select the cell or cells to be formatted.

2 On the Format menu, click Cells.

3 Click the Number tab, and click Custom on the Category list.

4 In the Type list, click a custom format, and in the Type box, modify the format.

Or

1 In the Type box, type a new custom format.

2 Click OK.

Using Conditional Formatting

Changing Data Appearance
Based on Value

THE BOTTOM LINE

You can specify a different format for cell entries that meet certain conditions in order to highlight them as noteworthy or significant.

You can set **conditional formats** for selected cells so that the values that meet a particular condition are uniquely formatted to make them stand out. For example, a company's inventory manager can set conditions in a worksheet so that if a quantity of a particular stock item falls below a certain number, a format of red and bold is applied to the entry. This makes it easy for the inventory manager to identify when a particular item needs to be reordered.

◆ **Open Sales Summer 2005 from the Excel Expert Practice/Lesson04 folder.**

Apply conditional formatting

In this exercise, you apply conditional formatting to a range of cells so that sales figures that equal or exceed $10,000 appear green and bold.

1 **Select the range C4:D8.**

2 **On the Format menu, click Conditional Formatting.**

The Conditional Formatting dialog box appears.

3 **Click the second down arrow in the Condition 1 section of the Conditional Formatting dialog box (which currently reads "between"), and click "greater than or equal" to on the list.**

4 **In the empty box to the right, type 10000.**

The Conditional Formatting dialog box should look like that shown in Figure 4-4.

FIGURE 4-4

Conditional Formatting dialog box

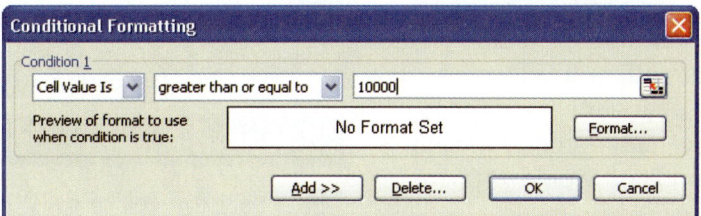

5 **Click the Format button.**

The Format Cells dialog box appears.

6 **In the Font style list, click Bold, and click the down arrow to the right of the Color box. Then click the Lime square (third row, third square) in the Color list.**

The Format Cells dialog box should look similar to that shown in Figure 4-5.

FIGURE 4-5

Setting conditional formats

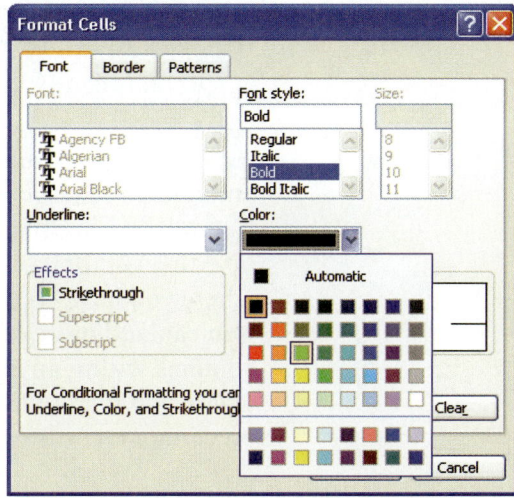

7 **Click OK in the Format Cells dialog box.**

You are returned to the Conditional Formatting dialog box.

8 **Click OK to close the Conditional Formatting dialog box.**

9 **Click outside the selected range to view the conditional formatting.**

Values in the Sales Figures columns that are greater than or equal to $10,000 appear bold and green. The values that are less than $10,000 appear in the regular format.

FIGURE 4-6

Conditional formats applied

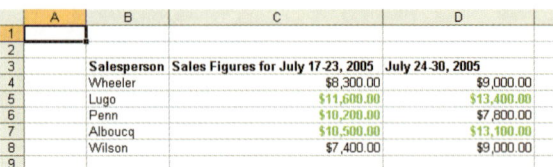

	Salesperson	Sales Figures for July 17-23, 2005	July 24-30, 2005
Wheeler		$8,300.00	$9,000.00
Lugo		$11,600.00	$13,400.00
Penn		$10,200.00	$7,800.00
Alboucq		$10,500.00	$13,100.00
Wilson		$7,400.00	$9,000.00

◆ **Save and close the workbook.**

QUICK REFERENCE ▼

Create a conditional format

1 Select the cell or cells to be formatted.

2 On the Format menu, click Conditional Formatting.

3 Set the desired conditions and formats in the Conditional Formatting dialog box, and click OK.

Subtotaling and Grouping Data

Performing Calculations on Filtered Data

THE BOTTOM LINE

In a list with a large number of records, you can review and assess the data easily if it is categorized into logical groups on which subtotals can be calculated.

Excel provides a number of features that enable you to organize large amounts of data into more manageable groups. You can sort data in a list and then insert subtotals at specified locations within the sorted list. Inserting subtotals essentially sets up your data in an outlined structure, where you have controls to hide and display certain levels of the outline. You can add more levels to the outline by grouping certain rows or columns within an existing level. This is especially useful in large lists where you might want to focus only on subtotals or certain groups or on certain records or fields within groups.

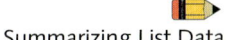

Summarizing List Data

Inserting Subtotals and Outlining Data

You can perform calculations on a list by subtotaling selected groups of values. You also can apply other calculations, such as the Count and Average function formulas, on subgroups of data. For instance, the CFO of Adventure Works has a list of AW employees, but she wants to know how many employees are in each department and how much each department spends on these employees' salaries. By using the Subtotals feature, she can organize her list so that it displays this information.

Before subtotaling values in a list, you must sort the records so that the values you want to subtotal are grouped together. You can customize the results of a subtotal calculation in several ways. If you have already created subtotals, you can replace the current subtotals with the new subtotals or you can display both the current subtotals and the new subtotals. You can insert page breaks between subtotaled groups so that when you print the worksheet, the subtotals appear on a different page. You also can add grand totals and summary information for the associated data.

Once you insert subtotals in a list, the groups on which the subtotals are based form an outline of the list data. Outlining controls, which you can use to manage the level of data that's displayed, appear to the left of the row numbers or above the column letters. For example, you might want only the rows that contain subtotals and a grand total to show on the worksheet. The numbered level buttons change the amount of detail that appears for all subtotal groups, while the Hide Detail and Show Detail buttons change the amount of detail for one specific group.

◆ **Open Personnel from the Excel Expert Practice/Lesson04 folder.**

Insert subtotals

In this exercise, you sort a list by department, subtotal the employee salaries by department, subtotal the number of employees by department, and insert summary rows below each department group. Then you change the level of detail displayed for the list.

TROUBLESHOOTING

If the active cell is outside the list when you attempt to sort, an alert box will appear, telling you that no list was found and that you should select a single cell within your list.

1 **Click any cell on the list. On the Data menu, click Sort.**

The Sort dialog box appears.

2 **Click the Sort By down arrow, click DEPARTMENT on the list, and click OK.**

The list is sorted by department.

3 **On the Data menu, click Subtotals.**

The Subtotal dialog box appears.

4 Click the At Each Change In down arrow, and click DEPARTMENT on the list.

5 In the Use Function box, make sure Sum is selected. If a different function is selected, click the down arrow, and click Sum on the list.

6 In the Add Subtotal To list, select the SALARY check box, and clear all other check boxes, if necessary.

7 Select the Summary Below Data check box, if necessary, and clear the Replace Current Subtotals and Page Break Between Groups check boxes, if necessary.

The Subtotal dialog box should look like that shown in Figure 4-7.

FIGURE 4-7

Subtotal dialog box

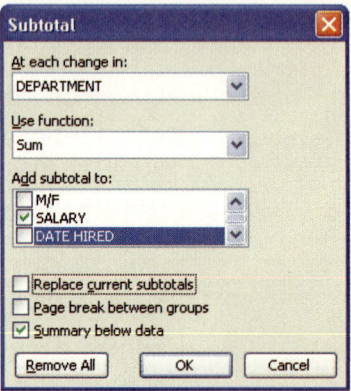

8 Click OK.

The salary subtotals for each department appear in the Salary column.

FIGURE 4-8

Subtotals inserted below groups

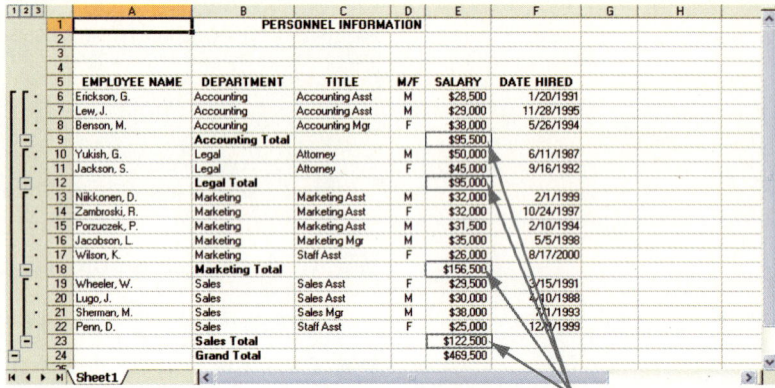

Salary subtotals for each department

TIP

Note that at the bottom of the list, a grand total appears in the SALARY column.

9 On the Data menu, click Subtotals.

10 In the Subtotal dialog box, click the Use Function down arrow, and click Count in the list. In the Add Subtotal To list, clear the SALARY check box, scroll down (if necessary), and select the DATE HIRED check box.

11 Click OK.

The Employee count for each department appears in the DATE HIRED column.

FIGURE 4-9

Adding another set of subtotals

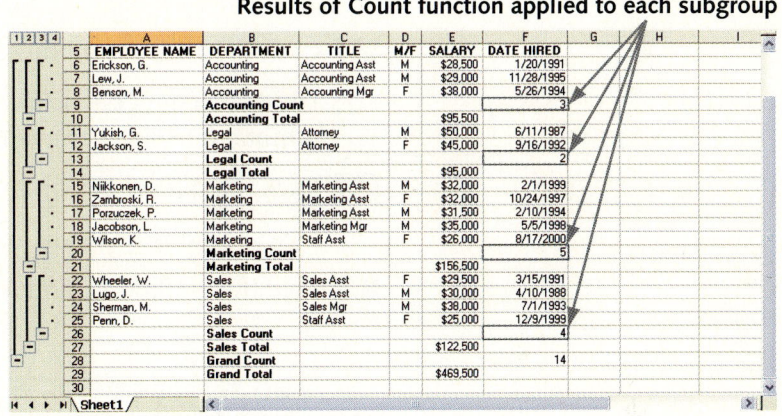

Results of Count function applied to each subgroup

12 Click the 1 level button in the top left corner of the worksheet.

The list displays only the first-level rows (Grand Count and Grand Total), as shown in Figure 4-10.

FIGURE 4-10

Displaying one level

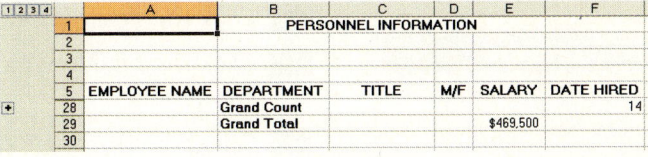

13 **Click the 2 level button in the top left corner of the worksheet.**

The rows are filtered so that only the first-level and second-level rows are visible. The departmental Totals appear in addition to the Grand Total and Grand Count, as shown in Figure 4-11.

FIGURE 4-11

Displaying two levels

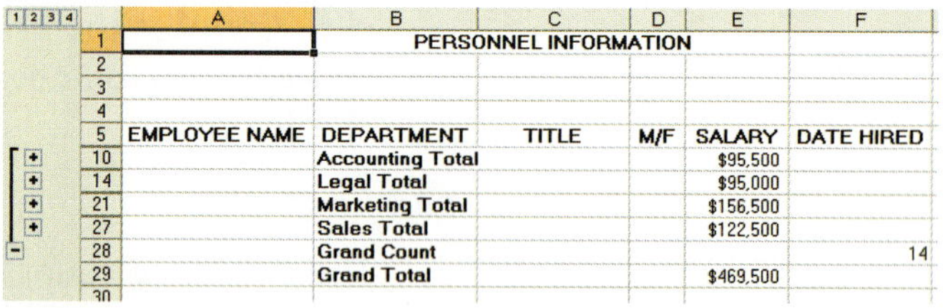

	A	B	C	D	E	F
1		PERSONNEL INFORMATION				
2						
3						
4						
5	EMPLOYEE NAME	DEPARTMENT	TITLE	M/F	SALARY	DATE HIRED
10		Accounting Total			$95,500	
14		Legal Total			$95,000	
21		Marketing Total			$156,500	
27		Sales Total			$122,500	
28		Grand Count				14
29		Grand Total			$469,500	
30						

14 **Click the Show Detail button to the left of row 10.**

The Accounting department records and Count subtotal are redisplayed.

15 **Click the Hide Detail button next to row 9.**

The Accounting department records are hidden, but the Count subtotal remains displayed.

16 **Click the 4 level button to redisplay all of the rows in the list.**

All rows in the worksheet appear.

◆ **Save the workbook, and leave it open for the next exercise.**

QUICK REFERENCE ▼

Insert subtotals, and outline data

1 Group the list using your desired criteria.

2 On the Data menu, click Subtotals.

3 Click the At Each Change In down arrow, and select the column by which you grouped the list.

4 Click the Use Function down arrow.

5 Click the desired function on the Use Function list.

6 Click the field in which you want the subtotal in the Add Subtotal To list.

7 Select or clear the Replace Current Subtotals, Page Break Between Groups, and Summary Below Data check boxes as desired. Click OK.

8 Click the numbered level buttons and the Show Detail and Hide Detail buttons to control the display of data in the list.

QUICK CHECK

Q. What does the Count function calculate?

A: It calculates the number of valid entries in a group or range.

Summarizing List Data

Grouping Data

You can further define the level of data that displays in a list by **grouping** rows or columns. You can group a single row or column or multiple rows or columns. You then use the detail buttons to hide the groups so that you can focus on the data that's most important.

Group data

In this exercise, you group columns in the list.

1 **Click the 3 level button in the top left corner of the worksheet.**

All of the records except for the subtotals rows are hidden, as shown in Figure 4-12.

FIGURE 4-12

Showing only subtotals

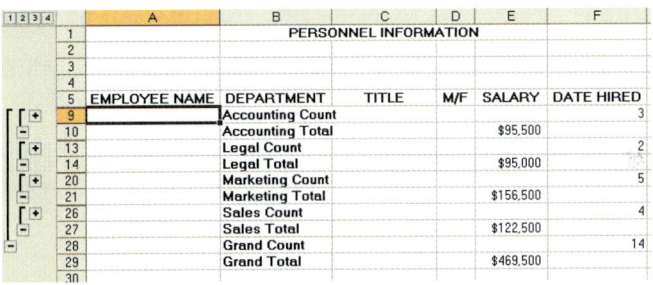

2 **Click cell A5, open the Data menu, point to Group and Outline, and click Group.**

The Group dialog box opens, as shown in Figure 4-13.

FIGURE 4-13

Group dialog box

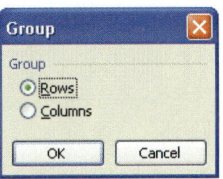

3 **Click Columns, and then click OK.**

The outline controls appear above the column letters.

4 **Click C5:D5, open the Data menu, point to Group and Outline, and click Group.**

5 **In the Group dialog box, click Columns, and then click OK.**

Outline controls appear above columns C and D. The worksheet should look like that shown in Figure 4-14.

FIGURE 4-14

Grouping columns

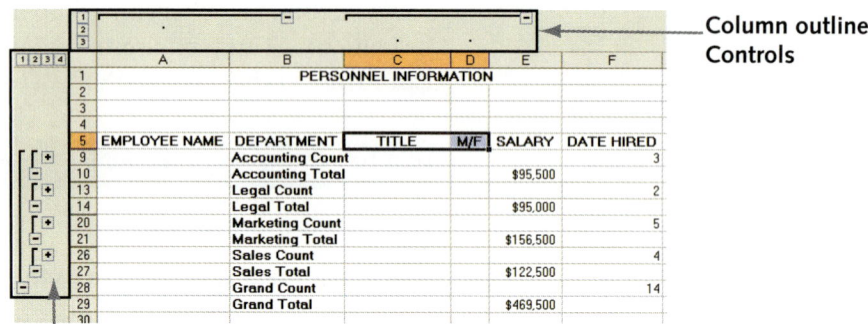

6 **In the column outline controls, click the Hide Detail button for columns C and D.**

The Title and M/F columns are hidden.

7 **In the column outline controls, click the Hide Detail button for column A.**

The Employee Name column is hidden. The worksheet should look like that shown in Figure 4-15.

FIGURE 4-15

Hiding columns

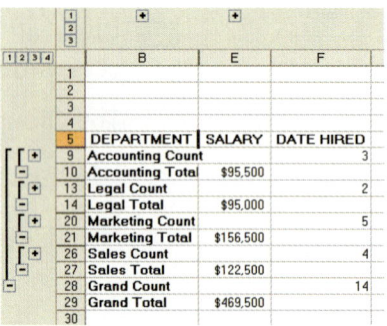

8 Click the Show Detail buttons for the hidden columns.

9 Click cell A5, open the Data menu, point to Group and Outline, and click Ungroup.

The Ungroup dialog box appears.

10 In the Ungroup dialog box, click Columns, and click OK.

The Employee Name column redisplays.

11 Select C5:D5, open the Data menu, point to Group and Outline, and click Ungroup.

12 In the Ungroup dialog box, click Columns, and click OK.

The Title and M/F columns redisplay.

13 On the Data menu, point to Group and Outline, and click Clear Outline.

All outline controls are removed.

◆ Save and close Personnel. If you are continuing to other lessons, leave Excel open. If you are not continuing to other lessons, save and close all open workbooks. Click the Close button in the top right corner of the Excel window.

QUICK REFERENCE ▼

Group and ungroup data

1 Select a cell in the row(s) or column(s) you want to group.

2 On the Data menu, point to Group and Outline, and click Group.

3 In the Group dialog box, click either Rows or Columns, and click OK.

4 Select a cell in the row(s) or column(s) you want to ungroup.

5 On the Data menu, point to Group and Outline, and click Ungroup.

6 In the Ungroup dialog box, click either Rows or Columns, and click OK.

Remove an outline

1 Click any cell in the data list.

2 On the Data menu, point to Group and Outline, and click Clear Outline.

QUICK CHECK

Q. Which detail button do you click to display all of the records in a group?

A: **You click the Show Detail button.**

Key Points

✔ *Applying accurate formatting to data makes it more useful and easier to interpret and analyze. Excel has many formats you can apply to data. If you need a special format, you can customize one of the existing formats or create your own.*

✔ *You can specify a different format for cell entries that meet certain conditions in order to highlight them as noteworthy or significant. This is referred to as conditional formatting.*

✔ *In a list with a large number of records, you can review and assess the data easily when it is categorized into logical groups on which subtotals can be calculated.*

✔ *When you apply an outline structure to a data list, you have access to controls that let you hide and display certain levels of the outline.*

✔ *You can add more levels to an outlined worksheet by grouping certain rows or columns within an existing level of the outline. This is especially useful in large lists where you want to focus only on subtotals or certain groups or on certain records or fields within groups.*

Quick Quiz

True/False

T F 1. The Number format treats text and numbers the same, with characters displayed exactly as they are typed.

T F 2. You can apply a custom format only to numbers.

T F 3. A pound sign (#) and a question mark (?) are examples of custom format symbols.

T F 4. A date formatted as *mmmm, yyy* would look like *Janu, 200*.

T F 5. You should sort a list before you insert subtotals.

T F 6. You can outline a list even if it does not contain subtotals.

Multiple Choice

1. Which number format displays numbers exactly as they are typed?
   a. General
   b. Number
   c. Standard
   d. Text

2. Which of the following is *not* a custom formatting symbol?
   a. @
   b. #
   c. 0
   d. ?

3. How would Oct. 2, 1963, appear if it were formatted as m/d/y?
   a. 10/2/63
   b. 10/02/1963
   c. Oct/2/1963
   d. Oct. 2, 1963

4. Which buttons let you control the levels of an outline that display?
   a. Page Up and Page Down
   b. Plus Detail and Minus Detail
   c. Close and Open
   d. Show Detail and Hide Detail

Short Answer

1. How would you apply a format to make a date entered as January 1, 2004, appear as 1/1?

2. What must you do before subtotaling data on a list?

3. How would you create a custom format so that 1-7-04 appears as Wed, Jan. 7, 2004?

4. Why would you apply conditional formatting to a cell or range of cells?

5. How do you change the level of detail for one specific group displayed on a list?

On Your Own

IMPORTANT

In the On Your Own section below, you must complete Exercises 1, 2, and 3 in sequence.

◆ **Open Human Resources from the Excel Expert Practice/Lesson04 folder.**

Exercise 1

Change the format of the salaries so that no decimal places appear. Change the format on the DateHired field so that the dates appear as *14-Mar-01*.

◆ **Save the workbook, and leave it open for the next exercise.**

Exercise 2

In the Human Resources workbook, apply conditional formatting to the dates in the DateHired field that are after Dec. 31, 1995. Select formats of your own choice. Apply conditional formatting to values in the Salary field that are less than or equal to $30,000. Again, select formats of your own choice.

◆ **Save the workbook, and leave it open for the next exercise.**

Exercise 3

In the Human Resources workbook, sort the list by Title. Subtotal the yearly salaries by job title. Add the subtotal to the Salary field, and include a summary below the data. Change the detail level so that only the subtotals appear.

◆ **Save and close Human Resources.**

One Step Further

IMPORTANT

You must have completed Exercise 1 in the One Step Further section of Lesson 3 in order to complete Exercise 1 below.

◆ **Open Household Inventory from the Excel Expert Practice/Lesson03 folder.**

Exercise 1

If necessary, apply appropriate number or custom formats to the list of household items. Sort the items by various fields. Determine which sort order provides you with the best assessment of the inventory's value. Then insert subtotals and show and hide details as you deem necessary.

◆ **Close Household Inventory.**

Exercise 2

This lesson discussed conditional formatting and how it can be used to highlight important or significant data. However, in a large worksheet with thousands of cells of data, the cells highlighted with conditional formatting might not be so easy to find. Use Excel's Help system to search for information on how you can find cells to which conditional formats have been applied. Write a short report on your findings, describing why these capabilities might be useful.

5

Auditing a Workbook

After completing this lesson, you will be able to:

✔ *Create a data entry list.*
✔ *Establish valid data entries.*
✔ *Trace errors.*
✔ *Trace precedent cells.*
✔ *Trace dependent cells.*
✔ *Watch and evaluate formulas.*

KEY TERMS

- data entry list
- dependents
- error code
- Formula Auditing toolbar
- input message
- precedents

When you create a data list or worksheet, you want it to be accurate, especially if you're using it for business purposes. Invalid data in a worksheet can lead to errors in performing day-to-day business duties. For instance, if an inventory list contains an Inventory-On-Hand column and valid inventory amounts should not exceed 100 and should not be less than 10, problems can result if a person accidentally enters an inventory amount that is outside this range. The inventory manager might order products when they are not needed, or the manager might think that a particular inventory item is well stocked when, in fact, it needs to be reordered.

Using Excel's data validation features, you can prevent inaccurate data from being entered in cells. For example, a sales manager can create a validation rule for sales amounts in his worksheets to prevent anyone from accidentally entering text into these cells (for instance, a salesperson's name or an employee ID instead of a sales amount).

You also can use Excel's Auditing features to check the accuracy of your data. For instance, you can trace errors in a formula, and you can trace cells that are used in formulas to ensure that the content of cells on which a formula depends is accurate. You also can evaluate each component of a formula to determine where errors are introduced. All of these safeguarding and data management tasks contribute to accurate and well-organized workbooks.

In this lesson, you create a data list of acceptable (valid) entries for particular cells in a worksheet, you specify a validation rule for a particular range of cells, and you create a data input message that will appear if a user tries to enter an invalid value in the range. You also learn how to use the Auditing toolbar to trace errors in formulas or in cells that affect formulas.

Working with Data Validation Tools

Validating Data

THE BOTTOM LINE

You can control the data that is entered in a cell or range and help ensure its accuracy by using data validation tools. These tools let you set parameters within which any data entered must fall.

Data entry can be a tedious task, and the margin for error is large. Excel's data validation tools enable you to set limits on which cells can contain data.

Creating a Data Entry List

A primary tool for validating Excel data is a **data entry list.** A data entry list dictates the accepted entries for a specified cell or range of cells. If a person entering data attempts to enter invalid data or data outside the approved values for the cell or range, an error message (which you can design) will appear. For example, the marketing manager has created a workbook that keeps track of calls made by the telemarketing staff. To aid in entering the names of telemarketers, she creates a data entry list of names. She then can enter a name by selecting from the list of valid telemarketer names rather than manually typing in (and possibly misspelling) the name.

When you create a data entry list for a field, a down arrow appears on a selected cell in the field. When you click the arrow, a menu opens displaying the data entry list.

IMPORTANT

A data entry list is different from a data list in that it limits the entries in cells to those values provided on the list. A data list is an organized collection of information displayed in row-and-column format so that it can be sorted, filtered, or manipulated in another way.

◆ **To complete the procedures in this lesson, you must use the files AW Reservation Stats and AW Marketing in the Lesson05 folder in the Excel Expert Practice folder located on your hard disk.**

◆ **Open AW Marketing from the Excel Expert Practice/Lesson05 folder.**

Create a data entry list

In this exercise, you create a list of valid entries for a range of cells.

1 Click the Telemarketing sheet tab, if necessary.

2 Hold down the Ctrl key, and click cells A7, A10, A13, A16, and A19.

Next, you establish the list of names that can be entered in the selected range of cells.

3 On the Data menu, click Validation.

The Data Validation dialog box appears.

4 Click the Settings tab, if necessary.

FIGURE 5-1

Settings tab in the Data Validation dialog box

5 Click the Allow down arrow, and click List.

6 Click in the Source box, and type Wendy, Scott, Matthew, Heather, Isabel.

7 Click OK.

8 Click cell A7, and then click its down arrow.

The data entry list appears, as shown in Figure 5-2.

FIGURE 5-2

Data entry list

9 **Click Wendy on the data entry list.**

10 **Repeat this process for cells A10, A13, A16, and A19, clicking the names Scott, Matthew, Heather, and Isabel, respectively.**

The names appear in the cells.

◆ **Save the workbook, and keep it open for the next exercise.**

QUICK REFERENCE ▼

Create a data entry list

1 Select the cell or cells to which the list should apply.

2 On the Data menu, click Validation and click the Settings tab, if necessary.

3 Click the Allow down arrow, and click List.

4 Click in the Source box, and type the entries to be included in the list.

5 Click OK.

Establishing Valid Data Entries

You can create additional data entry controls by setting a valid range of entries for a cell. For example, the Adventure Works sales manager wants to restrict the Commission Amount field in his sales worksheet to numbers between .05 and .15—the valid commission percentages for salespeople based on seniority. So he sets a data entry range to ensure that only entries within the specified range are accepted. Attempts to enter any other data in the specified cells will result in an error message.

The allowable data types in the Data Validation dialog box are described in the following table.

Data Type	Content That Can Be Entered
Any Value	Text, numbers, formulas
Whole Number	Any number with no decimal places
Decimal	Any number with decimal places
List	Any item from a list specified by the user
Date	Text and numbers in date format
Time	Text and numbers in time format
Text Length	Any text or numeric content that doesn't exceed a length you specify
Custom	Any text or numeric content that fits within a formula you specify

If you (or any user entering data in your validated worksheet) attempt to enter data that violates the validation settings, a standard error message appears, as shown in Figure 5-3.

FIGURE 5-3

Error message

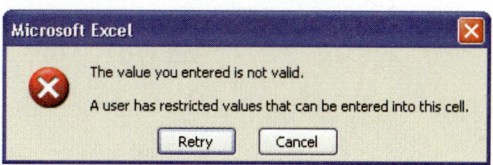

If you want, you can create your own error message. An error message that you create can contain more explanatory information, such as the type or range of entries that is acceptable. A custom error message, then, helps users make correct entries in cells that have validation rules applied. You also can choose which error icon appears in the error message dialog box. You can select one of these three icons:

Icon	Icon Name	What the Dialog Box Will Display
❌	Stop	Retry and Cancel buttons
⚠️	Warning	A Continue? prompt as well as Yes, No, and Cancel buttons
ℹ️	Information	OK and Cancel buttons

The icons appear with the custom message you create. Be careful to choose the icon that best represents the directions (if any) that your custom message imparts to the user.

You also can aid users in their data entry by providing an **input message**. An input message helps prevent users from entering incorrect values by informing the user about the type or range of entries that are acceptable for a particular cell or range of cells. Your customized input message can contain as many as 255 characters, but you should keep the message as clear and concise as possible so that users will take the time to read the message in its entirety.

> **TIP**
>
> An input message looks similar to an inserted comment, but it appears when a user clicks a cell that has an input message appended to it, not when the mouse pointer is positioned over the cell.

Apply valid data type settings and messages

In this exercise, you create an input message to assist users in making appropriate entries in a range of cells. You also establish a range of acceptable numeric entries for specified cells and create an error message that appears when incorrect data is typed in a cell or range of cells.

1 On the Telemarketing sheet tab, select the range C7:Z7.

2 On the Data menu, click Validation.

The Data Validation dialog box appears.

3 On the Settings tab, click the Allow down arrow, and click Whole Number.

4 Click in the Minimum box, type 1000, click in the Maximum box, and type 2500.

The Settings tab should look like that shown in Figure 5-4.

FIGURE 5-4

Setting validation criteria for the range

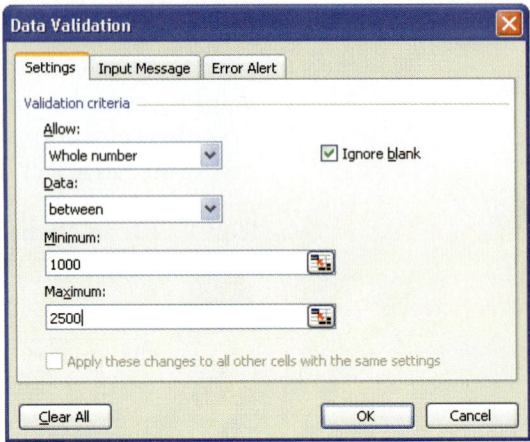

5 Click the Error Alert tab in the Data Validation dialog box.

6 Click the Style down arrow, and click Stop on the Style list, if necessary.

7 Click in the Title box, and type Invalid Amount.

8 Click in the Error Message box, and type Your entry must be between 1000 and 2500 calls per month.

The Error Alert tab should look like that shown in Figure 5-5.

FIGURE 5-5

Text for the error message

9 Click the Input Message tab in the Data Validation dialog box.

10 Click in the Title box, and type Calls Per Month.

11 Click in the Input Message box, and type Locate the number of calls for this telemarketer on his or her call sheet and type that number here.

The Input Message tab should look like that shown in Figure 5-6.

FIGURE 5-6

Text for the input message

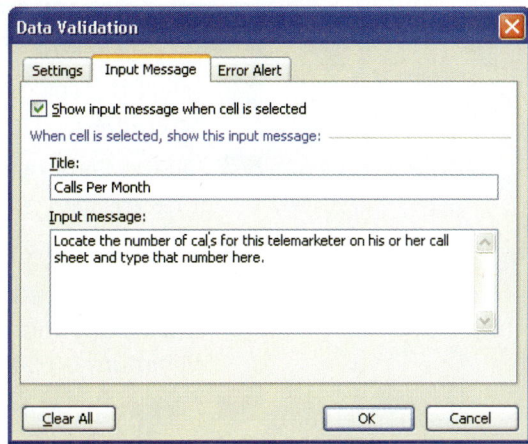

12 Click OK.

The input message you created appears below the active cell (C7).

13 Click cell D7.

The input message appears below the selected cell.

14 Type 3000, and press Enter.

The error message appears, as shown in Figure 5-7.

FIGURE 5-7

Entering invalid data produces error message

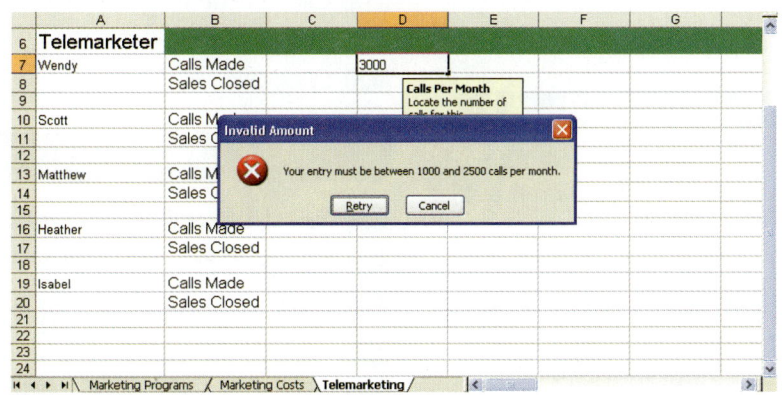

15 Click Retry.

16 Type **2152**, and press Enter.

No error message appears because the number you typed meets the requirements for the valid range of entries.

◆ **Save the workbook, and keep it open for the next exercise.**

QUICK REFERENCE ▼

Set a valid range of entries

1 Select the cell or range of cells into which the validated entries will be entered.

2 On the Data menu, click Validation, and click the Settings tab, if necessary.

3 Click the Allow down arrow.

4 Select the type of entry allowed for the selected cell or range. If you choose anything other than Any Value or Text Length, click in the Minimum box, and type the lowest value possible.

5 Click in the Maximum box, and type the greatest value possible.

6 Click OK.

Create a custom error message

1 Select the cell or range of cells to which the validation error message applies.

2 On the Data menu, click Validation.

3 Click the Error Alert tab.

4 Click the Style down arrow, and select the icon you want to accompany your error message.

5 Click in the Title box, and type the title for the error message.

6 Click in the Error Message box, and type the message you want to appear in the error message.

7 Click OK.

Create an input message

1 Select the cell or range of cells that should display the message.

2 On the Data menu, click Validation.

3 Click the Input Message tab.

4 Click in the Title box, and type your input message title.

5 Click in the Input Message box, and type your input message.

6 Click OK.

QUICK **CHECK**

Q. How does an error message differ from an input message?

A: An error message alerts you after you type the invalid entry, whereas an input message provides information before you type the entry.

Auditing Worksheets for Errors

Finding and Correcting Errors in Calculations

THE BOTTOM LINE

Excel's auditing features enable you to quickly identify the factors that produce erroneous calculation results and provide you with the tools to resolve those errors.

Formulas are often the most important part of a worksheet. Their calculations play an essential role in the display and interpretation of the rest of the data in the worksheet.

If you enter a formula that displays an error, your efforts to locate the source of the error may be difficult and time-consuming, especially if the formula references cells or ranges of cells in "distant" locations of large worksheets, other worksheets, or even other workbooks. In these situations, you can use Excel's auditing tools. These tools enable you to see how a worksheet's formulas are built, which cells are used in a formula, and how other formulas build on each other. They also help you identify cells that might be referenced incorrectly in the formula or that were selected by mistake.

A cell that contains an erroneous result displays an **error code**. The following table lists the most common error codes and what they mean.

Error Code	Description
#####	The column isn't wide enough to display the value.
#VALUE!	The formula has the wrong type of argument (such as text where a TRUE or FALSE value is required).
#NAME?	The formula contains text that Excel doesn't recognize (such as an unknown named range).
#REF!	The formula refers to a cell that doesn't exist (which can happen whenever cells are deleted).
#DIV/0!	The formula attempts to divide by zero.

When a cell with an erroneous formula is the active cell, an error button appears next to it. Click the button's down arrow to display a menu of error analysis options, as shown in Figure 5-8.

FIGURE 5-8

Options for evaluating an error

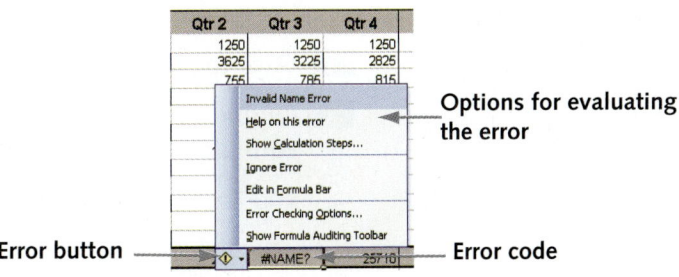

Error button — Error code

Options for evaluating the error

These options are explained in the following table.

Option	Description
Help On This Error	Connects you to the topic related to the error in Excel's Help system
Show Calculation Steps	Opens the Evaluate Formula dialog box in which each step in the calculation of the formula is displayed with an explanation of what will happen next
Ignore Error	Removes the error button from the cell
Edit In Formula Bar	Places the cursor in the Formula bar where you can modify the formula
Error Checking Options	Displays the Options dialog box, which contains various rules you can set to determine how Excel identifies and treats errors
Show Formula Auditing Toolbar	Displays the Formula Auditing toolbar

Working with the Auditing Toolbar

The **Formula Auditing toolbar** contains buttons that let you track down the cell references and data used in formulas so that you can quickly and easily identify the factor that's causing the error.

To display the Formula Auditing toolbar, on the Tools menu, point to Formula Auditing. Then click Show Formula Auditing Toolbar. The buttons on the toolbar are identified in Figure 5-9.

FIGURE 5-9

Formula Auditing toolbar

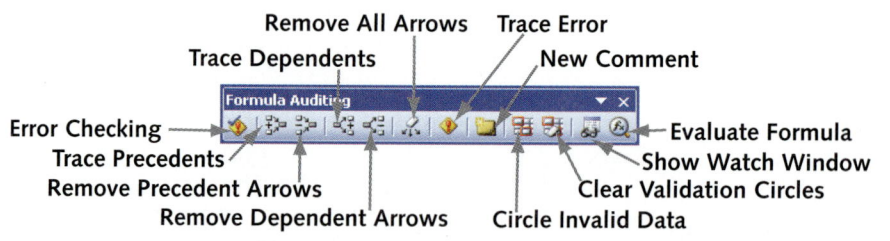

Trace errors

In this exercise, you edit a cell's content to create an error in one of the cell's formulas. Then you use the Trace Error feature to determine the nature of the error and to correct the error.

1 Click the Marketing Costs sheet tab.

2 On the Tools menu, point to Formula Auditing, and click Show Formula Auditing Toolbar.

The Formula Auditing toolbar appears.

TIP

The Formula Auditing toolbar is "floating." You can move it to other locations by dragging its title bar.

ANOTHER METHOD

On the View menu, point to Toolbars, and click Formula Auditing.

3 If necessary, move the Formula Auditing toolbar so that you can see the worksheet data.

4 Click cell D18.

5 Type Radio, and press Enter.

A #VALUE! error appears in cell D20.

FIGURE 5-10

#VALUE error

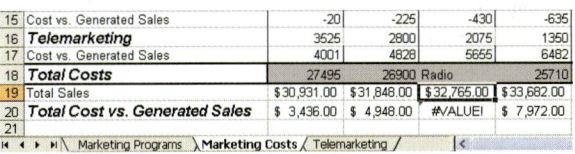

6 Click cell D20.

 7 On the Formula Auditing toolbar, click the Trace Error button.

The error is traced from cell D20 to the cell containing the value that has generated the erroneous result, as shown in Figure 5-11.

FIGURE 5-11

Tracing the error

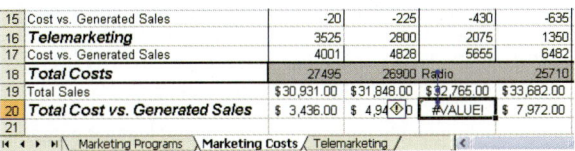

8 Click cell D18, type 26305, and press Enter.

 9 Click cell D20, and on the Formula Auditing toolbar, click the Remove Precedent Arrows button.

The trace arrows are removed.

◆ Save the workbook, and keep it open for the next exercise.

QUICK REFERENCE ▼

Display the Formula Auditing toolbar

On the Tools menu, point to Formula Auditing and click Show Formula Auditing Toolbar.

Or

On the View menu, point to Toolbars and click Formula Auditing.

Trace errors in a formula

1 Click the cell containing the error.

2 On the Formula Auditing toolbar, click the Trace Error button.

Tracing Precedent Cells

If you're working with your own worksheet, you probably know which cells are used in your formulas. But if you're looking at a worksheet that was created by another user or that you created a long time ago, you might not know or remember which cells were referenced in the worksheet's formulas. Using the Trace Precedents feature, you can see which cells are referenced in your formula, allowing you to troubleshoot your formula and make corrections easily.

A formula's **precedents** are those cells that the formula references. Of course, you can see these cells' addresses in the Formula bar when the cell containing the formula is selected. But the Trace Precedents tool on the Formula Auditing toolbar lets you see how the cells relate to the formula. When you view a formula's precedents, arrows lead from the formula's precedent cells to the cell containing the formula.

TIP

If your formula references cells in another worksheet or workbook, the arrow for precedent cells will point to a small grid icon, indicating an external reference. The names of the workbooks or worksheets that are referenced appear in the Formula bar.

Trace precedents

In this exercise, you trace a formula's precedents.

1 Click cell B18.

2 On the Formula Auditing toolbar, click the Trace Precedents button.

Arrows lead from the precedent cells to the cell containing the formula that references them.

FIGURE 5-12

Cells used in formula are identified

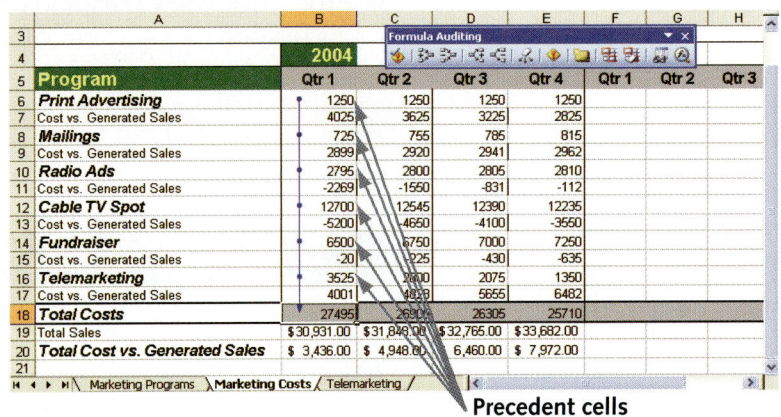

Precedent cells

3 **Click cell B20.**

4 **On the Formula Auditing toolbar, click the Trace Precedents button.**

The cells used in the formula found in cell B20 are identified with a precedent arrow.

5 **On the Formula Auditing toolbar, click the Remove Precedent Arrows button twice.**

The precedent arrows are removed.

◆ **Save the workbook, and keep it open for the next exercise.**

QUICK REFERENCE ▼

Trace a formula's precedents

1 Click the cell containing the formula you want to trace.

2 On the Formula Auditing toolbar, click the Trace Precedents button.

3 If your formula contains references to other formulas, continue to click the Trace Precedents button to view these formulas and the cells that are referenced in them.

Remove the displayed precedent arrows

On the Formula Auditing toolbar, click the Remove Precedent Arrows button.

QUICK CHECK

Q. If you trace a formula's precedents, do the trace arrows lead from the formula cell to the precedent cells or vice versa?

A: The trace arrows lead from the precedent cells to the formula cell.

Tracing Dependent Cells

When you trace precedents, you start with a cell that contains the formula and trace back to view the cells that are used in the formula. You can do the same trace in the opposite direction. You can start with a cell and trace the formulas that refer to it or are dependent on the cell's content. These are referred to as **dependents.** You might trace a cell's dependents if you change the value of a cell or want to delete it so that you can determine exactly which formulas are affected by that change.

Tracing the dependents saves you the trouble of scrolling through an entire worksheet looking for formula errors. For example, the accountant at Adventure Works creates formulas in budget workbooks to calculate totals for different account categories. The account category values are located in different parts of the budget worksheet, so if the accountant changes a value, scanning through the worksheet to determine which formulas are affected can be time-consuming. The accountant can more easily trace the dependent cells in which the cell is referenced.

Trace dependents

In this exercise, you trace the dependents of a formula.

1 **Click cell B12.**

2 **On the Formula Auditing toolbar, click the Trace Dependents button.**

The trace arrow leads from cell B12 to cells B13 and B18, which contain formulas that reference it.

3 **Click cell C18.**

4 **On the Formula Auditing toolbar, click the Trace Dependents button.**

The trace arrow leads from cell C18 to cell C20, which contains the formula that references it.

FIGURE 5-13

Tracing dependent cells to their formula cells

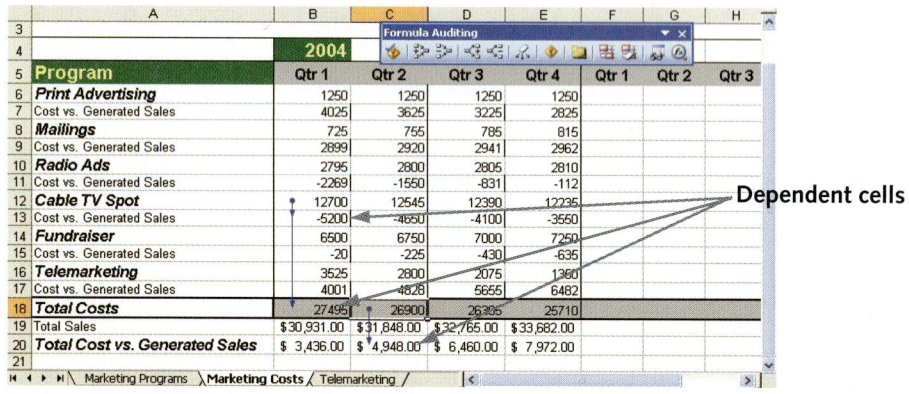

5 **On the Formula Auditing toolbar, click the Remove Dependent Arrows button.**

6 **Click cell B12, and click the Remove Dependent Arrows button.**

◆ **Save the workbook, and keep it open for the next exercise.**

QUICK CHECK

Q. If cell B3 contains a value and cell B10 contains a formula that references the value, which cell do you click to trace dependents?

A: **You click cell B3.**

Finding and Correcting Errors
in Calculations

QUICK REFERENCE ▼

Trace a formula's dependents

1 Click the cell whose reference you want to trace.

2 On the Formula Auditing toolbar, click the Trace Dependents button.

Remove the displayed dependent arrows

On the Formula Auditing toolbar, click the Remove Dependent Arrows button.

Watching and Evaluating Formulas

You can use the Watch Window and Evaluate Formula options on the Formula Auditing toolbar to further scrutinize formulas on the worksheet. With the Watch Window, you can select cells containing formulas to add to the window. As you make changes to cells referenced in the formula, you can view immediately in the Watch Window how the changes affect the formula cell.

With the Evaluate Formula option, the formula in the selected cell is evaluated part by part in the Evaluate Formula dialog box. You can readily see what each cell reference in the formula represents and where errors are introduced in the formula.

Watch and evaluate formulas

In this exercise, you introduce an error into a formula and view how changes to a cell appear immediately in the Watch Window. You then evaluate the formula.

1 **On the Formula Auditing toolbar, click the Show Watch Window button.**

2 **Click cell B20, and click the Add Watch button in the Watch Window.**

The Add Watch window opens, with cell B20 designated as the cell whose value you want to watch.

3 **Click Add.**

The Watch Window displays the selected cell, as shown in Figure 5-14.

FIGURE 5-14

Watch Window

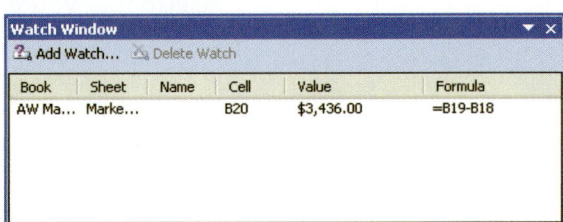

4 **Click the Marketing Programs sheet tab, and then click cell B14.**

You notice that the total in cell B14 is calculated by a formula that references each individual cell in the range. You decide that you want to replace that formula with the more efficient SUM function.

5 **In cell B14, type SUM(B8:B13), press Enter, and look at the Watch Window.**

The Watch Window shows that cell B20 on the Marketing Costs sheet now contains an error, as shown in Figure 5-15.

FIGURE 5-15

Error identified in Watch Window

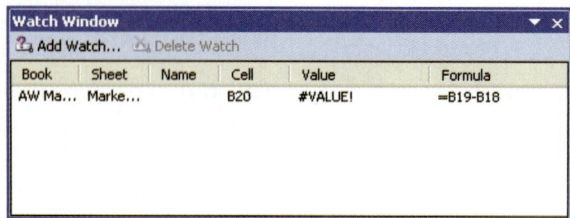

6 **Switch back to the Marketing Costs sheet, make sure that cell B20 is selected, and click the Evaluate Formula button on the Formula Auditing toolbar.**

The Evaluate Formula dialog box opens, as shown in Figure 5-16.

FIGURE 5-16

Evaluate Formula dialog box

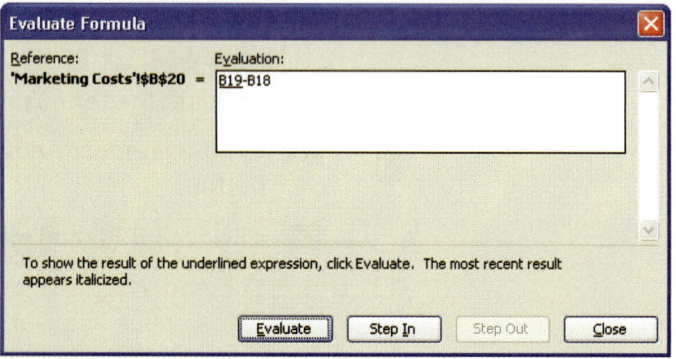

7 **Click the Evaluate button.**

The value of cell B19 appears. The value is the SUM function you just entered, instead of the formula result, as shown in Figure 5-17. You realize that you forgot to begin the function with the equal (=) sign.

FIGURE 5-17

Identifying where the error was introduced

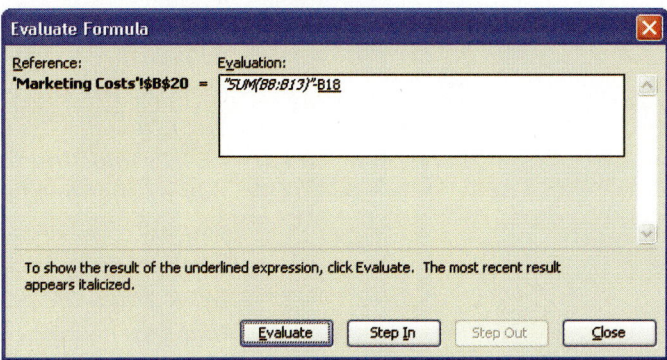

8 Click the Close button in the Evaluate Formula dialog box.

9 Switch to the Marketing Programs worksheet, and click cell B14.

10 Insert an equal (=) sign at the beginning of the function formula, and press Enter.

The Watch Window indicates that the error in cell B20 on the Marketing Costs worksheet has been removed.

11 In the Watch Window, click the item listed, and click Delete Watch.

12 Close the Watch Window and the Formula Auditing toolbar.

◆ Save and close AW Marketing. If you are continuing to other lessons, leave Excel open. If you are not continuing to other lessons, save and close all open workbooks. Click the Close button in the top right corner of the Excel window.

QUICK REFERENCE ▼

Watch a formula

1 Click the Show Watch Window button on the Formula Auditing toolbar.

2 Click the cell in the worksheet that you want to watch, and click the Add Watch button in the Watch Window.

3 In the Add Watch dialog box, click Add.

Evaluate a formula

1 Click the cell containing the formula you want to evaluate.

2 Click the Evaluate Formula button on the Formula Auditing toolbar.

3 In the Evaluate Formula dialog box, click the Evaluate button to step through each part of the formula.

4 When you are done, click the Close button to close the Evaluate Formula dialog box.

QUICK CHECK

Q. How do you add cells to the Watch Window?

A: Click the cell, and in the Watch Window, click the Add Watch button.

Key Points

✔ *You can control the data that is entered in a cell or range and help ensure its accuracy by using data validation tools. These tools let you set parameters within which any data entered must fall.*

✔ *Excel's auditing features enable you to quickly identify the factors that produce erroneous calculation results and provide you with the tools to resolve those errors.*

✔ *The Formula Auditing toolbar contains buttons that let you track down the cell references and data used in formulas so that you can quickly and easily identify the factor that's causing the error.*

✔ *Using the Trace Precedents feature, you can see which cells are referenced in your formula, allowing you to troubleshoot your formula and make corrections easily.*

✔ *Using the Trace Dependents feature, you can see how changing a cell's value affects any formulas that reference the cell.*

✔ *You can use the Watch Window and Evaluate Formula options on the Formula Auditing toolbar to further scrutinize formulas on the worksheet. With the Watch Window, you can view immediately in the Watch Window how changes to cells referenced in a formula affect the formula cell. With the Evaluate Formula option, a formula is evaluated part by part so that you can readily see what each cell reference in the formula represents and where errors are introduced in the formula.*

Quick Quiz

True/False

T F 1. A data entry list is defined as an organized collection of information displayed in row-and-column format so that it can be sorted, filtered, or manipulated in another way.

T F 2. You can create a data entry list only for a field that contains numeric values.

T F 3. You can create your own error message to appear when a user enters data that violates validation settings.

T F 4. An input message is designed to aid users in data entry.

T F 5. The #REF! error code indicates that the formula refers to a cell that doesn't exist.

Multiple Choice

1. Which type of error message includes Retry and Cancel buttons in its dialog box?
    a. Stop
    b. Warning
    c. Information
    d. Alert

2. Which data type would you use to validate numeric entries with no decimal places?
    a. Any Value
    b. Whole Number
    c. Decimal
    d. Text Length

3. Which error code indicates that the formula has the wrong type of argument?
    a. #####
    b. #VALUE!
    c. #NAME?
    d. #ARGUE!

4. If you want to trace an error from the formula cell to the cells that the formula references, what would you be tracing?
    a. precedents
    b. dependents
    c. absolutes
    d. relatives

5. If you want to trace a cell value to the formulas that reference the cell, what would you be tracing?
    a. precedents
    b. dependents
    c. absolutes
    d. relatives

Short Answer

1. How do you display the Formula Auditing toolbar?

2. How would you trace the precedents for a formula located in cell A8?

3. You want to restrict the value that can be entered into a cell to be between 0 and 1000, and you want to notify the user when an entry is not within this range. How would you do this?

4. What happens when you try to enter text in a cell that allows only numeric entries?

5. How do you validate a cell so that any whole number other than zero can be entered in the cell?

On Your Own

◆ **Open AW Reservation Stats from the Excel Expert Practice/Lesson05 folder.**

Exercise 1

On the Room Use sheet, create an input message for cells N5:Q7, stating that values entered should be greater than 0 but less than 300. Create a warning-style error alert stating that invalid data was entered. Test each message by entering values that do not fall within the valid range.

◆ **Save the workbook, and keep it open for the next exercise.**

Exercise 2

In the AW Reservation Stats workbook, click the Quarterly Comparisons sheet tab. Trace the dependents for cell I3. Trace the precedents for cell F8. Then trace the precedents for cell D8. What does the icon that appears when you trace this cell's precedents indicate? Remove the dependent and precedent arrows.

◆ **Save and close the workbook.**

One Step Further

Exercise 1

Explore the buttons on the Formula Auditing toolbar that were not discussed in this lesson (Error Checking, Circle Invalid Data, and Clear Validation Circles). Write a brief explanation on the use of each button. Use Excel's Help files, if necessary.

◆ **Open AW Marketing from the Excel Expert Practice/Lesson05 folder.**

Exercise 2

Re-create the #VALUE! error on the Marketing Costs sheet by typing some text into a cell in row 18. Point to the error button that appears alongside the cell containing the error, and click the down arrow. What can you find out about this error from the list that appears? What happens if you ignore the error? What dialog box do you see when you click Show Calculation Steps? What are the error-checking options available to you? Write a report outlining the options available from the Error button drop-down list.

◆ **Save and close the workbook.**

Exercise 3

In this lesson, you learned about the data types for which you can set validation rules. Refer to the table that listed the data types, and provide an example of when you might use each one.

Using Data Analysis Tools and Features

KEY TERMS

- constraints
- data analysis
- Goal Seek
- interactive Web format
- page fields
- PivotTable
- PivotTable list
- scenarios
- Solver

Microsoft Excel provides a rich set of features for analyzing data. **Data analysis** involves any steps that you take to reveal meaning behind the data in worksheets. Up to this point, the only true data analysis tools you've used in this book are the Excel charts that graphically represent data. But managers have other data analysis requirements that can't always be met by creating charts. For example, managers must be able to create "What if?" scenarios that describe how values can change under different business circumstances. A company's sales manager creates a sales quota for salespeople for each upcoming quarter. The sales manager doesn't want to simply guess at what these amounts should be. Instead, she uses Excel to determine what the sales quotas would be if sales grew at a rate of 15 percent per quarter. Then she creates another "What if?" scenario to determine what the quotas would be if sales grew at a rate of 20 percent per quarter.

In another example, an inventory manager likes to use the inventory records list stored in an Excel worksheet to create reports that summarize and organize inventory totals in different ways. Creating different summary reports in this way helps him to better understand future ordering requirements and trends and to identify current inventory problems. Excel provides several tools that you can use to analyze data quickly and effectively.

Working with PivotTables

Creating and Using PivotTables

THE BOTTOM LINE

With a PivotTable, you can experiment with different row and column arrangements in a data list. This tool enables you to analyze or interpret data in a different manner.

A **PivotTable** is a report created from an existing worksheet that summarizes worksheet data by rearranging it in different row-and-column layouts so that you can more easily identify the relationships among data—especially among totals. The easiest way to explain the value of a PivotTable is through an example.

At Adventure Works, the inventory manager uses an Excel worksheet to track inventory items supplied to guest rooms. Inventory items are organized into categories—bath items, bedding, clothing, and food. Columns include the amount for the current quantity ordered per inventory item, the amount for the current quantity on hand per item, and the total value of current inventory for each item. Following all rows for a particular category, the inventory manager has created a Totals row that summarizes the quantities for each category, as shown in Figure 6-1.

FIGURE 6-1

Inventory worksheet

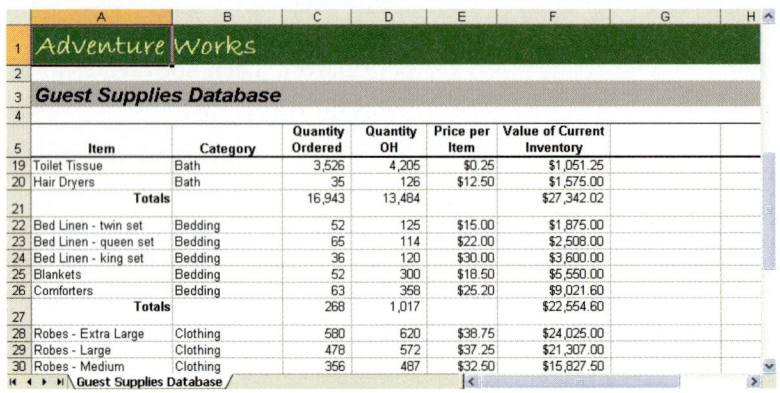

Although this worksheet is well organized, it isn't possible to see the totals for all categories at a single glance. The inventory manager must scroll the worksheet to view each Totals row. By creating a PivotTable, the inventory manager reorganizes the category and totals information so that he can easily view totals at a glance, as shown in Figure 6-2.

FIGURE 6-2

"Pivoting" the totals data so it's visible

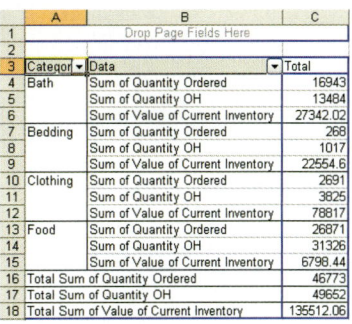

	A	B	C
1		Drop Page Fields Here	
2			
3	Category ▼	Data ▼	Total
4	Bath	Sum of Quantity Ordered	16943
5		Sum of Quantity OH	13484
6		Sum of Value of Current Inventory	27342.02
7	Bedding	Sum of Quantity Ordered	268
8		Sum of Quantity OH	1017
9		Sum of Value of Current Inventory	22554.6
10	Clothing	Sum of Quantity Ordered	2691
11		Sum of Quantity OH	3825
12		Sum of Value of Current Inventory	78817
13	Food	Sum of Quantity Ordered	26871
14		Sum of Quantity OH	31326
15		Sum of Value of Current Inventory	6798.44
16	Total Sum of Quantity Ordered		46773
17	Total Sum of Quantity OH		49652
18	Total Sum of Value of Current Inventory		135512.06

Creating a PivotTable

To create a PivotTable, you begin by displaying the PivotTable and PivotChart Wizard, which you use to define the range of data that you want to show in the PivotTable, the items that you want to include in the PivotTable, and the layout of rows and columns in the PivotTable.

◆ **To complete the procedures in this lesson, you must use the files AW Guest Supplies, AW Personnel, AW Reservation Stats, Quarterly Quota, and Sales Averages in the Lesson06 folder in the Excel Expert Practice folder located on your hard disk.**

◆ **Open AW Guest Supplies from the Excel Expert Practice/Lesson06 folder.**

Create a PivotTable

In this exercise, you use the PivotTable and PivotChart Wizard to create a PivotTable that displays a report of totals for each category in the AW Guest Supplies worksheet.

1 **Scroll through the Guest Supplies Database worksheet to locate the totals for each category.**

2 **On the Data menu, click PivotTable and PivotChart Report.**

The first PivotTable and PivotChart Wizard dialog box appears. Notice that the PivotTable option is selected by default.

TIP

If the Office Assistant appears, close it.

FIGURE 6-3

PivotTable and PivotChart Wizard – Step 1 of 3 dialog box

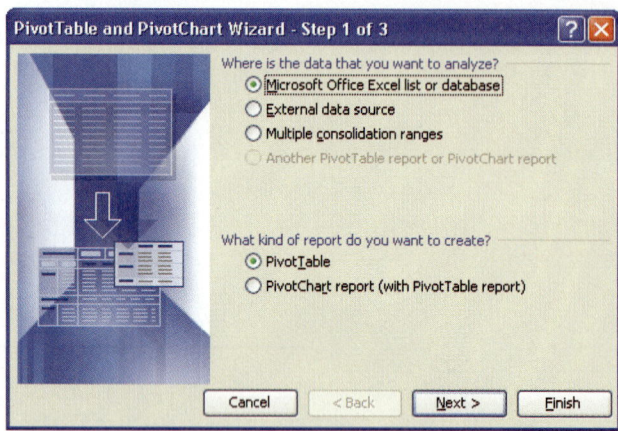

> **TIP**
>
> If you did not select a range of cells prior to starting the PivotTable and PivotChart Wizard, the dialog box will select the entire worksheet by default. This is indicated by the flashing marquee around the worksheet and by the range shown in the dialog box.

3 **Click Next.**

The next wizard dialog box appears. You use this dialog box to define the range for the data that will be summarized in the PivotTable.

FIGURE 6-4

PivotTable and PivotChart Wizard – Step 2 of 3 dialog box

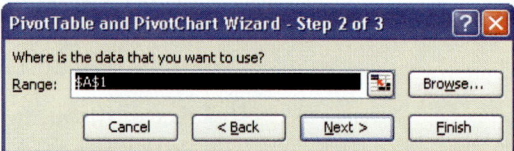

> **TIP**
>
> You can verify the range you selected by clicking the Back button and looking at the flashing marquee around the selected cells and the range reference that appears in the dialog box.

4 **In the Range box, type B5:F37, and click Next.**

The range of cells is selected, and the next dialog box appears.

FIGURE 6-5

PivotTable and PivotChart Wizard – Step 3 of 3 dialog box

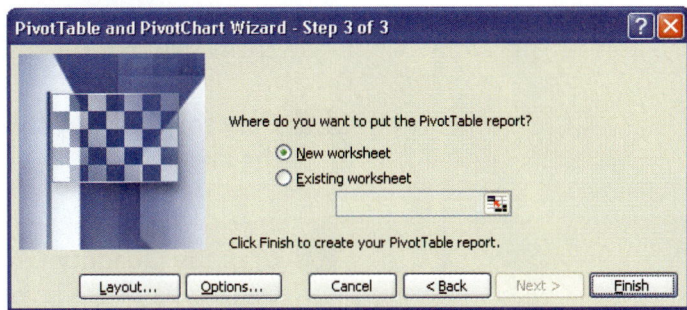

In this dialog box, you specify whether you want the PivotTable to appear in the same worksheet or in a new worksheet. If the PivotTable is small, you might want to place it in the same worksheet so you can compare the PivotTable with the worksheet contents. However, because the reason for creating PivotTables is often to isolate and format totals, it's generally preferable to place PivotTables in different worksheets. You can switch back to the original worksheet at any time.

TIP

The names on the field buttons depend on the names you use for column headings.

5 **If necessary, click the New Worksheet option, and click the Layout button.**

The PivotTable will be created in a separate worksheet, and the PivotTable and PivotChart Wizard – Layout dialog box appears. In this dialog box, you organize the fields that you want to include in the PivotTable. The field buttons appear along the right side of the dialog box. You can drag these buttons to the desired positions in the layout.

FIGURE 6-6

PivotTable and PivotChart Wizard – Layout dialog box

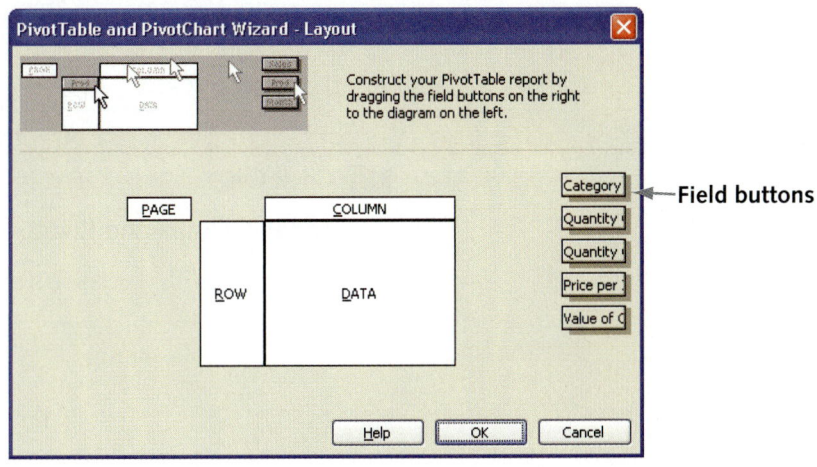

TIP

You can see the complete name of each field by holding the pointer over the field button until a ScreenTip appears.

6 **Drag the Category field button (the first button) to the ROW area of the layout.**

The PivotTable will display summary rows grouped by category.

7 **Drag the Quantity Ordered field button (the second button) to the DATA area of the layout.**

The PivotTable will display a Quantity Ordered sum for each category.

8 **Drag the Quantity OH field button (the third button) to the DATA area of the Layout, below the Quantity Ordered button.**

The PivotTable will display a Quantity OH sum for each category.

9 **Drag the Value of Current Inventory field button (the last button) to the DATA area of the layout, below the Quantity OH button.**

The PivotTable will display a Value of Current Inventory sum for each category. Your dialog box should match the one shown in Figure 6-7. If your dialog box looks different, drag the field buttons until they match the buttons in the figure.

FIGURE 6-7

Positioning fields

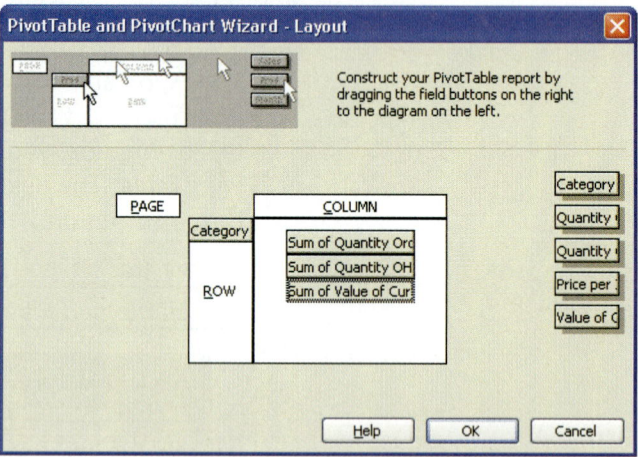

10 **Click OK.**

The PivotTable and PivotChart Wizard dialog box reappears.

11 **Click the Finish button.**

The wizard closes and displays your PivotTable in a new worksheet, along with the PivotTable toolbar and the PivotTable Field List dialog box. Notice that a category field named *(blank)* appears near the bottom of the report. This category field was created erroneously because the wizard found blank category entries for the category totals in the worksheet. The *(blank)* category also causes the grand totals at the bottom of the PivotTable to be calculated incorrectly. You'll learn how to remove this category field in the next exercise.

FIGURE 6-8

Completed PivotTable

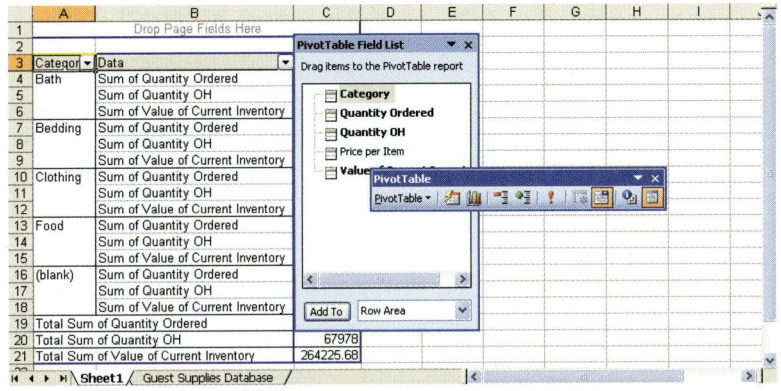

◆ **Save the workbook, and keep it open for the next exercise.**

TIP

Click anywhere in a PivotTable to delete it. On the PivotTable toolbar, click the PivotTable button to open the menu, point to Select, and click Entire Table. On the Edit menu, point to Clear, and click All.

QUICK REFERENCE ▼

Create a PivotTable using the PivotTable and PivotChart Wizard

1 On the Data menu, click PivotTable And PivotChart Report.

2 Click Next to accept the default settings and to proceed with the wizard.

3 Click the first cell containing the data you want to use, and drag to select the range of cells you want to analyze.

Or

In the Range box, type the range of cells that you want to analyze.

1 Click Next.

2 Click New Worksheet to create a new sheet in the workbook for the PivotTable.

Or

Click Existing Worksheet to place the PivotTable on the currently active sheet.

1 Click the Layout button.

2 Drag the field buttons from the right side of the dialog box (one for each of the fields in your list) onto the layout, placing them in the PAGE, ROW, COLUMN, or DATA areas.

3 Click OK.

4 Click the Finish button to create the PivotTable.

Modifying a PivotTable

 Editing PivotTables

The advantages of creating a PivotTable include the ability to reorganize the row-and-column layout, add or remove the fields and categories that appear, and change the format of table data. Excel provides dozens of techniques for modifying a PivotTable. Many of the options for modifying a PivotTable are available from the PivotTable toolbar.

FIGURE 6-9

PivotTable toolbar

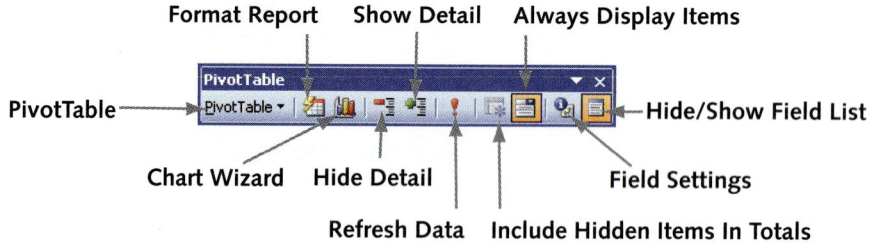

The following table explains the more commonly used buttons on the PivotTable toolbar.

Button Name	Description
PivotTable	Displays a menu of PivotTable options; the menu provides convenient access to most PivotTable options, especially if you have difficulty remembering what the other buttons do
Format Report	Displays a dialog box of AutoFormats, which are designs that you can apply to your PivotTable report
Chart Wizard	Displays the PivotTable as a column chart; you can modify a PivotChart (change the chart type, chart options, and so on) just as you can any chart that you create for a worksheet

Hide Detail	Hides detail lines; if your PivotTable contains detail rows in addition to summaries, you can use this button to hide the detail lines
Show Detail	Displays details for a selected field; normally you use the Show Detail button with the PivotTable to view details that appear only in the worksheet and then use the Hide Detail button to remove the details after you have reviewed them
Refresh Data	Updates the PivotTable with your changes; if you make any changes in the worksheet that affect the contents of the PivotTable, clicking this button refreshes the PivotTable so that it reflects your changes
Field Settings	Displays a dialog box that you can use to change the way PivotTable fields are totaled; totals are summed by default, but you can change the setting for one or more fields to display a total count of all rows for a field, the maximum value in a group, the minimum value in a group, and other mathematical and statistical totals
Hide/Show Field List	Displays the Table Field List dialog box on top of your worksheet; if you don't plan to add any fields to the PivotTable, you can hide the list to increase the viewing area in the PivotTable; if you choose to hide the list, the Hide Field List button becomes the Show Field List button, which you can click to display the list

The PivotTable Field List displays the fields that are available for the PivotTable. The fields shown on the list depend on the range of cells that you selected when you created the PivotTable. You can drag any of these buttons to the PivotTable to add fields. When you want to remove a field from your PivotTable, you can drag the column heading for the field from the PivotTable onto the PivotTable Field List. You also can use the down arrows that appear in each column-heading cell of your PivotTable to add or remove fields in the PivotTable.

You can further summarize data in a PivotTable by creating **page fields.**
When you add a page field to a PivotTable, the report displays summary
information for that field only. In this sense, a page field works like a
filter—by filtering out all summary information except for the page field.
You add page fields by dragging a field heading from the PivotTable Field
List to the page field area at the top of the PivotTable. In Figure 6-10, the
Category field button is being dragged from the PivotTable Field List to the
page field area. You'll see the result of adding this page field in the following
exercise.

FIGURE 6-10

Adding a page field

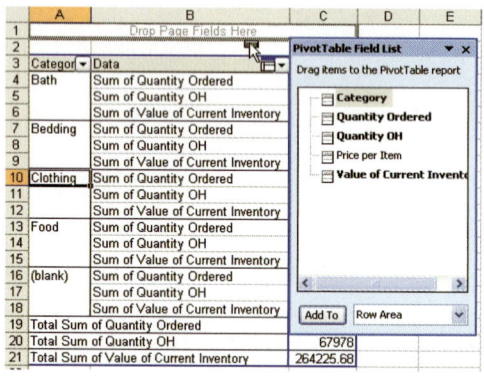

Modify a PivotTable

In this exercise, you remove the *(blank)* field from the PivotTable,
change the layout of your PivotTable to view summary information in
different ways, and use AutoFormat to format a PivotTable attractively.

1 **In cell A3, click the Category heading down arrow.**

A list of fields displayed in the Category column appears.

FIGURE 6-11

Field list

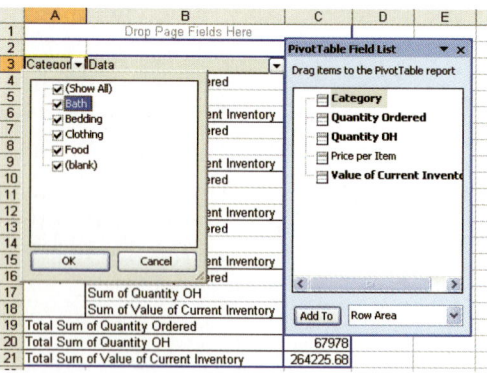

2 On the list of fields that appears, clear the check mark to the left of the (blank) field, and click OK.

The *(blank)* Category field is removed from the PivotTable. The three Total Sum rows at the bottom of the PivotTable are now calculated correctly.

FIGURE 6-12

Removing a field from a PivotTable

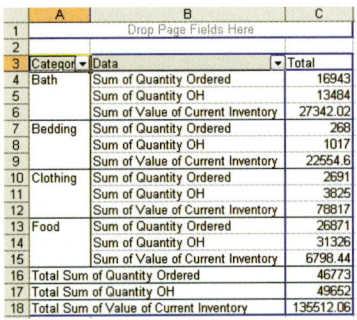

3 On the PivotTable toolbar, click PivotTable, and then click PivotTable Wizard.

The final PivotTable and PivotChart Wizard dialog box appears.

4 Click the Layout button.

The PivotTable and PivotChart Wizard – Layout dialog box appears.

5 Drag the Category field button to the COLUMN area of the layout.

The categories in the PivotTable will be displayed in columns.

FIGURE 6-13

Displaying categories in columns

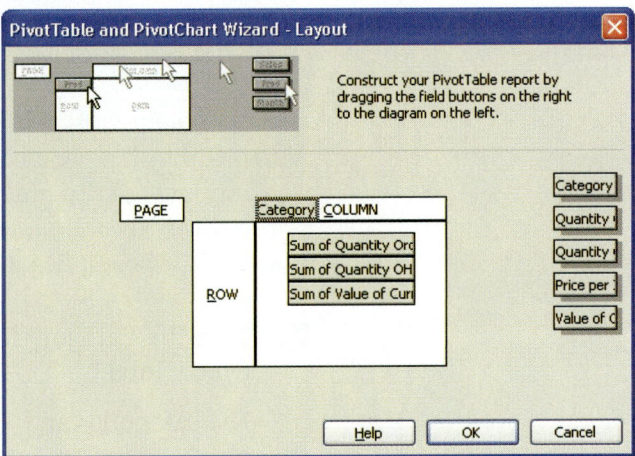

6 Click OK.

The PivotTable and PivotChart Wizard dialog box reappears.

7 **Click the Finish button.**

Excel displays the modified PivotTable in the same worksheet. The new PivotTable rotates the rows and columns. Because you placed the Category field button in the COLUMN section of the layout, the categories now appear as columns and the Data sums appear as rows.

FIGURE 6-14

Modified PivotTable

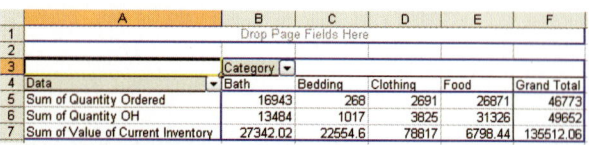

	A	B	C	D	E	F
1		Drop Page Fields Here				
2						
3		Category ▾				
4	Data ▾	Bath	Bedding	Clothing	Food	Grand Total
5	Sum of Quantity Ordered	16943	268	2691	26871	46773
6	Sum of Quantity OH	13484	1017	3825	31326	49652
7	Sum of Value of Current Inventory	27342.02	22554.6	78817	6798.44	135512.06

TIP

Note that the PivotTable Field List is visible only when the PivotTable is selected.

8 **Drag the Category field button from the PivotTable Field List to cell A1 in the page field area, which contains the gray text "Drop Page Fields Here."**

The PivotTable filters the data so that only Category summaries appear.

FIGURE 6-15

Displaying only Category summaries in the PivotTable

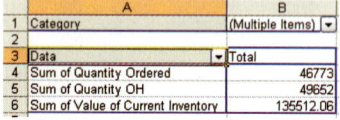

	A	B
1	Category	(Multiple Items) ▾
2		
3	Data ▾	Total
4	Sum of Quantity Ordered	46773
5	Sum of Quantity OH	49652
6	Sum of Value of Current Inventory	135512.06

TIP

If you find that the PivotTable toolbar is frequently in the way of your PivotTable data, you can drag the title bar of the toolbar to anchor it to any edge of the window. Likewise, you can drag the PivotTable Field List to any location on the screen or drag it to the right side of the window where it becomes a task pane.

9 **Drag the Category field button from the page field area onto the word "Total."**

The categories and their summaries reappear.

 10 **On the PivotTable toolbar, click the Format Report button.**

The AutoFormat dialog box appears and displays more than 20 AutoFormat designs that you can apply to your PivotTable.

FIGURE 6-16

AutoFormat dialog box

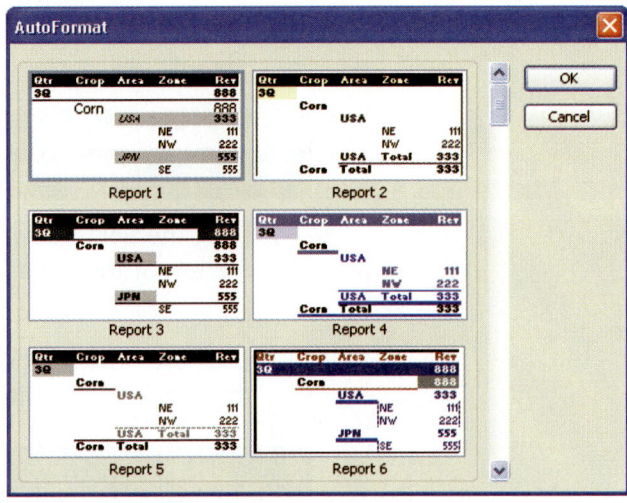

TROUBLESHOOTING TIP

If you click outside the PivotTable, the PivotTable toolbar is deactivated. To activate the toolbar again, click anywhere in the PivotTable.

11 Scroll down through the dialog box to view the complete list of AutoFormats.

12 Scroll to the Report 10 AutoFormat design, click it, and click OK. Click any blank cell outside the PivotTable to deselect it.

Excel formats the PivotTable using the Report 10 AutoFormat. Because this design displays summaries in columns, the rows and columns in your PivotTable are rotated to fit the AutoFormat.

FIGURE 6-17

Applying a format to the PivotTable

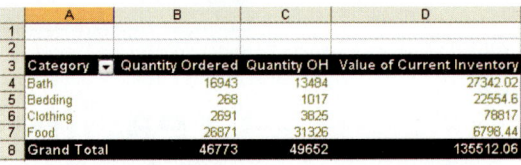

13 Double-click the sheet tab for the current worksheet, type Category Summary, and press Enter.

The worksheet is renamed.

ANOTHER METHOD

Right-click the sheet tab, click Rename on the shortcut menu, type the new name, and press Enter.

14 Save the workbook as Guest Supplies with PivotTable.

◆ Keep this file open for the next exercise.

QUICK REFERENCE ▼

Add a field to a PivotTable

Drag the field from the PivotTable Field List to the page field area at the top of the PivotTable.

Or

Click the down arrow that appears on the column heading, and select the check box of the field you want to add.

Remove a field from a PivotTable

Drag the field heading out of the PivotTable layout diagram.

Or

Click the down arrow that appears on the column heading, and clear the check box of the field you want to remove.

Change the layout of a PivotTable using the wizard

1 On the PivotTable toolbar, click the PivotTable button.

2 Click PivotTable Wizard on the PivotTable menu.

3 Click the Layout button.

4 Drag field headings to the desired ROW, COLUMN, DATA, or PAGE area.

Use AutoFormat to format a PivotTable

1 On the PivotTable toolbar, click the Format Report button.

2 Select an AutoFormat from the list, and click OK.

Creating and Modifying a PivotChart

Creating a Dynamic Chart Using PivotCharts

THE BOTTOM LINE

A PivotChart provides a more graphic and visual representation of the data and summaries in a PivotTable, enabling you to make deductions and identify trends effectively.

Just as you can create a chart for data in a worksheet, you also can create a PivotChart for data in a PivotTable. Like a PivotTable, a PivotChart gives you the flexibility to experiment with different arrangements and representations of data.

You can create a PivotChart from an existing PivotTable, or you can create a PivotChart from worksheet data. Then the PivotTable and PivotChart Wizard automatically creates the PivotTable for you.

You can modify a PivotChart by dragging field buttons to column and row areas on the chart. This approach adds fields and rotates column and row data on different axes, which you can do by dragging field buttons in a PivotTable. You can either drag a field button that appears on the PivotChart (to move data to a different axis) or drag a field button from the PivotTable Field List onto the PivotChart (to add fields to the chart). You also can make other modifications to PivotCharts, such as changing the chart type and formatting chart parts.

Create and modify a PivotChart

In this exercise, you create a PivotChart from your existing PivotTable. Then you rotate data on the chart and modify the chart type.

1 **Click any cell in the PivotTable.**

The buttons on the PivotTable toolbar are activated, and the PivotTable Field List reappears.

TIP

You can specify page fields in a PivotChart just as you do in a PivotTable, and you can drag field buttons around in the PivotChart to reorganize the way data appears in the chart.

2 **On the PivotTable toolbar, click the Chart Wizard button.**

Excel displays the PivotTable as a stacked column chart.

FIGURE 6-18

Creating a PivotChart

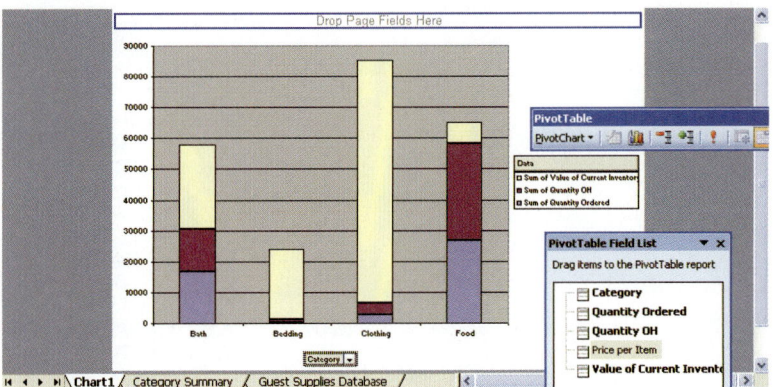

3 **Locate the Category field button in the bottom center of the PivotChart, and drag this button above the Data button along the right side of the PivotChart.**

The chart now shows each category amount and each summary amount as a separate section in one stacked column.

4 **Drag the Data field button into the "Drop Category Fields Here" box along the bottom of the PivotChart.**

The chart axes are now rotated so that each column displays summaries for each category.

FIGURE 6-19

Arranging chart elements

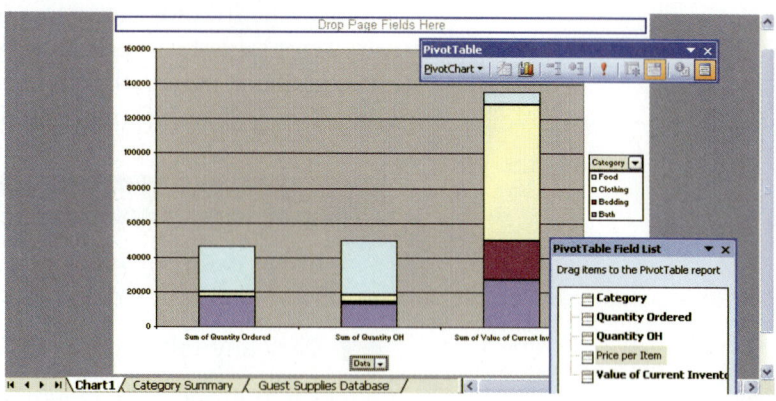

TIP

If you have experience working with charts created from worksheets, you'll notice that the Chart Type dialog box shown here is identical to the Chart Type dialog box you've used in the past.

---

5 **Right-click on the background of the chart, and click Chart Type from the menu.**

The Chart Type dialog box appears.

FIGURE 6-20

Chart Type dialog box

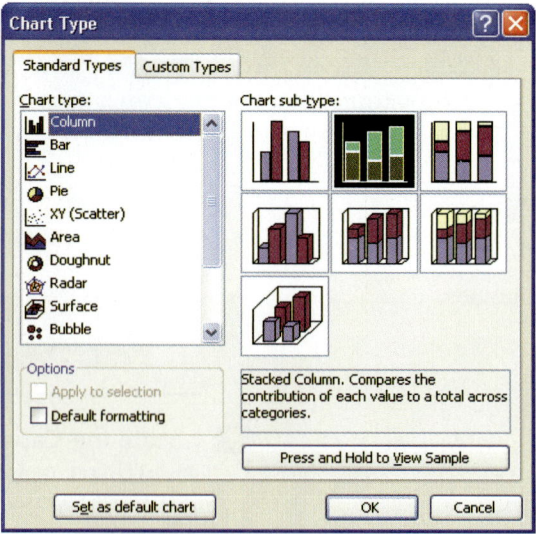

6 In the Chart Sub-type section, click the third chart in the second row (a stacked column chart with a 3-D effect), and click OK.

The PivotChart changes to the selected chart sub-type.

FIGURE 6-21

Changing the chart type

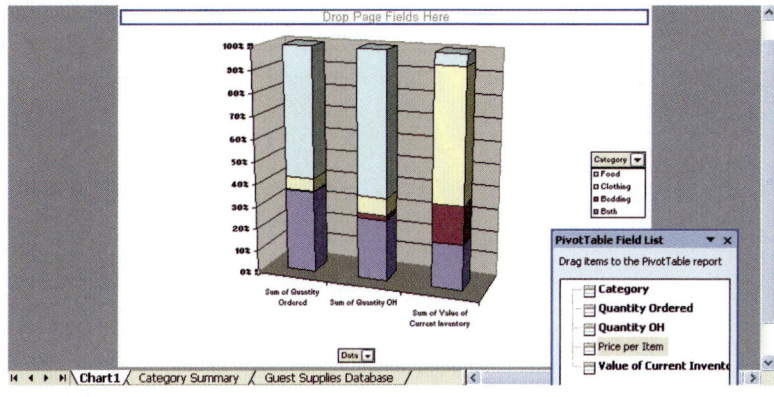

7 Right-click the Value Axis labels (the percentages on the Y axis), and click Format Axis on the shortcut menu.

The Format Axis dialog box opens.

8 Click the Font tab, and in the Font Style box, click Bold; then click OK.

The labels are bolded.

◆ Save the workbook, and keep it open for the next exercise.

QUICK REFERENCE ▼

Create a PivotChart from an existing PivotTable

1 Click any cell in the PivotTable.

2 On the PivotTable toolbar, click the Chart Wizard button.

3 Drag fields to axes, as desired.

Using Goal Seek

THE BOTTOM LINE

With Excel's powerful Goal Seek feature, you can create a quick analysis of how a particular cell value must change in order to generate a desired result for a formula. This eliminates the timely task of building complex formulas that test various values.

When you know the expected outcome or goal for a situation but don't know the values to use to arrive at that goal, you can implement Excel's **Goal Seek** feature. For example, you want to determine the growth rate

QUICK CHECK

Q. How do you add a field to a PivotChart?

A: You drag a field button from the PivotTable Field List onto the PivotChart.

Working with Goal Seek and Solver

your business must achieve in order to reach total sales of $225,000 for the coming year. Your sales for the previous year were $190,000. Using Goal Seek, you can quickly determine what your growth rate must be in order to increase total sales from $190,000 to the goal of $225,000.

To use Goal Seek, you open the Goal Seek dialog box, as shown in Figure 6-22.

FIGURE 6-22

Goal Seek dialog box

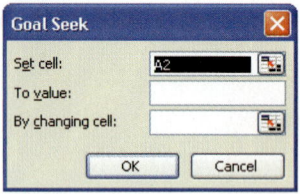

You need to provide the following three pieces of information:

- In the Set Cell box, you specify the cell that contains the current end result, which will be changed to the goal amount once the Goal Seek function is completed. This cell must contain a formula.
- In the To Value box, you specify the goal for the cell entered in the Set Cell box.
- In the By Changing Cell box, you specify the cell whose value can be adjusted in order to meet the goal. This cell must be referenced in the formula that's in the cell that you specified for the Set Cell box.

When you run the Goal Seek, a message box appears in which you can specify whether you want to accept the change made to achieve the goal or reject the change, leaving the worksheet as is.

In the following exercise, you use Goal Seek to help the Adventure Works inventory manager negotiate a better price per unit on blankets. The current price per unit, based on the number of units that the inventory manager expects to order for the year, is higher than some competitive vendors, so the inventory manager will use Goal Seek to convince the blanket vendor to lower the price-per-unit cost. The inventory manager believes that if the vendor does not negotiate a lower price, he will have to switch to a different vendor.

Use Goal Seek

In this exercise, you use Goal Seek to determine the appropriate decrease in price-per-unit cost for blankets in order to meet a total inventory valuation goal of $4,300.

1 Click the Guest Supplies Database sheet tab.

2 Click cell D25.

There are 300 blankets on hand.

3 Click cell F25, and on the Tools menu, click Goal Seek.

The Goal Seek dialog box appears, with F25 entered as the set cell.

4 Click in the To Value box, and type **4300**.

5 Click in the By Changing Cell box, and type **E25**.

The Goal Seek dialog box looks like that shown in Figure 6-23.

FIGURE 6-23

Setting the values for Goal Seek

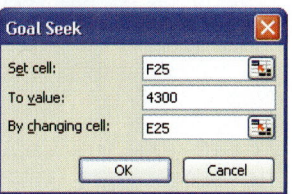

6 Click OK.

The Goal Seek Status dialog box appears, indicating that a solution was found, as shown in Figure 6-24.

FIGURE 6-24

Goal Seek Status dialog box

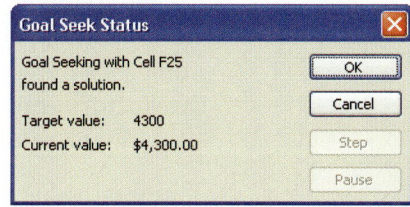

7 Click OK.

Note that the value in cell E25 has changed from $18.50 per unit to $14.33 per unit. The inventory manager will use this price to attempt to negotiate a better price per unit with the blanket vendor.

◆ Save the workbook, and keep it open for the next exercise.

QUICK REFERENCE ▼

Use Goal Seek

1 On the Tools menu, click Goal Seek.

2 In the Set Cell box, specify the cell that currently contains the formula that you want to resolve.

3 In the To Value box, enter the desired result.

4 In the By Changing Cell box, enter the reference for the cell that you want to change in order to achieve the desired result.

5 Click OK.

6 In the Goal Seek Status dialog box, click OK.

QUICK CHECK

Q. In the Goal Seek dialog box, what do you enter in the To Value box?

A: You enter the goal in the To Value box.

Analyzing Data with the Scenario Manager

Defining and Editing Alternative Data Sets

THE BOTTOM LINE

The Scenario Manager lets you quickly formulate different versions of a calculation so that you can evaluate results and determine the best outcome for a situation.

If you anticipate that a situation may have several different outcomes, you can create and store **scenarios** for each of the outcomes and display them as needed. This allows you to perform "What if?" analyses simply by switching between the different outcomes. Using the growth rate example from the previous section, you might create a scenario to determine total sales for the coming year if your growth rate is 15 percent, another if your growth rate is 18 percent, and so on.

With Excel's Scenario Manager, you specify values that can change in cells that are referenced in a formula. The formula is then recalculated based on the different values that you specify for those cells. You can change the values in more than one cell to generate an outcome, and you can create numerous outcomes, or scenarios, that can help you determine the most satisfactory result. In most cases, you should try different assumptions to see how the results of a formula will change.

You use the Scenario Manager to create and run different scenarios. With the Scenario Manager, you specify a name for each scenario and then specify cells whose values you want to change. You can choose to display the values of a scenario in the worksheet, or you can maintain the original values and simply store the scenarios for viewing as needed.

Use the Scenario Manager

In this exercise, you create two scenarios that allow you to change the values in cells D25 and E25 and view the outcome in cell F25.

1 **Click cell D25.**

You will include this cell in your scenarios.

2 **On the Tools menu, click Scenarios.**

The Scenario Manager dialog box appears, as shown in Figure 6-25.

FIGURE 6-25

Scenario Manager dialog box

3 **Click the Add button.**

The Add Scenario dialog box appears. You use this dialog box to name and create your scenario. Your name and the date you created a scenario are also added to the dialog box.

FIGURE 6-26

Add Scenario dialog box

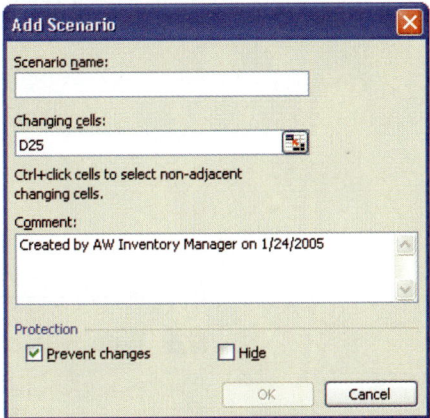

4 **Type 500 Blankets in the Scenario Name field, and click in the Changing Cells box.**

Excel displays a flashing marquee around cell D25, indicating that it is currently included in the scenario.

ANOTHER METHOD

Specify cells for a scenario by clicking in the Changing Cells box and typing the cell references or by selecting cells or a range of cells in the worksheet.

5 **Hold down Shift, and click cell E25.**

Cells D25 and E25 are included in the Changing Cells box.

FIGURE 6-27

Specifying the changing cells

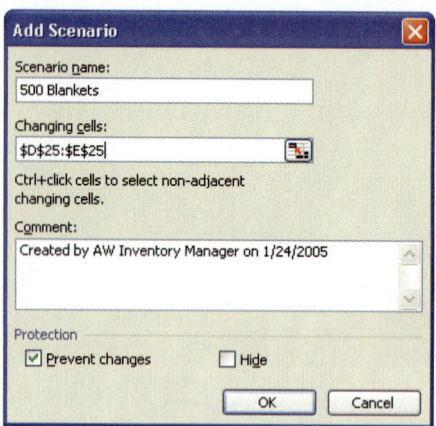

6 **Click OK.**

The Scenario Values dialog box appears.

FIGURE 6-28

Scenario Values dialog box

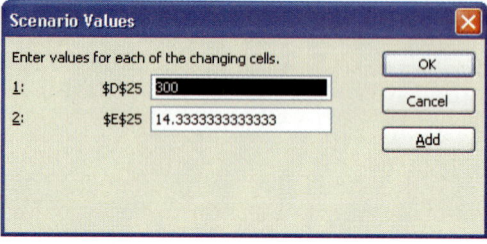

7 **Type 500, and press Tab.**

The Scenario value for cell D25 is entered, and the second scenario value box is selected.

8 **Type 17.25, and click the Add button.**

The scenario is created, and the Add Scenario dialog box is displayed again. The dialog box shows that cells D25 and E25 are the cells to change for the next scenario. In other words, Excel assumes that you want to create a different scenario for the same cells.

9 **In the Scenario name box, type 400 Blankets, and click OK.**

The Scenario Values dialog box appears.

10 **Type 400, and press Tab.**

The Scenario value for cell D25 is entered, and the second scenario value box is selected.

Defining Multiple Alternative Data Sets

11 Type **17.75**, and click **OK**.

The Scenario Manager dialog box reappears, now showing the names of the two scenarios you created.

FIGURE 6-29

New scenarios listed in the Scenario Manager dialog box

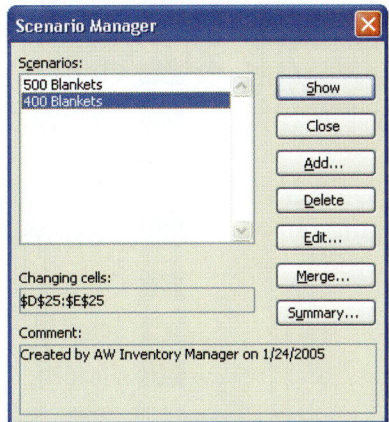

> **TIP**
>
> You should create a scenario for the original values in case you decide that none of your new scenarios are suitable.

12 On the Scenarios list, click **500 Blankets**, and click **Show**.

The values that you specified for cells D25 and E25 are inserted in the worksheet, and the formula in cell F25 is recalculated.

13 On the Scenarios list, click **400 Blankets**, and click **Show**.

The values that you specified for cells D25 and E25 are inserted in the worksheet, and the formula in cell F25 is recalculated.

> **TIP**
>
> When you want to modify a scenario, select it in the Scenarios box and click the Edit button. You can change the name of the scenario, the changing cells, or the values for the changing cells.

14 In the Scenario Manager dialog box, click **Close**.

The Scenario Manager dialog box closes.

> **TIP**
>
> You can generate a report that summarizes the scenarios on a different worksheet within the workbook. In the Scenario Manager dialog box, click Summary. The Scenario Summary dialog box opens, where you can choose to create a summary report or a PivotTable report.

◆ Save and close the workbook.

QUICK REFERENCE ▼

Use the Scenario Manager

1 On the Tools menu, click Scenarios.

2 Click the Add button.

3 In the Scenario Name box, type a name.

4 In the Changing Cells box, type the cells to be modified.

5 Click OK.

6 Change the current values to the desired values.

7 Click OK.

Switch between scenarios

1 On the Tools menu, click Scenarios.

2 Select the scenario to be displayed.

3 Click the Show button.

Using Solver

 Working with Goal Seek and Solver

THE BOTTOM LINE

With the Solver tool, you can set parameters for the values in multiple cells that are used to formulate a desired outcome. Like Goal Seek, the Solver eliminates the time-consuming trial-and-error method for finding satisfactory results.

Solver is similar to Goal Seek and scenarios, but it is more sophisticated because you can restrict the allowable range of values for different cells that can affect the goal. Consider that the sales manager at Adventure Works is trying to determine quotas for different salespeople for the upcoming quarter. Suppose that he wants next quarter's total sales for a particular salesperson to equal $125,000. He uses Solver to modify the assumed values for each sales month to achieve the desired goal, but he places **constraints** on the amounts that can be entered for different months.

For example, the sales manager knows that the first month of the new quarter will be a slower sales month than other months in the quarter. So he uses Solver to restrict the maximum value for that month's sales to $30,000. He then assumes that the maximum value for the second month will not exceed $50,000 and that the maximum amount for the third month will not exceed $60,000. Solver would then resolve the amounts in the range of cells by distributing values for the three months, based on the specified maximum amount restrictions, to achieve the goal of $125,000.

Solver is also useful for predicting how results might change over time. For example, suppose that you use Solver to create a solution when you first create the sales quota worksheet for the upcoming quarter. During the first quarter, as sales for the month accumulate, you can modify the assumptions and constraints to see how much the sales quotas for the second and third months can be redistributed to meet the goal of $125,000.

◆ **Open Quarterly Quota from the Excel Expert Practice/Lesson06 folder.**

Use Solver

In this exercise, you use Solver to create a scenario that recalculates monthly sales quotas for a particular salesperson based on a desired quarterly sales total of $125,000.

1 **Click cell F6.**

IMPORTANT

If Solver is not installed on your system, you can add it by selecting Add-Ins on the Tools menu, selecting Solver Add-In in the Add-Ins dialog box, and clicking OK.

2 **On the Tools menu, click Solver.**

The Solver Parameters dialog box appears.

FIGURE 6-30

Solver Parameters dialog box

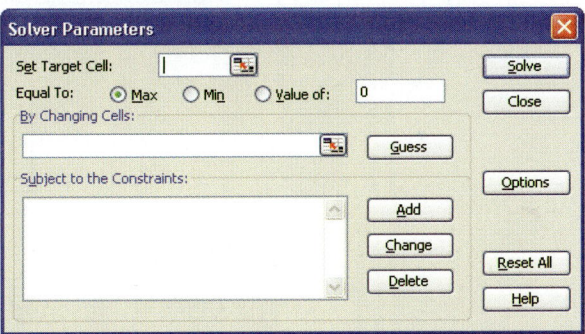

3 **Click cell F6 to set the target cell.**

4 **In the Equal To section, click the Value Of option, and type 125000 in the box.**

You will solve a calculation so that the value in cell F6 is equal to $125,000.

TIP

If you want Solver to include all possible cells that can be adjusted based on the target cell, click the Guess button rather than entering the cell references in the By Changing Cells box.

5 **Click in the By Changing Cells box.**

The target cell amount is set for $125,000, and you can now select cells whose values you want to change.

6 Select the range C6:E6.

The Solver Parameters dialog box collapses as you select the range of cells, and the selected cell range appears in the By Changing Cells box.

FIGURE 6-31

Specifying the cell range to change

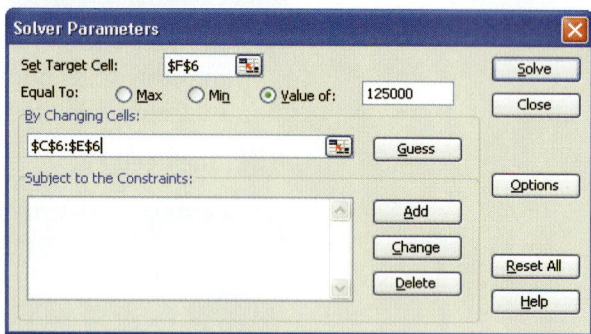

7 In the Subject To The Constraints section of the dialog box, click the Add button.

The Add Constraint dialog box appears. Notice that the <= (less than or equal to) constraint operator is selected by default.

FIGURE 6-32

Add Constraint dialog box

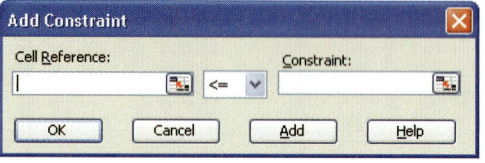

8 Click cell C6.

Cell C6 is inserted in the Cell Reference box.

9 Click in the Constraint box, type 30000, and click the Add button.

The first constraint, cell C6 <= 30000, is entered, and the Add Constraint dialog box reappears so that you can create the next constraint.

10 Click cell D6, click in the Constraint box, type 50000, and click the Add button.

The second constraint, cell D6 <= 50000, is entered, and the Add Constraint dialog box reappears so that you can create the next constraint.

11 Click cell E6, click in the Constraint box, type 60000, and click OK.

The third constraint, cell E6 <= 60000, is entered, and the Solver Parameters dialog box appears. The Subject To The Constraints section of the dialog box contains the constraints that you created.

FIGURE 6-33

Solver Parameters dialog box

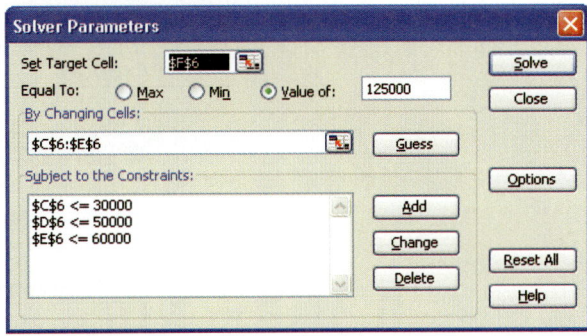

12 **Click Solve.**

The Solver Results dialog box appears, indicating it has found a result, and the values in cells C6, D6, and E6 are recalculated in cell F6 to achieve the goal of $125,000.

FIGURE 6-34

Solving the problem

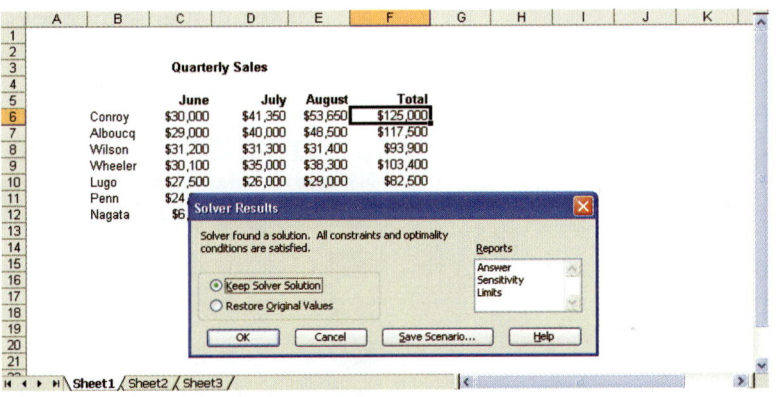

13 **On the Reports list, click Answer, and click OK. (The default Keep Solver Solution option is accepted.)**

The answer report is saved to a separate worksheet.

TIP

If you want to retain the original worksheet values, click the Restore Original Values option in the Solver Results dialog box.

14 **Click the Answer Report 1 sheet tab.**

The answer report appears in the worksheet.

FIGURE 6-35

Answer report

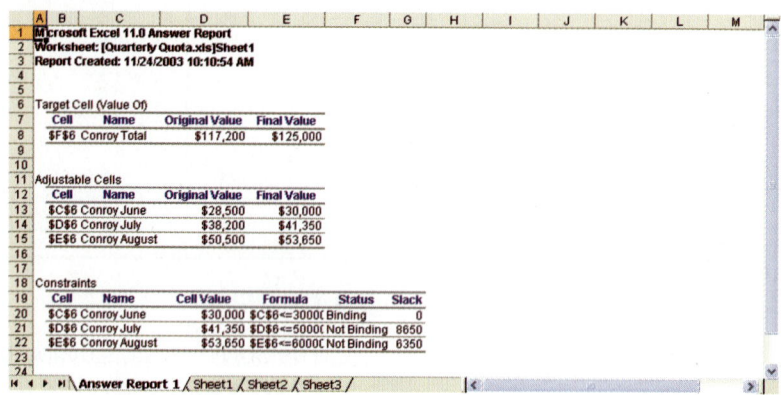

◆ **Save and close the workbook. If you are continuing to other lessons, leave Excel open. If you are not continuing to other lessons, save and close all open workbooks. Click the Close button in the top right corner of the Excel window.**

QUICK REFERENCE ▼

Use Solver

1 Click the cell you want to use as the target cell.

2 On the Tools menu, click Solver.

3 Verify that the correct cell appears in the Set Target Cell field.

4 Click the Min, Max, or Value Of option. If you select Value Of, type the value in the box.

5 In the By Changing Cells box, specify the cells that you want to change to meet the new target cell value.

6 In the Subject To The Constraints box, enter constraints as needed.

7 Click Solve.

8 To keep the new values, click OK in the Solver Results dialog box. To restore the original data, click the Restore Original Values option, and click OK.

9 To save the Solver results, click Save Scenario, type a name in the Scenario Name box, and click OK.

10 In the Solver Results dialog box, click OK.

QUICK CHECK

Q. In a Solver problem, what does the target cell contain?

A: **The target cell contains the value of the desired outcome or goal.**

Key Points

✔ *With a PivotTable, you can experiment with different row and column arrangements in a data list. This tool enables you to analyze or interpret data in a different manner.*

✔ *A PivotChart provides a more graphic and visual representation of the data and summaries in a PivotTable, enabling you to make deductions and identify trends.*

✔ *With the Goal Seek feature, you can create a quick analysis of how a particular cell value must change in order to generate a desired result for a formula. This eliminates the timely task of building complex formulas that test various values.*

✔ *The Scenario Manager lets you quickly formulate different versions of a calculation so that you can evaluate results and determine the best outcome for a situation.*

✔ *With the Solver tool, you can set parameters for the values in multiple cells that are used to formulate a desired outcome.*

Quick Quiz

True/False

T   F   1. A PivotTable can be placed on the same worksheet as the data it analyzes or on a separate worksheet.

T   F   2. You can add fields to a PivotTable, but you cannot delete them.

T   F   3. A page field in a PivotTable displays summary information for a particular field.

T   F   4. To create a PivotChart, you always create a PivotTable first.

T   F   5. With the Goal Seek tool, you can have multiple changing cells.

T   F   6. With the Scenario Manager, you can place constraints on the values that are in changing cells.

T   F   7. With the Solver tool, you can set a maximum or minimum value for the target cell.

Multiple Choice

1. Which element in a PivotTable displays summary information for a particular field?
   a. row
   b. column heading
   c. page field
   d. field button

2. Which data analysis tool would you use when you know the expected outcome but aren't sure how to achieve it?
   a. PivotTable
   b. Goal Seek
   c. Scenario Manager
   d. Solver

3. Which data analysis tool lets you create and store different versions of a calculation?
   a. PivotTable
   b. Goal Seek
   c. Scenario Manager
   d. Solver

Short Answer

1. How do you apply an AutoFormat to a PivotTable?

2. How does a PivotTable help you analyze totals in a worksheet?

3. If you have one answer in mind for a problem but you aren't sure how a cell value should change to achieve the desired result, should you use Goal Seek or the Scenario Manager?

4. How can you create a PivotChart from a PivotTable?

5. What basic feature does Solver provide that can't be performed by creating scenarios in the Scenario Manager or by using Goal Seek?

6. How do you access the Scenario Manager?

On Your Own

◆ **Open AW Reservation Stats from the Excel Expert Practice/Lesson06 folder.**

Exercise 1

Create a PivotTable using the data on the Room Use worksheet. The PivotTable should enable you to view each room type and the number of reservations for January, February, and March for each type. Use the PivotTable to create a PivotChart. Working with the Quarterly Comparisons worksheet, use Goal Seek to determine what percentage increase would be required for the projected number of guests to be 750 for the fourth quarter of 2005.

◆ **Save and close the workbook.**

◆ **Open AW Personnel from the Excel Expert Practice/Lesson06 folder.**

Exercise 2

Determine how much Robert Fuller's salary would need to increase (with the other salaries unchanged) for the average salary of all employees to increase to $54,000.

◆ **Save and close the workbook.**

◆ **Open Sales Averages from the Excel Expert Practice/Lesson06 folder.**

Exercise 3

Create scenarios that show what the average sales for all sales reps would be if Nagata's averages were $8,000, $10,000, and $12,000. Name the scenarios as desired.

◆ **Save and close the workbook.**

One Step Further

◆ **Open AW Guest Supplies from the Excel Expert Practice/Lesson06 folder.**

Exercise 1

The inventory manager at Adventure Works wants to reduce the overall total spent on supplies to $265,000. Determine what each category's total should be in order to achieve this goal.

◆ **Save and close the workbook.**

◆ **Open Guest Supplies with PivotTable from the Excel Expert Practice/Lesson06 folder.**

Exercise 2

If necessary, switch to the PivotTable worksheet. On the PivotTable toolbar, click PivotTable, and then click Table Options. Explore this dialog box. Use Excel's Help files to learn more about the options within this table. Write a brief description of your findings.

Sharing Workbooks

After completing this lesson, you will be able to:

✔ *Track changes in a workbook.*
✔ *Accept or reject changes to a worksheet.*
✔ *Create a shared workbook.*
✔ *Merge workbooks.*
✔ *View and change workbook properties.*
✔ *Apply and remove password protection.*
✔ *Protect worksheets and workbooks.*

KEY TERMS

- change tracking
- locked
- password
- properties
- shared workbook
- unlock

Creating and updating workbooks is often a collaborative process. A worksheet in a workbook might go through many review processes. Or it might be routed to other employees so that they can verify data or make changes of their own. Microsoft Excel has several features that facilitate collaborative work on workbooks and worksheets. For example, you can track and review changes that you and others made to the worksheet. If more than one person needs to update the same worksheet, you can share the worksheet, allowing each person to make separate changes and comments. Later you can selectively accept and reject changes to create the final version of the worksheet.

In this lesson, you will learn how to track changes made to a workbook, merge different versions of a workbook, password-protect workbooks, protect a worksheet and a workbook, and share a workbook so that multiple users can simultaneously make changes to it.

IMPORTANT

Before you can use the practice files in this lesson, you must install them from the book's companion CD to their default location. For additional information on how to find and open files used in this book, see the "Using the CD-ROM" section at the beginning of this book.

Tracking Changes and Sharing a Workbook

Tracking and Managing Changes

THE BOTTOM LINE

The Track Changes and sharing features make it easy to identify what content has been changed in a worksheet, when the content was changed, and what user made the change. These features allow you to focus on data that's been modified and pinpoint who made the change in case you have questions.

Excel's Track Changes feature allows several people (or one person performing distinct worksheet development tasks) to enter and edit worksheet content in a single workbook. For example, at Adventure Works, the budget worksheet will be routed to each department manager for review. Each manager can change values in the worksheet, but because **change tracking** (or simply tracking) is turned on for the worksheet, each person's edits will be tracked and the name and date of each person's entry will be recorded. When the process of editing the workbook is complete, one person can go through everyone's changes and selectively accept or reject them, either making them a permanent part of the worksheet (accepting the change) or deleting the changes entirely (rejecting the change). You can turn change tracking on or off at any time. When change tracking is on, Excel stores information about every change made to the range of cells you specified when you turned on change tracking.

TIP

If you are familiar with the Track Changes command in Microsoft Word, you might know that Word indicates that tracking is turned on by displaying TRK in bold on the status bar. However, you will not see this indicator in an Excel workbook.

When you activate the Track Changes feature, you also save and share the workbook, giving other people access to it through your network.

TIP

If you want to allow only certain people to open the workbook, you can protect the file with a password, as described later in this lesson.

When a cell in the tracked range is edited, the edited cell displays a blue triangle in the top left corner, as shown in Figure 7-1.

FIGURE 7-1

Blue triangle identifies edited cell

Quarter 2	Quarter 3
$ 1,876,600.00	$ 6,897,600.00
$ 460,250.00	$ 363,250.00
$ 450,350.00	$ 5,480,050.00
$ 345,250.00	$ 363,050.00
$ 620,750.00	$ 691,250.00

— Blue triangle identifies cells that have been edited

To find out what edits have been made, point to the cell. The Track Changes information about that cell appears in a yellow box, similar to the way a comment appears.

◆ **To complete the procedures in this lesson, you must use the files AW Budget, AW Budget Tracking, SalesSummer, AW Budget Final, Employees, AW Marketing TC, and AW Departmental Expenses in the Lesson07 folder in the Excel Expert Practice folder located on your hard disk.**

◆ **Open AW Budget from the Excel Expert Practice/Lesson07 folder.**

Track changes

In this exercise, you activate Track Changes for the Resort Budget worksheet of the AW Budget workbook. You then edit cells in the worksheet and view the track changes information.

1 **Save the workbook as AW Budget Edited.**

2 **On the Tools menu, point to Track Changes, and then click Highlight Changes.**

The Highlight Changes dialog box appears, as shown in Figure 7-2.

FIGURE 7-2

Highlight Changes dialog box

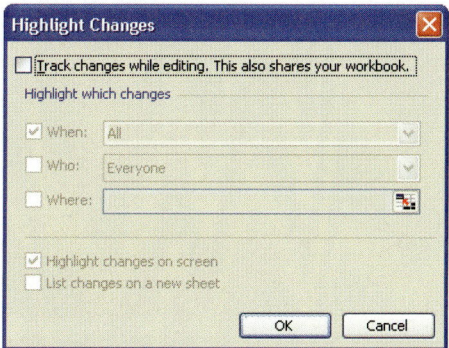

3 **Click the "Track Changes While Editing. This Also Shares Your Workbook" check box to activate the Track Changes feature.**

IMPORTANT

A reviewed change is one in which you have accepted or rejected a user's edits. You will learn how to accept and reject changes in the next section of this lesson.

4 **Click the When down arrow, and click Not Yet Reviewed.**

Excel will track all changes that have been made but not reviewed.

5 **Click the Who check box. If necessary, click the Who down arrow, and click Everyone.**

A check mark appears in the Who check box. Selecting Everyone causes Excel to track all changes made to the worksheet, including changes you make.

 6 **Click the Collapse Dialog button on the right side of the Where box.**

The dialog box collapses to expose the worksheet cells.

TROUBLESHOOTING TIP

If you do not specify a range in the Where box, Excel will track changes for the entire contents of all worksheets in the workbook.

7 **Select the range C7:F17.**

A flashing marquee surrounds the range you selected. The address for the range appears in the Highlight Changes dialog box.

ANOTHER METHOD

To specify the track changes range, you also can type the addresses for a cell or range of cells in the Where box.

 8 **In the Highlight Changes dialog box, click the Expand Dialog button.**

The dialog box returns to full size, the range appears in the Where box, and the Where check box is selected.

FIGURE 7-3

Specifying the content to track

9 **Click OK.**

A dialog box appears telling you that the workbook will be saved.

IMPORTANT

You will learn more about shared workbooks later in this lesson.

10 **Click OK.**

Tracking is activated for the selected range of cells, and the workbook is saved. Notice that the title bar now indicates that the workbook is shared.

11 **Click cell C8, which contains the Quarter 1 payroll for the Guest Services Staff, and type 327125.**

12 **Click cell D8, and press Delete to delete the contents of the cell.**

The blue triangles in the top left corners of cells C8 and D8 indicate that changes have been made to those cells.

13 **Point to cell C8.**

The Track Changes information appears, showing your user name, the date and time you made the change to the cell, and a description of the change you made.

FIGURE 7-4

Tracked changes

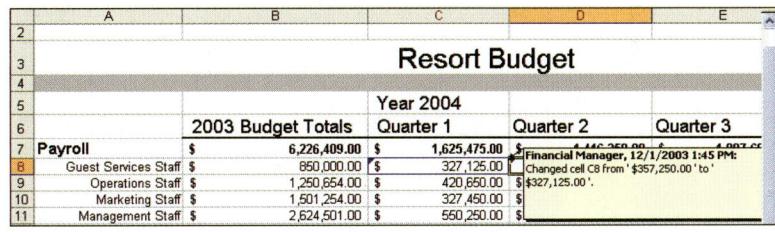

14 **Point to cell D8.**

The Track Changes information appears.

◆ **Save the workbook, and then close it.**

QUICK REFERENCE ▼

Activate Track Changes

1 On the Tools menu, point to Track Changes, and click Highlight Changes.

2 Select the *Track Changes While Editing. This Also Shares Your Workbook* check box.

3 Click the When down arrow to choose from which point in the worksheet's development you want to track changes.

4 Click the Who down arrow to choose whose changes will be tracked.

5 Click the Collapse Dialog button to the right of the Where box.

6 Select the range of cells for which you want to track changes.

7 Click the Expand Dialog button.

8 Click OK.

Accepting or Rejecting Changes to a Worksheet

After a workbook has been edited, you can easily identify which cells have been changed and determine whether you want to keep or reject the changes. You can choose to accept or reject all changes at one time without reviewing each change, or you can accept or reject them individually.

◆ **Open AW Budget Tracking from the Excel Expert Practice/Lesson07 folder.**

Accept and reject changes

In this exercise, you turn on change tracking in a version of the AW Budget workbook that contains tracked changes made by two managers at the resort. You also create a history of changes in a new worksheet. You then accept and reject changes that have been made to the worksheet.

1 Save the workbook as **AW Budget Tracking Edited**.

2 On the Tools menu, point to Track Changes, and click Highlight Changes.

The Highlight Changes dialog box appears.

3 If necessary, select the "Track Changes While Editing. This Also Shares Your Workbook" check box to activate the Track Changes feature.

4 Click the When down arrow, and click Not Yet Reviewed.

Excel will display all tracked changes that have not yet been reviewed.

5 Select the Who check box, click the Who down arrow, if necessary, and click Everyone.

 6 Click the Collapse Dialog button on the right side of the Where box.

The dialog box collapses to expose the worksheet cells so that you can select a range.

7 Select the range C7:F17.

A flashing marquee surrounds the range you selected. The address for the range appears in the Highlight Changes dialog box.

8 In the Highlight Changes dialog box, click the Expand Dialog button.

The dialog box returns to full size, the range appears in the Where box, and the Where check box is selected.

9 Select the "List Changes On A New Sheet" check box, make sure the Highlight Changes On Screen check box is selected, and click OK.

Excel displays a worksheet that contains a history list of all changes that have been made to the Resort Budget worksheet. Notice that two changes have been made by the facilities manager and one change has been made by the operations manager. In the Range column, make a note of the cells that have been changed.

FIGURE 7-5

History of changes listed on a new worksheet

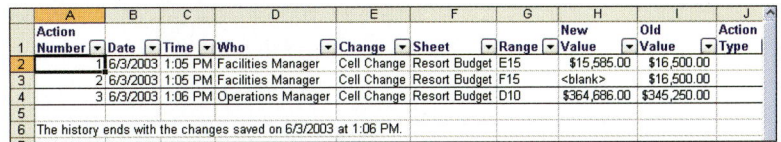

10 **Click the Resort Budget sheet tab.**

Notice that the three cells listed in the Range column (E15, F15, and D10) in the History worksheet contain tracking indicators in the Resort Budget worksheet. Each user's changes are outlined in a different color.

11 **On the Tools menu, point to Track Changes, and then click Accept Or Reject Changes.**

The Select Changes To Accept Or Reject dialog box appears. You can use the options to determine which changes you want to review, or you can accept the defaults.

FIGURE 7-6

Select Changes To Accept Or Reject dialog box

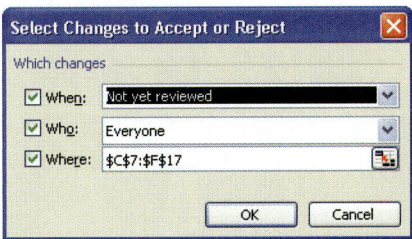

> **TIP**
>
> The Accept Or Reject Changes dialog box displays changes in the order in which they were made, not the order in which they appear in the worksheet.

12 **Click OK.**

The Accept Or Reject Changes dialog box appears, displaying the first edit that was made to the worksheet (cell E15 was changed from $16,500.00 to $15,585.00 by the facilities manager).

FIGURE 7-7

Accept Or Reject Changes dialog box

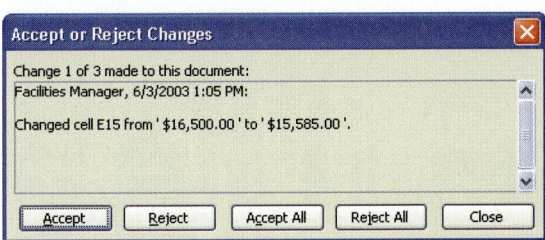

13 **Click the Accept button.**

The change is made to cell E15, and the Accept Or Reject Changes dialog box displays the next edit that was made in the Resort Budget worksheet (the contents of cell F15 were deleted by the facilities manager).

14 **Click the Reject button.**

The contents of cell F15 revert to the original entry ($16,500.00) prior to when change tracking was turned on, and the Accept Or Reject Changes dialog box displays the third and final edit that was made in the Resort Budget worksheet (cell D10 was changed from $345,250.00 to $364,686.00 by the operations manager).

ANOTHER METHOD

You can click Accept All to make all edits a part of the worksheet without your reviewing them individually, or you can click Reject All to reject all changes.

15 **Click the Accept button.**

The change is made to cell D10, and the Accept Or Reject Changes dialog box closes.

16 **Save the workbook as AW Budget Reviewed.**

◆ **Close the workbook.**

QUICK REFERENCE ▼

Accept or reject changes

1 On the Tools menu, point to Track Changes, and click Accept Or Reject Changes.

2 Click the When down arrow to choose the time frame for which you want to accept or reject changes.

3 Click the Who down arrow to choose whose changes will be accepted or rejected.

4 Click the Collapse Dialog button to the right of the Where box.

5 Select the range of cells for which you want to track changes.

6 Click the Expand Dialog button.

7 Click OK.

8 Click Accept to make and edit a permanent part of the worksheet, or click Reject to revert to the cell's previous condition.

Or

Click Accept All to make all edits a permanent part of the worksheet without your reviewing them individually, or click Reject All to get rid of all edits and return the cells to their previous content.

QUICK CHECK

Q. How are tracked changes that were made by more than one user identified?

A: **The cell(s) containing each user's changes are outlined in a different color.**

Turn off change tracking

1 On the Tools menu, point to Track Changes, and click Highlight Changes.

2 Clear the *Track Changes While Editing. This Also Shares Your Workbook* check box, and click OK.

3 Click Yes.

Creating a Shared Workbook

When you turn on change tracking for a workbook, the workbook is automatically shared. However, you also can share a workbook without turning on change tracking. If you want two or more users to have access to a workbook so that all users can make changes simultaneously, you must save the workbook as a **shared workbook.** When you do this, you can choose how edits within a shared workbook will be handled, when changes can occur, and how to resolve conflicts when two or more people make changes to the same cells (or to different cells that are used by the same formula).

To share a workbook, on the Tools menu, click Share Workbook to display the Editing tab of the Share Workbook dialog box, as shown in Figure 7-8. Select the *Allow Changes By More Than One User At The Same Time. This Also Allows Workbook Merging* check box.

FIGURE 7-8

Share Workbook dialog box

The Advanced tab of the Share Workbook dialog box contains four sections you can use to customize the shared use of the workbook.

FIGURE 7-9

Advanced tab in the Share Workbook dialog box

The following table describes the options on the Advanced tab.

Option	Result
Track Changes	Determines whether and how long change history information will be kept; for history information to be maintained, change tracking must be turned on
Update Changes	Controls when changes made to the shared workbook are incorporated into the workbook; changes can be updated when the file is saved or at a specified time, such as every 15 minutes
Conflicting Changes Between Users	Determines whose edits become part of the file if two or more people are attempting to edit the same portion of a shared workbook; you can determine whether you want to be prompted to choose the edits to keep (*Ask Me Which Changes Win*), or you can specify that the person who saves the workbook will have his or her changes reflected whenever the workbook is saved (*The Changes Being Saved Win*); if you select *The Changes Being Saved Win*, the workbook is updated each time any user saves the workbook—with that user's changes overwriting any existing changes
Include In Personal View	Enables each person who edits the workbook to see a personal view of the workbook; you can choose to have each person's print settings and filter settings preserved as part of his or her personal view

QUICK REFERENCE ▼

Share a workbook

1 On the Tools menu, click Share Workbook.

2 Select the *Allow Changes By More Than One User At The Same Time. This Also Allows Workbook Merging* check box.

3 Click OK.

Merging Workbooks

THE BOTTOM LINE

You can merge data from different workbooks or from different versions of the same workbook to quickly compile a summary.

Being able to track changes is an effective way to gather and manage input from several users to a single workbook. There may be instances when you want to compile input or content changes that are made to different workbooks or multiple versions of a single workbook. For example, you might have sales managers working in remote locations who are required to submit a weekly sales report by 9 a.m. every Monday. You've provided each manager with a copy of the workbook that contains a specified section for each manager's sales numbers. When the managers send you their version of the workbook, you can merge the workbooks to create a single worksheet that summarizes all of the sales numbers for the previous week.

When you work with multiple versions of a workbook, you might want to have individual users turn on the track changes feature so that you can easily identify who is changing what and when the changes were made.

◆ **Open SalesSummer from the Excel Expert Practice/Lesson07 folder.**

Merge workbooks

In this exercise, you make copies of a worksheet and merge the copies into a single worksheet.

1 **On the Tools menu, point to Track Changes, and click Highlight Changes.**

The Highlight Changes dialog box appears.

2 **Select the "Track Changes While Editing. This Also Shares Your Workbook" check box, and click OK.**

An alert box appears, warning you that this action will save the workbook and asking you if you want to continue.

3 **Click OK.**

The title bar indicates that the workbook is now shared.

4 **Save the workbook as SalesSummer2.**

TIP

After you have created copies of the original workbook, you can distribute them to the people who will be working on the files.

5 In cell B10, type Penn. In cell C10, type 8600. Then press Enter.

Because worksheet changes are being tracked, the new entries appear with the blue triangle in the top left corners of the cells and the cells are outlined in a different color.

FIGURE 7-10

Tracking changes

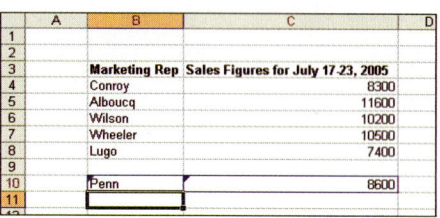

6 Save SalesSummer2, and close it.

7 Open SalesSummer, which is the master workbook.

Notice that the title bar indicates that the workbook is currently shared.

8 On the Tools menu, click Compare And Merge Workbooks.

The Select Files To Merge Into Current Workbook dialog box appears, as shown in Figure 7-11.

FIGURE 7-11

Select Files To Merge Into Current Workbook dialog box

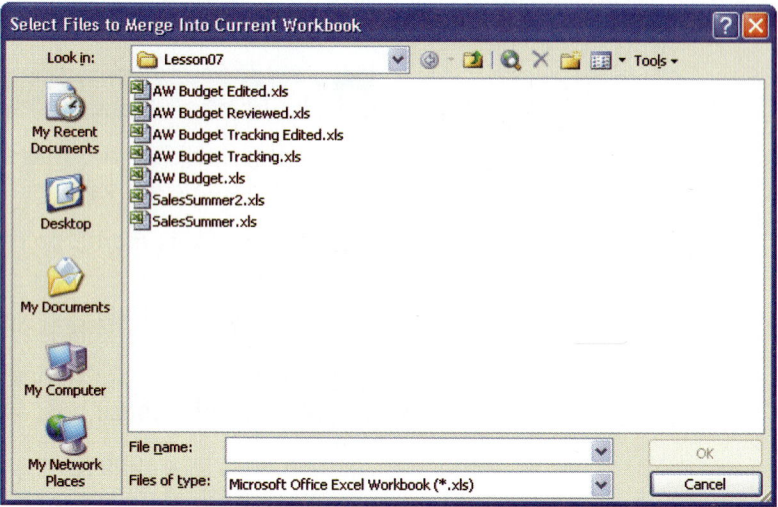

IMPORTANT

As a precautionary measure, Excel saves the current workbook before merging it with another workbook, even if no changes have been made to the workbook.

9 **Click the SalesSummer2 workbook, and then click OK.**

The two workbooks are merged, and the changes you made in SalesSummer2 appear in SalesSummer. Note that SalesSummer is saved automatically when the merge occurs, and you can't undo the changes except by manually deleting the new entries or manually changing the data back to its original state.

10 **Point to either of the cells with the triangle mark.**

A ScreenTip appears with the name of the user who made the changes, the date and time of the change, and a description of the change made.

◆ **Close SalesSummer.**

IMPORTANT

If there is a conflict in data between the master workbook and the workbook copy selected to merge into it, the data in the copy will overwrite the master workbook.

QUICK REFERENCE ▼

Prepare a worksheet so that copies can be merged later

1 On the Tools menu, point to Track Changes, and click Highlight Changes.

2 In the Highlight Changes dialog box, select the *Track Changes While Editing. This Also Saves Your Workbook* check box.

3 Save the file when you're prompted.

4 On the File menu, click Save As.

5 Type the new name of the copy in the File Name box, and click Save.

Merge workbooks

1 Open the workbook that you want to preserve as the master.

2 On the Tools menu, click Compare And Merge Workbooks.

3 Type the name of the copy you want to merge into the master in the File Name box. Or browse to find the file, and double-click it.

4 Click OK.

Viewing and Changing Workbook Properties

Modifying Workbook Settings

THE BOTTOM LINE

Defining a clear and comprehensive set of properties for a workbook is an effective way to document its creation, development, and history.

Workbook **properties** are the characteristics that help define the workbook and provide useful information about it. For example, if you have the Details view selected in the Open dialog box, you see information about a workbook, such as where it's stored, its size, and the date on which it was last updated. There are many other properties that you can define or modify. For example, you can assign properties that detail who has opened or reviewed the workbook, what the workbook is to be used for, who should view the workbook next, and so on.

To define properties that provide information about a workbook, you use the Properties dialog box, which you open by clicking Properties on the File menu. The Properties dialog box has five tabs, but the Summary and Custom tabs provide you with the most flexibility in defining workbook properties and other information. The other three tabs contain information that cannot be edited.

Some of the properties that you might change are described in the following table.

Tab	Property	Description
Summary	Title	A name that you can use when searching for the file in Windows Explorer; the title can be different from the file name and is useful especially when the file name is not very descriptive; for example, a budget workbook might be saved with the file name *FIN2005V1* to conform with a company's file naming conventions; to facilitate locating workbooks that are not descriptively named, you can create a title, such as *Budget 2005*
Summary	Subject	The reason the workbook has been created; for example, you might use Budget 2005 as the subject for each workbook that is used to create a budget for the year 2005; you can then use the Find dialog box to search for workbooks by subject
Summary	Author	Typically the person who created the file

Summary	Manager	The person to whom the author reports or the person who is responsible for the contents of the workbook
Summary	Company	The company that created the workbook or the company for which the workbook was created
Summary	Category	A designation that can be used to include a workbook as part of a related group; for instance, you could specify a department as the category or use a customer name as the category
Summary	Keywords	Any additional words that might help when you search for a workbook; a keyword should be unique to the workbook or to only a few workbooks
Summary	Comments	Additional information that you want to add to a workbook to describe what its contents are, who created and revised it, who the workbook should be sent to, and so on
Summary	Hyperlink Base	The base URL or folder location for links contained within a workbook
Summary	Save Preview Picture	The option to store a picture of the first page of the workbook in the file; if you create a workbook template and then store it in the Templates folder, Excel can display a preview picture of the workbook when a user clicks New on the File menu; for example, if you create a purchase order template, you can create a preview picture of the template so that users quickly identify it on the list of templates
Custom	Name	Any one of 27 available field names you can choose for additional properties that you want to describe; some available field names are Department, Checked By, Editor, Date Completed, and Telephone Number
Custom	Type	The field type for a field that you choose on the Name list; a field can be text, a number, a date, or a logical yes/no field
Custom	Value	The content of a field; for example, you could add a Date Completed field and assign it the value 12/04/05
Custom	Properties	A list of the field names and values that you've created

TIP

To change your user name in Excel, on the Tools menu, click Options. In the Options dialog box that opens, click the General tab, and type your preferred user name in the User Name box at the bottom of the tab. You can change other default settings by making selections on the various tabs within the Options dialog box.

◆ **Open AW Budget Final from the Excel Expert Practice/Lesson07 folder.**

Review and change properties

In this exercise, you view workbook properties and change the author name to your name. You also record the date on which the workbook was completed.

1   On the File menu, click Properties.

The Properties dialog box appears.

TROUBLESHOOTING TIP

You cannot change the properties of a workbook if it is currently being shared. You must turn off workbook sharing before you can modify any properties.

2   Click the Summary tab, if necessary.

The Properties dialog box lists summary properties that have been previously defined.

FIGURE 7-12

Properties dialog box for the workbook

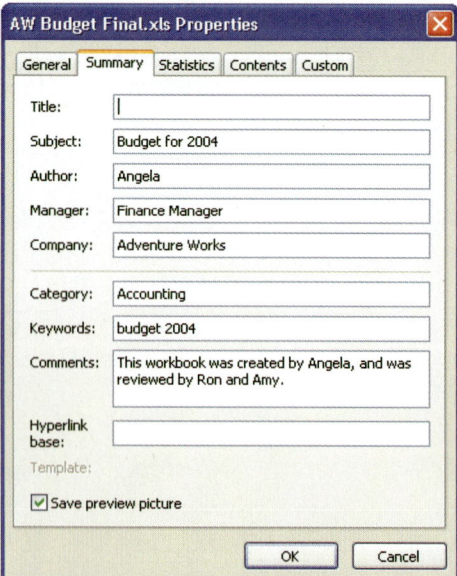

3 Click in the Author box, select the existing text, and type your name.

4 Click the Custom tab.

The Custom tab shows that two properties—Checked By and Department—have already been defined.

FIGURE 7-13

Custom tab in the Properties dialog box

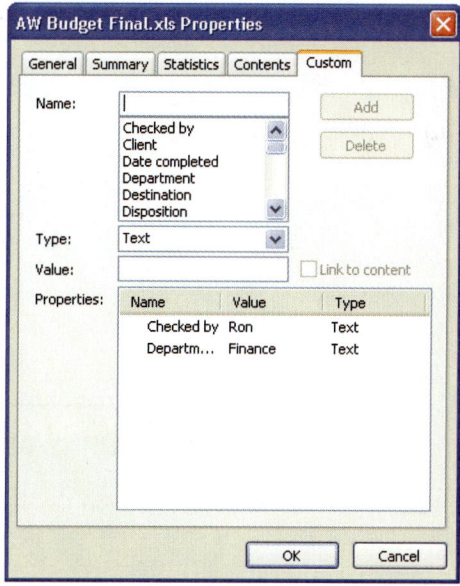

5 On the Name list, click Date Completed.

6 Click the Type down arrow, and click Date to indicate that the new property is a date.

7 Click in the Value box, and type today's date in mm/dd/yy format (for example, 11/15/03).

8 Click the Add button to add the new property to the Properties box.

The date the worksheet was completed appears as a property for the workbook.

CHECK THIS OUT ▼

Using Properties for Searches
The properties defined for a workbook can be valuable tools in locating a workbook. This can be extremely useful when you quickly need to find a workbook on a network or on a hard disk that contains hundreds or even thousands of workbook files. To search for a workbook using a work-book property, click the Open button on the Standard toolbar to display the Open dialog box. On the toolbar in the Open dialog box, click the down arrow on the Tools button, and click Search. Click the Advanced tab in the Search dialog box. You can run a search that's based on any of the more than 50 prop-erties listed. For example, you might want to locate any workbook on a network that was completed on a certain date by a certain author. Select the property, specify the con-dition and the value it must meet, and click Search. The file names of those workbooks that meet the criteria of the search are listed in the Results window of the Search dialog box. Point to the file name in the Results window to display a ScreenTip that contains the complete path for the file.

QUICK CHECK

Q. What does the Author property for a workbook define?

A: **The Author property typically defines the person who created the file.**

FIGURE 7-14

Defining a property

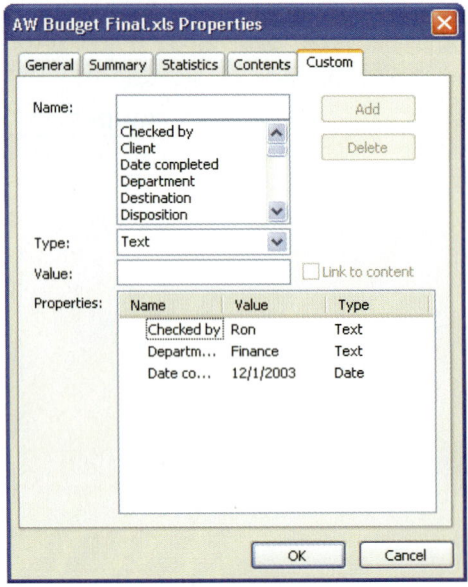

TIP

If you can't see all of the text in a cell, you can widen a column in the Properties area just as you widen a column in a workbook. Drag the right edge of a column selector to the right to widen it.

9 **Click OK.**

The Properties dialog box closes.

◆ **Save the workbook, and then close it.**

QUICK REFERENCE ▼

Access workbook properties

1 On the File menu, click Properties.

2 Click the tab for the workbook's properties you want to view or edit.

3 When you finish making changes, click OK.

Applying Protection Features

Protecting Workbooks and
Worksheets

> **THE BOTTOM LINE**
>
> Excel's protection features enable you to control who accesses and
> modifies the data in a workbook and minimize the risk of unautho-
> rized users gaining access to sensitive or classified information.

If your computer is part of a network and your folders are set up as shared
in Windows, everyone on the network can open, read, and change your
workbooks. If all of your workbooks are stored in one folder (and in
subfolders of the main folder) and the folder is not shared, other people
cannot access your workbooks—with one exception: if you are currently
logged on to your computer and you step away from your desk, anybody
can access your workbooks from your computer. Although it would be
nice to think that you can trust everyone in your organization, some workbook information might be too sensitive for you to take any chances.

Using Password Protection

Assigning a **password** to a workbook is an effective way to keep any
user who does not know the password from accessing the workbook. At
Adventure Works, the human resources manager has created a workbook
that includes information about all employees, including their salaries.
The resort has a strict policy that forbids employees from disclosing their
salaries to other employees. The human resources manager doesn't want
to take any chances that an employee might be tempted to open the workbook from her computer to view the salaries of everybody at the resort.
So she assigns a password to the workbook, which makes it impossible
for anyone to open the workbook—even from her computer—without
knowing the password.

> **TIP**
>
> To prevent other people from editing your comments, you can apply
> worksheet protection. On the Tools menu, point to Protection, and
> click Protect Sheet. Select the Objects check box. Because a comment
> is an object, worksheet protection prevents others from making any
> changes to your comments, but it still allows others to make changes
> to worksheet content.

There are other reasons for password-protecting a workbook or even an
individual worksheet within a workbook. For instance, after the budget for
the year has been finalized, the accountant at Adventure Works wants to
ensure that nobody makes changes to the budget workbook without au-
thorization. But he still wants others on the network to be able to open
and view or print the budget. In this case, the accountant uses Excel to
password-protect the workbook so that it can be opened, but not modified, by others on the network.

TIP

If you want some people to be able to open a workbook but not modify it and you want other people to be able to open and modify the workbook, you should use separate passwords for opening the workbook and modifying the workbook.

◆ **Open Employees from the Excel Expert Practice/Lesson07 folder.**

Apply password protection

In this exercise, you protect a workbook by requiring passwords to open it and to modify it. Then you remove the password protection.

1 **On the File menu, click Save As.**

IMPORTANT

If you want to allow everybody to open a workbook but want to recommend that the workbook not be modified, select the Read-Only Recommended check box without entering passwords. Excel will display a message indicating that the file should be opened as read-only whenever somebody attempts to open the workbook. Users will have the option to open the workbook as read-only or with full privileges for making changes to the workbook.

2 **On the toolbar of the Save As dialog box, click the Tools button. On the menu that appears, click General Options.**

The Save Options dialog box appears.

FIGURE 7-15

Save Options dialog box

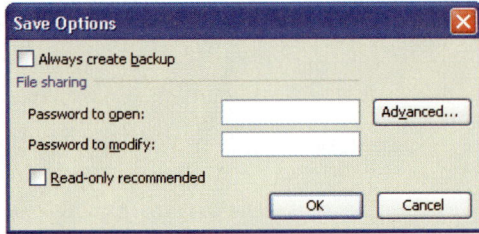

3 **In the Password To Open box, type t82y65A.**

IMPORTANT

Passwords are case-sensitive.

4 **In the Password To Modify box, type B23cd49, and click OK.**

A Confirm Password dialog box appears, prompting you to reenter the password. This dialog box applies to the first password you entered, the password to open the workbook.

5 Type the password for opening the workbook (t82y65A), and click OK.

The Confirm Password dialog box appears again. This time it applies to the second password, for modifying the workbook.

6 Type the password for modifying the workbook (B23cd49), and click OK.

7 In the Save As dialog box, click Save.

8 When you are asked if you want to replace the file, click Yes.

9 Close the workbook.

◆ Open Employees from the Excel Expert Practice/Lesson07 folder.

FIGURE 7-16

Password dialog box

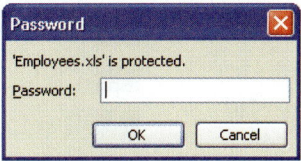

10 In the Password dialog box, type the password for opening the workbook (t82y65A), and click OK.

Another Password dialog box appears.

11 Type the password for modifying the workbook (B23cd49), and click OK.

The workbook opens.

12 On the File menu, click Save As.

13 Click the Tools button, and click General Options to display the Save Options dialog box.

14 Delete the passwords that appear in the Password To Open and Password To Modify boxes, and click OK.

15 In the Save As dialog box, click Save.

16 When you are asked if you want to replace the existing workbook, click Yes.

The passwords are removed from the workbook.

◆ Close the workbook.

TIP

Even if you don't have the password necessary to modify a workbook, you can save the workbook using another name and make changes in your copy of the workbook.

QUICK REFERENCE ▼

Apply a password to a workbook

1 On the File menu, click Save As.

2 Click the Tools button, and click General Options.

3 In the Password To Open or Password To Modify boxes, type your desired password, and click OK.

4 In the Confirm Password dialog box, retype your password, and click OK.

5 In the Save As dialog box, click Save.

6 When you are asked if you want to replace the existing workbook, click Yes.

Remove a password from a workbook

1 On the File menu, click Save As.

2 Click the Tools button, and click General Options.

3 Delete the passwords that appear in the Password To Open and Password To Modify boxes, and click OK.

4 In the Save As dialog box, click Save.

5 When you are asked if you want to replace the existing workbook, click Yes.

Protecting Worksheets and Workbooks

Excel provides other protection features in addition to password protection. You can protect an individual worksheet so that it cannot be changed without the user providing a password, or you can protect a complete workbook so that individual worksheets cannot be moved or deleted and new worksheets cannot be inserted. You can even protect a range of cells within a worksheet so that only those cells can't be changed.

At Adventure Works, the accountant wants to protect the budget worksheet so that formulas can't be changed but budget values can. This ensures that all totals will be calculated correctly if other managers make changes to any budget values. To apply this kind of protection, select all of the cells that other users will be allowed to change. Then in the Format Cells dialog box, click the Protection tab, and click the option to **unlock** the selected cells. By default, all cells in a worksheet are **locked** so that no changes can be made when the worksheet is protected. By unlocking selected cells and then protecting the worksheet, only the unlocked cells can be changed.

When applying protection to a worksheet, you can choose to protect the following components in a worksheet. By default, all three types of protection are activated when you protect a worksheet.

Component	How the component is protected
Contents	Protects the text and numbers in the worksheet's cells; data in locked cells on a protected sheet cannot be deleted, edited, or reformatted
Objects	Protects graphics, charts, text boxes, and maps; any object that has been inserted, pasted, or embedded in the worksheet cannot be edited or deleted
Scenarios	Protects any scenarios created in the open worksheet; scenarios cannot be edited or deleted

When you protect a workbook, Excel protects all of the sheets in the workbook (but not their content). The following protection options can be applied to a workbook.

Component	How the component is protected
Structure	Prevents any user from moving, renaming, or deleting all worksheets in the workbook
Windows	Prevents any user from resizing, hiding, unhiding, or closing a workbook's windows

By default, neither Structure protection nor Windows protection is activated when you open a workbook. You can apply either type or both types of protection to the open workbook.

◆ **Open AW Budget from the Excel Expert Practice/Lesson07 folder.**

Protect worksheets and a workbook

In this exercise, you unlock selected cells in a worksheet and then protect the worksheet so that worksheets can't be moved, inserted, or deleted. Finally, you remove workbook and worksheet protection.

1 **Select the range B8:F11.**

You will unlock the selected range so that the cells can be changed following protection of the worksheet.

2 **Hold down Ctrl, and select the range B13:F17.**

You also will unlock this range so that the cells can be changed following protection of the worksheet.

3 **On the Format menu, click Cells, and then click the Protection tab in the Format Cells dialog box.**

ANOTHER METHOD

- Right-click the selection, and select Format Cells on the shortcut menu.
- Press Ctrl+1.

FIGURE 7-17

Protection tab in the Format Cells dialog box

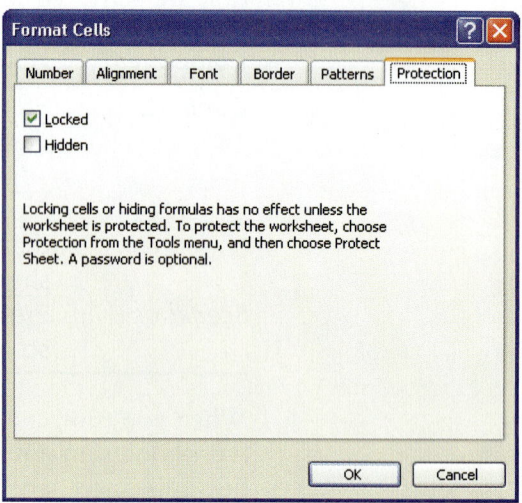

TIP

A password is optional for protecting a worksheet. When a password is not provided, anyone can change locked cells by unprotecting the worksheet.

4 **Clear the Locked check box, and then click OK.**

The selected ranges are now unlocked. Cells that contain formulas remain locked.

5 **On the Tools menu, point to Protection, and click Protect Sheet.**

The Protect Sheet dialog box appears. You can elect to protect the contents of cells, objects in the worksheet (such as comments and pictures), and scenarios that you have created. All three levels of protection are selected by default.

FIGURE 7-18

Protect Sheet dialog box

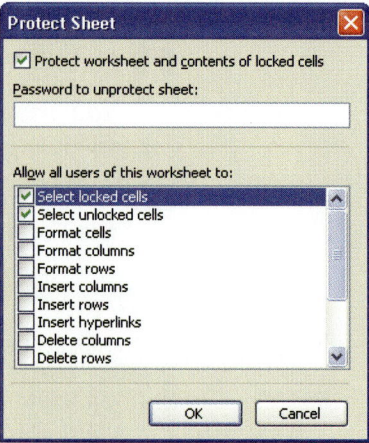

6 **Click OK.**

The worksheet is protected, except for the cells that you have unlocked.

7 **Click cell B7, and type =.**

Excel displays a message notifying you that the cell you are trying to change is protected.

FIGURE 7-19

Message box explains that cell is protected

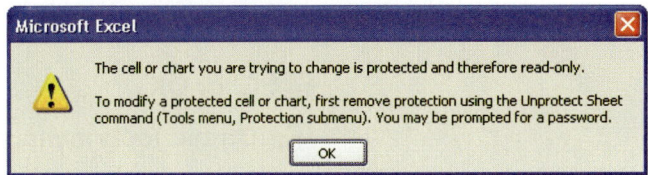

8 **Click OK.**

9 **Click cell B8, type 800,000, and press Enter.**

Excel allows you to make the change because this cell has been unlocked.

TIP

You also can protect a shared workbook so that change tracking cannot be turned off. On the Tools menu, point to Protection, and click Protect And Share Workbook. Select the Sharing With Tracked Changes check box.

10 **On the Tools menu, point to Protection, and click Protect Workbook.**

The Protect Workbook dialog box appears. If you protect the workbook structure, other users cannot delete, move, hide, unhide, or rename worksheets in the workbook. If you protect the workbook windows, other users cannot move, resize, hide, unhide, or close any windows in the workbook.

FIGURE 7-20

Protect Workbook dialog box

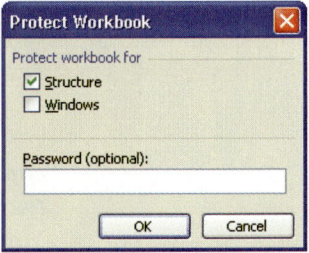

11 **Make sure the Structure check box is selected and the Windows check box is cleared, and then click OK.**

Users cannot make changes to the structure of worksheets.

12 **Double-click the Resort Budget sheet tab.**

Excel notifies you that the workbook is protected. You cannot rename the worksheet.

FIGURE 7-21

Message box explains that workbook is protected

13 **Click OK.**

14 **On the Tools menu, point to Protection, and click Unprotect Sheet.**

The worksheet is no longer protected, and changes can be made to all cells in the worksheet.

15 **On the Tools menu, point to Protection, and click Unprotect Workbook.**

The workbook is no longer protected, and worksheets can now be moved, inserted, deleted, and renamed.

◆ **Close the workbook without saving changes. If you are continuing to other lessons, leave Excel open. If you are not continuing to other lessons, save and close all open workbooks. Click the Close button in the top right corner of the Excel window.**

QUICK REFERENCE ▼

Protect a workbook

1 On the Tools menu, point to Protection, and click Protect Workbook.

2 Select the type of protection you desire, type a password in the Password box if you desire, and click OK.

3 If necessary, retype the password in the Confirm Password dialog box.

Key Points

✔ *The Track Changes and sharing features make it easy to gather input from various users. You can easily identify what content has been changed in a worksheet, when the content was changed, and what user made the change.*

✔ *You can merge data from different workbooks or from different versions of the same workbook to quickly compile a report that summarizes data.*

✔ *Workbook properties are the characteristics that help define the workbook and provide useful information about it. Defining a clear and comprehensive set of properties for a workbook is an effective way to document its creation, development, and history.*

✔ *Excel's protection features enable you to control who accesses and modifies the data in a workbook.*

✔ *Assigning a password to a workbook is an effective way to keep any user who does not know the password from accessing the workbook.*

✔ *You can protect an individual worksheet so that it cannot be changed without the user providing a password, or you can protect a complete workbook so that individual worksheets cannot be moved or deleted and new worksheets cannot be inserted. You also can protect a range of cells within a worksheet so that only those cells can't be changed.*

Quick Quiz

True/False

T F 1. When a cell in a tracked range is edited, a blue triangle appears in its top left corner.

T F 2. The change tracking feature allows for a maximum of two users to make edits to a workbook.

T F 3. The date that a workbook was last modified is an example of a workbook property.

T F 4. You cannot modify the Title property for a workbook.

T F 5. Workbook passwords are case-sensitive.

T F 6. You can assign one password to open a workbook and a different password to modify an open workbook.

Multiple Choice

1. Which of the following identifies that a cell in a tracked range has been edited?
   a. red triangle in the top right corner
   b. blue triangle in the top left corner
   c. moving marquee that outlines the cell
   d. yellow highlight in the cell

2. Which workbook property typically identifies the person who created the file?
   a. Title
   b. Subject
   c. Author
   d. Developer

3. If you wanted to provide additional information about a workbook, such as a description of its contents or who created and revised it, which workbook property would you use?
    a. Subject
    b. Category
    c. Comments
    d. Keywords

4. If you established *EXcEL* as a workbook's password, which of the following would you enter to open the workbook?
    a. EXcEL
    b. EXCEL
    c. Excel
    d. All of the above

Short Answer

1. Why might you want to share a workbook without turning on change tracking?

2. Why would you use the Title property on a workbook?

3. Why might you want to create separate passwords for modifying and opening a workbook?

4. If you're using change tracking, how do you create a history list of changes in a separate worksheet?

5. What two protection options do you have for a workbook?

On Your Own

◆ **Open AW Marketing TC from the Excel Expert Practice/Lesson07 folder.**

Exercise 1

Display the Marketing Costs sheet, if necessary. Turn on change tracking for all changes that have not yet been reviewed, for all users, and for the range B6:F17. In cell F12 of the Marketing Costs worksheet, type 13010. Reject all changes except the one you've made.

◆ **Save and close the workbook.**

◆ **Open AW Departmental Expenses from the Excel Expert Practice/Lesson07 folder.**

Exercise 2

Specify that the file can be opened only with the password Lmarket and can be modified only with the password q458ty. Close the file. Then reopen it, specifying both passwords. Delete the passwords.

◆ **Save and close the file.**

◆ **Open AW Budget from the Excel Expert Practice/Lesson07 folder.**

Exercise 3

Protect the worksheet, but leave column B unprotected. Verify worksheet protection by attempting to make a change in column C. Turn off worksheet protection.

◆ **Close the workbook without saving changes.**

One Step Further

Exercise 1

This lesson discussed the Search dialog box (accessible from Excel's Open dialog box) and how it can be used to look for files with specific properties. Open the Search dialog box. What can be done from the Basic tab of the Search dialog box? Can you perform this same search from the Advanced tab? Given the options that are available in the Search dialog box, does it seem likely that this Search feature would be available in the other Office 2003 applications?

Exercise 2

What does the Contents tab of the Properties dialog box contain for an Excel file? Can you perform a search based upon the contents?

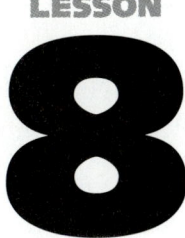

LESSON

8

Exchanging Information Using the Web

After completing this lesson, you will be able to:

✔ *Publish worksheets on the Web.*
✔ *Publish a PivotTable on the Web.*
✔ *Retrieve data from the Web using queries and Smart Tags.*
✔ *Import and export workbooks as structured data.*

KEY TERMS

- browser
- Extensible Markup Language (XML)
- Hypertext Markup Language (HTML)

- PivotTable list
- round-trip
- Smart Tags
- tags

The World Wide Web is a dynamic, interactive vehicle through which volumes of information are exchanged. You can save Excel workbooks and worksheets as files that can be accessed and interacted with via the World Wide Web. This feature empowers you with the capabilities and flexibility to share and exchange information with many users—even those who don't work with Excel. All the user needs is a Web browser. You also can bring data from the Web into your workbooks.

Excel offers **Extensible Markup Language (XML)** technology. XML is a content markup language, meaning that an XML file has information about the data contained within it (as compared with Hypertext Markup Language, which tells a Web browser how to display a file's contents). Saving Excel workbooks as XML files means that your Excel data is readable by a wide range of programs. One application of XML is **Smart Tags,** a technology that recognizes certain types of information, such as stock symbols, and looks up related information on the Web or opens another program so that you can execute a related action.

In this lesson, you'll learn how to save workbooks on the Web, publish worksheets and PivotTables on the Web, retrieve data from the Web, and move data from one application to another.

Publishing Data on the Web

Publishing Worksheets and PivotTables on the Web

THE BOTTOM LINE

You can save workbooks and individual worksheets in a format that enables anyone with Internet access to open and view them using a Web browser. You also can apply the interactivity element to these files so that others can edit, change formatting, and manipulate the data from within their browser.

One of the strengths of Excel is that you can save workbooks as Web documents, allowing you and your colleagues to view them over the Internet or a corporate intranet. This capability represents an effective way to share workbook data, charts, and tables with others who might not use Excel.

For a document to be viewed via the World Wide Web, the document must be saved as a **Hypertext Markup Language (HTML)** file. HTML files, which end with either the .htm or the .html extension, include **tags** that tell a Web **browser** such as Microsoft Internet Explorer how to display the contents of the file.

To create HTML files in Excel, you use the Save As Web Page command on the File menu. There are a number of options you can apply when you save a workbook as a Web page. For example, you can change the title that appears on the title bar of the file when it is opened in a Web browser. You can set the interactivity feature so that viewers have the capability to interact with the file after it is published on the Web. This includes editing cell values; sorting, filtering, or calculating values with formulas; and changing cell formatting. And with the AutoRepublish feature, you can have the Web file automatically updated whenever the file on which it is based is updated.

Once you have saved a workbook as a series of HTML documents, the data is automatically tagged to be readable by a Web browser such as Internet Explorer.

Publishing Worksheets on the Web

You also can save individual worksheets as HTML documents. For example, you might have a workbook that contains worksheets for individual department budgets and a summary worksheet that contains budget information for the entire company. You want to publish only the summary worksheet for others to review. To save a single worksheet as an HTML document, you use the Save As Web Page command on the File menu. In the Save As dialog box, you select the Selection: Sheet option to save the active worksheet as an HTML document.

◆ To complete the procedures in this lesson, you must use the files **Publish, Pivot, WebData, Financial.htm, Smart, Structured,** and **PivotXML** in the **Lesson08** folder in the **Excel Expert Practice** folder located on your hard disk.

◆ Open **Publish** from the **Excel Expert Practice/Lesson08** folder.

Publish a worksheet to the Web

In this exercise, you publish a worksheet to the Web, set a title for the worksheet, make the worksheet interactive, change the format of worksheet elements in a Web browser, and turn on AutoRepublish so that any changes in the original document will be reflected in the Web document created from it.

1 If necessary, click the January sheet tab to display the January worksheet.

2 On the File menu, click Save As Web Page.

The Save As dialog box appears.

3 In the Save section of the dialog box, select the Selection: Sheet button to publish only the active worksheet on the Web.

TIP

If the Office Assistant appears, close it.

4 In the Save section of the dialog box, select the Add Interactivity check box, and then click Publish.

The Publish As Web Page dialog box appears.

FIGURE 8-1

Publish As Web Page dialog box

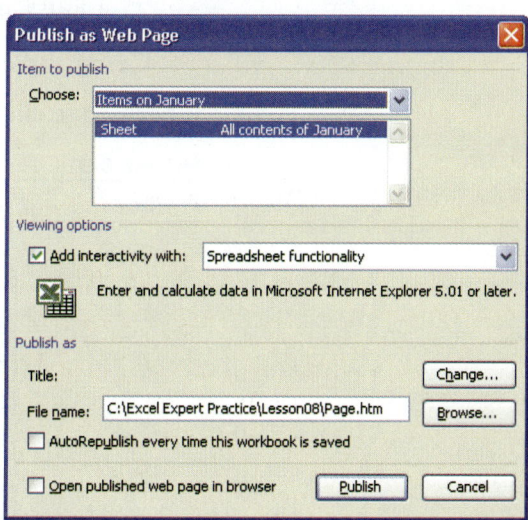

5 In the Publish As section of the dialog box, click the Change button.

The Set Title dialog box appears.

6 In the Title box, type January Sales Data, and then click OK.

The Set Title dialog box closes, and *January Sales Data* appears as the title of the Web page.

7 Select the AutoRepublish Every Time This Workbook Is Saved check box.

8 Select the Open Published Web Page In Browser check box, if necessary, and then click Publish.

The workbook appears in Internet Explorer, as shown in Figure 8-2.

FIGURE 8-2

Worksheet opens in Internet Explorer

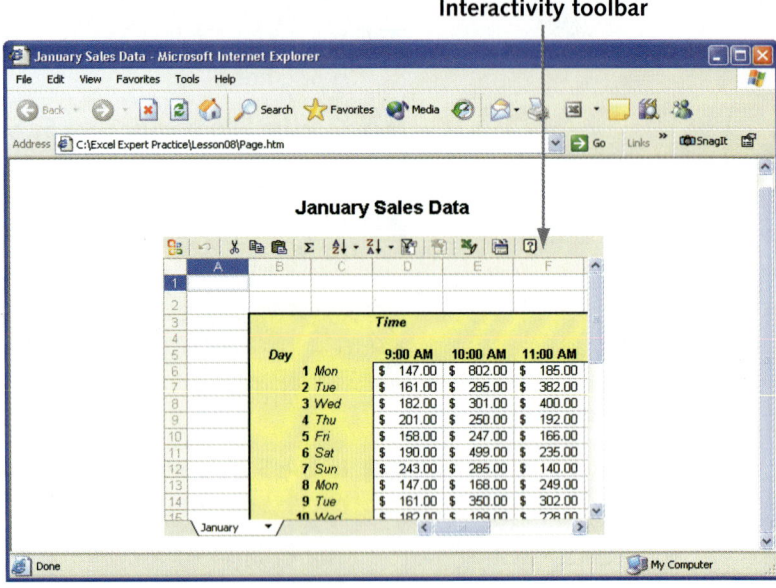

9 Click cell B5, and on the Interactivity toolbar, click the Commands And Options button.

The Commands And Options dialog box appears.

10 If necessary, click the Format tab.

FIGURE 8-3

Format tab in the Commands And Options dialog box

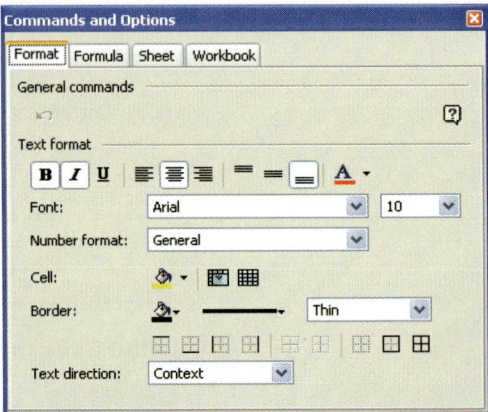

11 In the Text format section of the dialog box, click the Align Left button.

The contents of cell B5 are aligned at the left edge of the cell.

 12 In the Commands And Options dialog box, click the Close button.

The Commands And Options dialog box closes.

 13 In Internet Explorer, click the Close button to close the program.

◆ **Close the Publish workbook without saving changes.**

QUICK REFERENCE ▼

Save a workbook as an HTML document

1 On the File menu, click Save As Web Page.

2 If necessary, in the Save section, select the Entire Workbook option button.

3 Verify that the desired file name appears in the File Name box, and then click Save.

Publish a worksheet on the Web

1 On the File menu, click Save As Web Page.

2 In the Save section of the dialog box, select the Selection: Sheet button to publish the active worksheet on the Web.

3 To allow others to make changes to the worksheet, click the Add Interactivity check box in the Save section of the dialog box, and then click Publish.

4 In the Publish As Web Page dialog box, change the title of the worksheet, if desired, by clicking the Change button in the Publish As section, typing the new title in the Title box, and clicking OK.

5 Select the AutoRepublish Every Time This Workbook Is Saved check box if you want the Web page to be updated when the original file is updated.

6 Select the Open Published Web Page In Browser check box, and then click Publish.

Publishing a PivotTable on the Web

In Lesson 6, "Using Data Analysis Tools and Features," you learned how to rearrange data in different row-and-column formats to create a PivotTable report. Just as you can publish a workbook or worksheet to the Web, you can publish a PivotTable report, thus giving users the capability to rearrange rows and columns to meet their own needs or to generate other analyses.

Round-tripping Worksheets
You can **round-trip** data between Excel and the Web. Round-tripping refers to the process of saving an Excel worksheet as a Web page, saving the Web page to a Web site, viewing the page in a Web browser, saving the page in your Web browser, and reopening the file in Excel. When you round-trip a file in this manner, Excel retains the original Excel formatting as a set of XML tags stored in the Web page. When you convert the Web page back to Excel, the XML tags are used to return the worksheet to its original Excel format. Round-tripping is useful when you want to display an Excel worksheet as an HTML table so that others can view the table on the Web. Web site visitors can use their Web browsers to save the Web page to a file on their hard disk. They can then open the files in Excel—retaining all of the formatting of the original Excel worksheet that you created.

When you save a PivotTable as a Web page in interactive format, the PivotTable appears in users' Web browsers as a **PivotTable list**. The main difference between a PivotTable in a workbook and a PivotTable list on the Web is that the PivotTable list data is independent of any worksheet data; that is, the PivotTable list is no longer linked to the data in a particular worksheet. When other people open a PivotTable list in Internet Explorer, they can drag field buttons to different columns and rows to create different PivotTable views.

For example, if the owner of Adventure Works is on vacation but wants to participate in a meeting, she can use her laptop to connect to the company's Web site, view a PivotTable report saved there, and manipulate the data as desired.

> **TIP**
>
> If you publish an entire workbook, rather than just the PivotTable, viewers will not be able to interact with the PivotTable.

◆ Open Pivot from the Excel Expert Practice/Lesson08 folder.

Publish a PivotTable to the Web

In this exercise, you publish a PivotTable on the Web and then filter the PivotTable's contents using Internet Explorer.

1 If necessary, click the Pivot sheet tab, and then click any cell in the PivotTable.

2 On the File menu, click Save As Web Page.

The Save As dialog box appears.

3 In the Save section of the dialog box, click the Selection: Sheet button, and then click the Add Interactivity check box.

4 In the File Name text box, change the name of the file to Page2, and then click Publish.

The Publish As Web Page dialog box appears.

5 If necessary, click the arrow on the Choose box, and click Items On Pivot.

Items On Pivot appears in the Choose box, and the items on the Pivot worksheet appear in the list below the Choose box.

FIGURE 8-4

Publish As Web Page dialog box

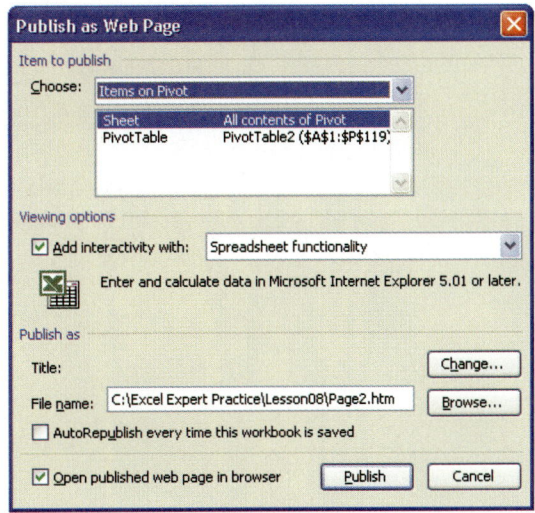

6 In the list below the Choose box, click the item beginning with "PivotTable."

In the Viewing options section of the dialog box, the value in the Add Interactivity With box changes to PivotTable Functionality.

7 If necessary, in the bottom section of the dialog box, select the Open Published Web Page In Browser check box.

8 Click Publish.

The PivotTable is saved as a Web page and opens in Internet Explorer.

9 Click the Show Details button.

The PivotTable expands to show every cell.

FIGURE 8-5

Changing views in the PivotTable

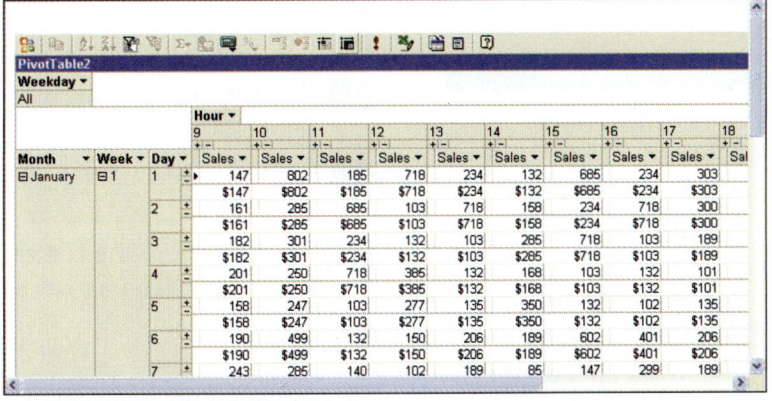

10 In the top left section of the PivotTable, click the Weekday down arrow, and clear the Mon, Tue, Wed, Thu, and Fri check boxes.

11 Click OK.

The PivotTable is filtered so that only Saturday and Sunday sales are shown.

FIGURE 8-6

Modifying a PivotTable in Internet Explorer

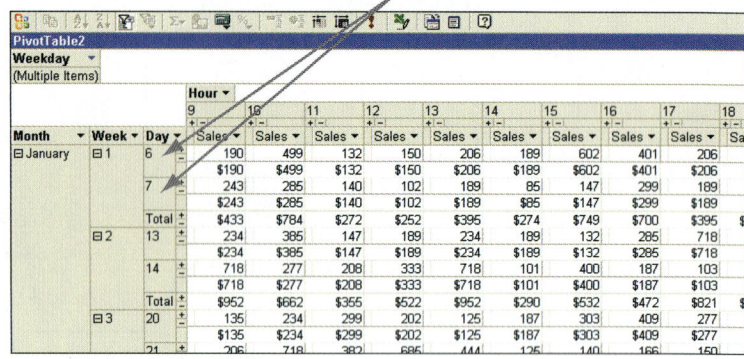

12 Click the Weekday down arrow again, click the All check box, and click OK.

The filter is removed.

 13 Click the Close button to close Internet Explorer.

◆ Close the Pivot workbook without saving changes.

QUICK REFERENCE ▼

Save a PivotTable as a PivotList

1 Click any cell in the PivotTable.

2 On the File menu, click Save As Web Page.

3 In the Save section of the dialog box, select the Selection: Sheet button.

4 If desired, click the Add Interactivity check box, and then click Publish.

5 If necessary, click the arrow on the Choose box, and click Items On Pivot.

6 In the list below the Choose box, click the item beginning with *PivotTable*.

7 If necessary, in the bottom section of the dialog box, select the Open Published Web Page In Browser check box.

8 Click Publish.

Work with a PivotList via the Web

1 In Internet Explorer, open the Web page with the PivotList.

2 Use the down arrows and column heads to modify the PivotList's organization.

Retrieving Data from the Web

Using XML Data Capabilities and
Retrieving Web Data

THE BOTTOM LINE

Tabular data that's commonly found on the Web is ideal for copying to a worksheet, where it can be calculated, formatted, and analyzed just like the raw data you enter in a worksheet.

The World Wide Web is a great source of information. From stock quotes to product descriptions, many companies publish useful information on their Web sites. The most common HTML structure used to present financial information is the table, which, like a spreadsheet, organizes the data into rows and columns, as shown in Figure 8-7.

FIGURE 8-7

Table on a Web page

Indexes		
Dow	10,220.67	+172.44
Nasdaq	1,965.72	+56.24
S&P	1,109.83	+18.50
10-Yr Note	102.13	-0.22
	Yield:	3.730%

You can copy data from a Web page and paste it in a workbook. Then you can create a query to retrieve data from the HTML table you copied. To create a Web query, open the target Web page in Internet Explorer, copy the data to the Clipboard, click a cell in the Excel workbook, and paste the data in the workbook. The data appears in the worksheet with a Paste Options button next to it. Click the Paste Options button, as shown in Figure 8-8, and then click Create Refreshable Web Query. The New Web Query dialog box opens, in which you can easily select a table to import.

FIGURE 8-8

Paste Options menu

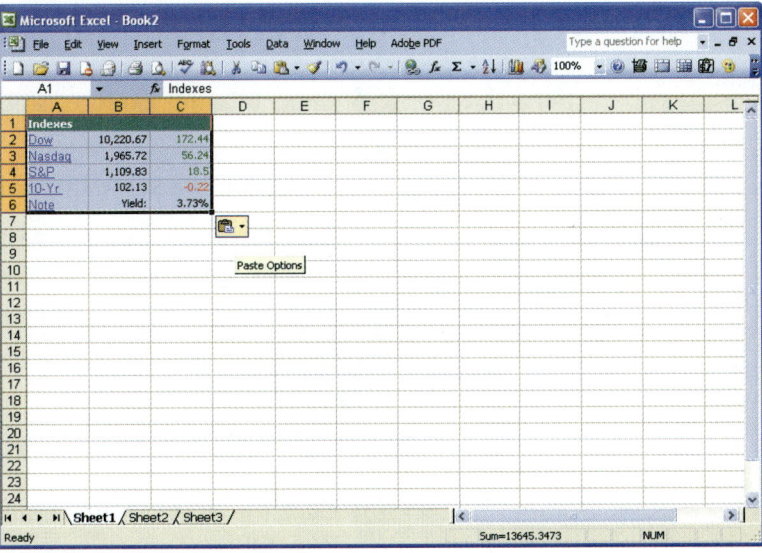

After you select the table, click Import to copy the data to the worksheet. To refresh data, right-click any cell in the imported table. Then from the shortcut menu, click Refresh Data (or click the Refresh Data button on the External Data toolbar). The query mechanism automatically checks the Web page from which the table came and makes any updates to it in your workbook.

> **TIP**
>
> You can select an entire Web page by clicking the top table icon in the display pane.

◆ **Open WebData from the Excel Expert Practice/Lesson08 folder.**

Use a Web query to retrieve data

In this exercise, you create a Web query to retrieve data.

1 Start Internet Explorer, and on the File menu, click Open.

The Open dialog box appears.

2 Click Browse.

The Microsoft Internet Explorer dialog box appears.

3 Navigate to the C:\Excel Expert Practice\Lesson08 folder, and then double-click Financial.htm.

4 Click OK.

Financial.htm appears in Internet Explorer.

5 Select the table data, and then on the Edit menu, click Copy.

The data is copied to the Clipboard.

> **ANOTHER METHOD**
>
> ■ Press Ctrl+C.

6 Close Internet Explorer, and return to the Excel window.

 7 In the WebData workbook, click cell A1, and then click the Paste button on the Standard toolbar.

The HTML table data is pasted in the worksheet, and the Paste Options button appears next to the data.

> **ANOTHER METHOD**
>
> ■ On the Edit menu, click Paste.
> ■ Press Ctrl+V.

8 Click the Paste Options button, and then click Create Refreshable Web Query.

The New Web Query dialog box appears, with Financial.htm displayed.

FIGURE 8-9

New Web Query dialog box

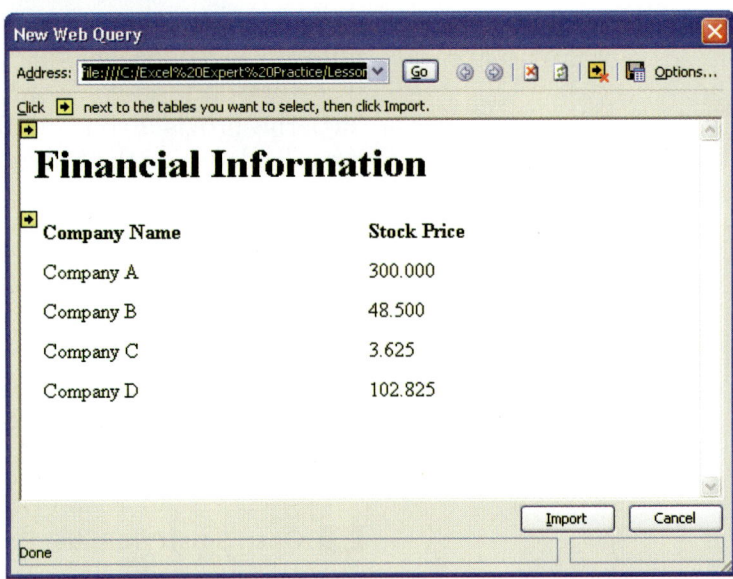

9 **Click the table icon next to "Company Name," and then click Import.**

The HTML table data appears in the worksheet, with its original HTML formatting.

FIGURE 8-10

Table imported to a worksheet

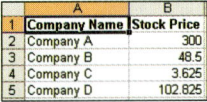

◆ Save and close the WebData workbook.

QUICK REFERENCE ▼

Link to Web data

1 In Internet Explorer, open the Web page with the table data to which you want to link.

2 Select the table data, and then click Copy on the Edit menu to copy the data to the Clipboard.

3 In Microsoft Excel, click the desired cell, and click the Paste button.

4 Click the Paste Options button, and then click Create Refreshable Web Query.

5 Click the table icon next to the object or file to import, and then click Import.

QUICK CHECK

Q. How do you refresh table data that you've imported from a Web page using a Web query?

A: You refresh the data by right-clicking any cell within the table data that you've imported and selecting Refresh Data on the shortcut menu or by clicking the Refresh Data button on the External Data toolbar.

Acquiring Web Data with Smart Tags

Excel, like other Office programs, offers Smart Tags technology, which enables you to execute certain actions or gather information that you normally must open another program to do. For example, a date entered in a worksheet (or in a Word document as well) is labeled with a Smart Tag. This provides you with the options to schedule a meeting or display the calendar using the Microsoft Outlook program.

The clearest example of how Smart Tags work is with stock symbols—the abbreviations of company names on stock market tickers—that are entered in a worksheet. When you turn on Smart Tags, many of the stock symbols are identified with a Smart Tags indicator (a small purple triangle in the lower right corner of the cell). Pointing to a cell with an indicator displays the indicator button. You click the button, select Financial Symbol, and choose the information related to the company that you want to retrieve. With Smart Tags technology, the information is automatically retrieved from the location, such as a Web site, that contains the information.

◆ **Open Smart from the Excel Expert Practice/Lesson08 folder.**

Work with Smart Tags

In this exercise, you turn on Smart Tags, check a worksheet for Smart Tags, and use the Smart Tag you find to get stock information about the company represented by a stock symbol.

1 **On the Tools menu, click AutoCorrect Options.**

The AutoCorrect dialog box appears.

2 **Click the Smart Tags tab.**

The Smart Tags tab appears, as shown in Figure 8-11.

FIGURE 8-11

Smart Tags tab in the AutoCorrect dialog box

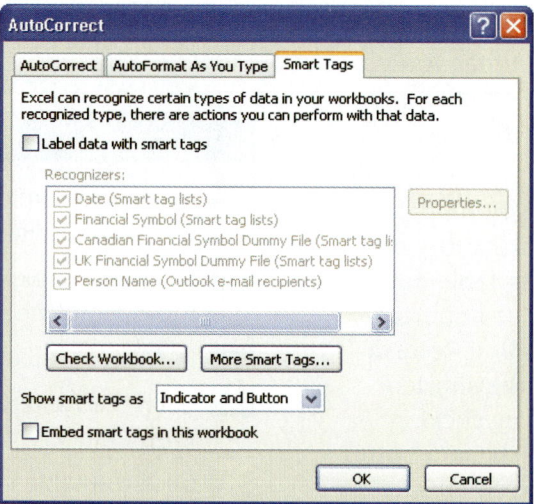

3 **Select the Label Data With Smart Tags check box.**

The Recognizers box becomes active.

4 Select the Embed Smart Tags In This Workbook check box.

Smart Tags will now be saved as part of the workbook file.

5 Click Check Workbook.

The AutoCorrect dialog box closes, and a message box appears, telling you that the Smart Tags check is complete.

6 Click OK.

A Smart Tag indicator appears in cell B3.

7 Move the mouse pointer over cell B3.

A Smart Tag Actions button appears next to the cell.

8 Click the Smart Tag Actions button, click Financial Symbol, and click Insert Refreshable Stock Price.

The Insert Stock Price dialog box appears.

FIGURE 8-12

Insert Stock Price dialog box

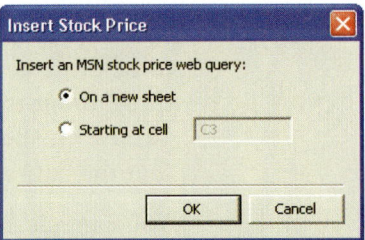

IMPORTANT

If you must manually establish your connection to the Internet, do so before clicking OK in the Insert Stock Price dialog box.

9 Select the Starting At Cell option, verify that C3 appears in the Starting At Cell box, and click OK.

Depending on the speed of your Internet connection, the stock quote appears in the workbook within moments.

10 If desired, turn off Smart Tags by selecting AutoCorrect Options on the Tools menu, clicking the Smart Tags tab, clearing the Label Data With Smart Tags check box, and clicking OK.

◆ Save and close the Smart workbook.

QUICK REFERENCE ▼

Acquire data with Smart Tags

1 On the Tools menu, click AutoCorrect Options.

2 Click the Smart Tags tab.

3 Select the Label Data With Smart Tags check box.

QUICK CHECK

Q. How do you know if data in a cell has been labeled with a Smart Tag?

A: The cell contains a small purple triangle in the lower right corner.

4 Select the Embed Smart Tags In This Workbook check box.

5 Click Check Workbook, and then click OK in the message box.

6 Move the mouse pointer over a cell with the Smart Tag indicator.

7 Click the Smart Tag Actions button, and then, from the list that appears, click the desired action.

8 Select the Starting At Cell option button, verify that the proper cell appears in the Starting At Cell box, and click OK.

Using XML Data Capabilities and Retrieving Web Data

Working with Structured Data

THE BOTTOM LINE

XML technology enables you to save worksheet data in a format and structure that can be read by programs other than Excel, thus giving you the flexibility to share workbook data in a variety of formats.

As you have learned, HTML is the format applied to documents that are to be displayed in a Web browser. However, HTML doesn't tell you anything about the meaning of data in a document. Internet Explorer might "know" it should display a set of data in a table, but it doesn't "know" that the data represents an Excel spreadsheet.

You can add metadata, or data about data, to Web documents using Extensible Markup Language (XML). While a full discussion of XML is beyond the scope of this book, the following bit of XML code shows how to identify an Excel workbook in XML:

```
<?xml version="1.0"?>
<Workbook xmlns="urn:schemas-microsoft- com:office:spreadsheet"
xmlns:o="urn:schemas-microsoft- com:office:office"
xmlns:x="urn:schemas-microsoft-com:office:excel"
xmlns:ss="urn:schemas-microsoft-com:office:spreadsheet"
xmlns:html="http://www.w3.org/TR/REC-html40">
```

Also, XML can identify rows and cells within the spreadsheet, as in the following example:

```
<Row>
    <Cell><Data ss:Type="String">January</Data></Cell>
    <Cell><Data ss:Type="Number">1</Data></Cell>
    <Cell><Data ss:Type="String">Tue</Data></Cell>
    <Cell><Data ss:Type="Number">2</Data></Cell>
    <Cell><Data ss:Type="Number">9</Data></Cell>
    <Cell><Data ss:Type="Number">161</Data></Cell>
</Row>
```

This represents the worksheet row identified in Figure 8-13.

FIGURE 8-13

XML-coded worksheet

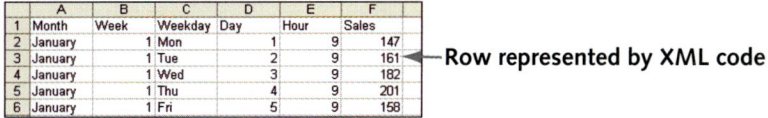

← Row represented by XML code

The goal of XML is to be a universal language, allowing data to move freely from one application to another. In this case, saving an Excel workbook as an XML document allows any other spreadsheet program to read the XML file, separate out the cell data, and use the metadata to decide how to structure a worksheet to contain that data.

Converting an Excel Workbook to XML

To save an Excel document as an XML file, click Save As on the File menu to open the Save As dialog box. In the Save As dialog box, click the Save As Type down arrow, click XML Spreadsheet (*.xml), and click Save. You can open Excel spreadsheets saved as XML documents by clicking the Open button, displaying all Excel files, and clicking Open.

◆ **Open Structured from the Excel Expert Practice/Lesson08 folder.**

Work with XML documents

In this exercise, you save an Excel workbook as an XML document and then import an XML document into Excel.

1 **On the File menu, click Save As.**

The Save As dialog box appears.

2 **Click the Save As Type down arrow, and click XML Spreadsheet (*.xml).**

The file type changes to XML.

3 **Click Save.**

A message box appears, indicating that any Microsoft Visual Basic projects or header or footer image associated with the workbook will not be saved.

4 **Click Yes to clear the message box and save the workbook as an XML spreadsheet.**

5 **Click the Close Window button to close Structured.xml.**

6 **On the Standard toolbar, click the Open button.**

The Open dialog box appears.

7 **Navigate to the C:\Excel Expert Practice\Lesson08 folder, and double-click PivotXML.xml.**

PivotXML.xml, which contains a PivotTable, opens.

◆ **Save and close the workbook. If you are continuing to other lessons, leave Excel open. If you are not continuing to other lessons, save and close all open workbooks. Click the Close button in the top right corner of the Excel window.**

QUICK CHECK

Q. What is the difference between HTML and XML?

A: HTML is the format used on files that are to be viewed and read in a Web browser, whereas XML allows data to be formatted so that it can be read in a wide range of programs.

QUICK REFERENCE ▼

Export Excel documents as XML

1 On the File menu, click Save As.

2 Click the Save As Type down arrow, and click XML Spreadsheet (*.xml).

3 Click Save.

4 Click Yes to clear the message box and save the workbook as an XML spreadsheet.

Import an XML file into Excel

1 On the Standard toolbar, click the Open button.

2 Navigate to the target folder, and double-click the target file with the .xml extension.

Key Points

✔ *You can save workbooks and individual worksheets in a format that enables anyone with Internet access to open and view them using a Web browser. You also can apply the interactivity element to these files so that others can edit, change formatting, and manipulate the data from within their browser.*

✔ *Tables and tabular data that are commonly found on the Web are ideal for copying to a worksheet, where they can be calculated, formatted, and analyzed just like the raw data you enter in a worksheet.*

✔ *Excel, like other Office programs, offers Smart Tags technology, which enables you to execute certain actions or gather information that you normally must open another program to do.*

✔ *XML technology enables you to save worksheet data in a format and structure that can be read by programs other than Excel, thus giving you the flexibility to share workbook data in a variety of formats.*

Quick Quiz

True/False

T   F   1.   For a workbook to be viewed via the World Wide Web, it must be saved in HTTP format.

T   F   2.   You can publish a workbook to the Web, but not individual worksheets.

T   F   3.   When you publish a workbook to the Web, you can change the title so that it's different from the file name.

T   F   4.   XML is an example of a Web browser.

T   F   5.   You can use a Web query to refresh data in a table that you've copied from the Web.

T   F   6.   You must turn on the Smart Tags feature; it is not activated by default.

Multiple Choice

1.   Which feature enables you to update a Web version of a workbook file whenever the original workbook file is saved?
   a.   Round-tripping
   b.   AutoRepublish
   c.   Add Interactivity
   d.   Smart Tags

2.   Which feature allows you to save a worksheet as a Web page, save the page to a Web site, view and save the page in a Web browser, and reopen the file in Excel with all of the formatting intact?
   a.   Round-tripping
   b.   AutoRepublish
   c.   Add Interactivity
   d.   Smart Tags

3.   Which feature do you apply so that other Internet users can make changes to workbook files that you publish to the Web?
   a.   Round-tripping
   b.   AutoRepublish
   c.   Add Interactivity
   d.   Smart Tags

4.   What identifies a cell that is recognized by Smart Tags technology?
   a.   small red triangle in lower left corner
   b.   small purple triangle in lower right corner
   c.   small blue square in upper right corner
   d.   flashing marquee outlining the cell

Short Answer

1. Why would you want to publish a worksheet on the Web?

2. What does adding interactivity mean when you are publishing an Excel worksheet on the Web?

3. What is the main difference between a PivotTable in a workbook and a PivotTable list on the Web?

4. What is the name of the feature that lets you copy data directly from a Web page into Excel and then create a query to retrieve data from the HTML table that you copied?

5. What are Smart Tags?

On Your Own

◆ **Open Pivot from the Excel Expert Practice/Lesson08 folder.**

Exercise 1

Publish the entire workbook as a Web page (name it Page3). Open this page in Internet Explorer, and then open the Page2 file that you created from the Pivot workbook in the exercises in this lesson. How are the two pages similar? How are they different? What is the cause of the differences?

◆ **Leave the Pivot workbook open for the next exercise.**

Exercise 2

Create an XML document from the Pivot workbook. Open Internet Explorer, and then open the Pivot.xml document from within Internet Explorer. What information do you see at the beginning of the file? What can you learn about the document from this view?

◆ **Close all open workbooks and Internet Explorer.**

One Step Further

◆ **Open Publish from the Excel Expert Practice/Lesson08 folder.**

Exercise 1

In this lesson, you learned how to enable and disable AutoRepublish. In the Publish workbook, is the AutoRepublish feature enabled? Is there a way to temporarily disable the AutoRepublish feature so that it does not republish at this particular time? Use Excel's Help files, if necessary, to learn more about the AutoRepublish feature.

◆ **Close Publish without saving changes.**

Exercise 2

Create a new workbook, and insert Smart Tags for several stocks in which you are interested. (You might want to use the stock symbols for local companies or for companies in which you or someone you know owns stock.) Use the Smart Tags options to get current stock price information.

Exercise 3

In this lesson, you learned how to use Smart Tags to retrieve information on stocks. What other data can be retrieved using Smart Tags? Use Excel's Help files, if necessary, to answer this question. Open a new workbook, and use a Smart Tag to retrieve data of this type.

9

Creating, Customizing, and Using Templates

After completing this lesson, you will be able to:

✔ *Customize a standard template.*
✔ *Understand where templates are stored.*
✔ *Open and modify a customized template.*
✔ *Create a template from an existing workbook.*

KEY TERMS

- placeholders
- print area
- template

A **template** is a document that can be used as the basis for creating another document. A worksheet based on a template retains any formulas, formatting, text, and other characteristics that were stored in that template. Microsoft Excel comes with several ready-made templates, which you can customize or use as is. These templates enable you to create a specialized worksheet, such as an invoice, without having to design the worksheet yourself. You also can create your own templates from scratch.

In this lesson, you'll learn how to customize the templates that come with Excel, use the Templates dialog box to open existing templates, create your own templates, and establish a print area in a template.

IMPORTANT

Before you can use the practice files in this lesson, you must install them from the book's companion CD to their default location. For additional information on how to find and open files used in this book, see the "Using the CD-ROM" section at the beginning of this book.

Working with Standard Templates

THE BOTTOM LINE

Templates serve as the framework for workbooks that you use over and over again and are useful for standardizing the appearance and functionality of workbooks. You can customize a standard template so that it suits your needs.

Customizing one of the templates that comes with Excel is as easy as opening the template file and making changes to the template's settings or content. For example, you can customize the standard invoice template with your company's name, address, and phone number, and you can change the state tax rate and shipping charges to those your company uses. By customizing the template, you won't need to type this information each time you create an invoice.

After you make changes to one of the standard templates, you simply save the template with a new name or the original name. In either case, the original template remains as is (it cannot be overwritten), and your custom template is saved in a separate place.

IMPORTANT

Your instructor may make these templates available to you so that you do not need to install them from the Office 2003 or Excel 2003 CD-ROM. See your instructor for directions.

Most templates include **placeholders** at different locations in the template. The placeholder typically indicates what you can enter at a location, and it is not intended to remain there permanently. When you click a placeholder, a ScreenTip usually appears to give further directions on what to enter in that area as well as how to do it.

◆ **To complete the procedures in this lesson, you must use the files AW Logo.tif, 2005 Timesheet, and Purchase Order 185 in the Lesson09 folder in the Excel Expert Practice folder located on your hard disk.**

IMPORTANT

The template used in the following procedure might not be available if Excel was installed using the Typical installation option. The Spreadsheet Solutions templates are not installed by default. You might be prompted to insert the Excel 2003 or Office 2003 CD at the start of this exercise so that the templates can be installed.

◆ **Start Excel.**

Open and customize a template

In this exercise, you open the invoice template and customize several entries.

1 **On the File menu, click New to open the New Workbook task pane, if necessary.**

The New Workbook task pane appears.

2 **On the New Workbook task pane, in the Templates section, click On My Computer.**

The Templates dialog box opens.

3 **Click the Spreadsheet Solutions tab.**

The dialog box displays templates in the Spreadsheet Solutions category.

FIGURE 9-1

Templates dialog box

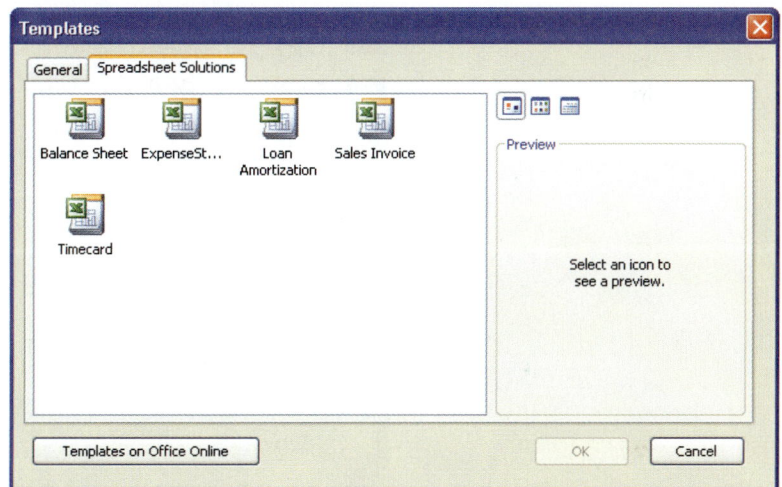

4 **Click the Sales Invoice icon.**

A preview of the template appears on the right side of the dialog box. You can use these previews as you examine templates to determine which template you want to use—without having to open each template that you want to consider.

5 **Click OK.**

The Sales Invoice template opens as a spreadsheet named Sales Invoice1.

IMPORTANT

You might see a warning that the numbering add-in must be loaded for optimal numbering and toolbar behavior. If you see this alert box, click OK. For more information on add-ins, use the Ask A Question text box to search for information on "Add-in programs for Microsoft Excel."

6 **Click the text "Insert Company Information Here."**

A ScreenTip appears detailing how to enter company information.

FIGURE 9-2

Inserting text in the template

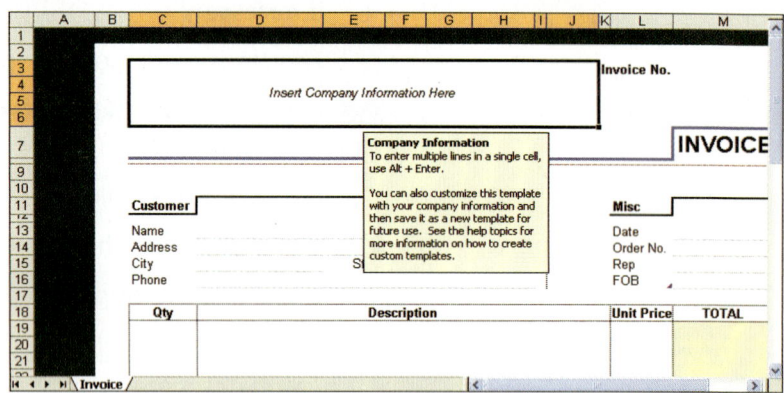

7 **Type Adventure Works, and press Alt+Enter.**

8 **Type 1501 Bryant's Gap Trail, and press Alt+Enter.**

9 **Type Erewhon, California 94501, and press Enter.**

The company name and address is entered, and the first *Qty* cell becomes the active cell.

10 **Scroll down and click the cell next to Tax Rate(s), type 6, and press Enter.**

A sales tax rate of 6.00% is entered.

TIP

You may need to type .06 to enter a tax rate of 6.00%.

---

11 **Click the Tools menu, point to Protection, and click Protect Workbook.**

The Protect Workbook dialog box opens, giving you the option to enter a password for the workbook.

12 **Click OK.**

 13 **Click the Save button to save your modified template with the suggested name (probably Sales Invoice1).**

TIP

Excel will automatically save your template to the Templates folder.

---

14 **Click the Save As Type down arrow, and select Template (*.xlt) from the list.**

15 **Click Save, and then close the template.**

QUICK REFERENCE ▼

Open a template

1 On the File menu, click New.

2 On the New Workbook task pane, in the Templates section, click On My Computer.

3 Select the tab that contains the template you want to use.

4 Double-click the template you want to open.

Understanding Where Templates Are Stored

Excel's built-in templates and the customized templates that you save are stored in different locations. Usually, the ready-made templates are stored in the path *C:\Program Files\Microsoft Office\Templates*. Customized templates and templates that you create are typically stored in *C:\Documents and Settings\<USERNAME>\Application Data\Microsoft\Templates*, although this path might be different if you didn't install Excel or Office using the default folder. The precise storage location for your customized templates depends on the operating system and the name you use to log on to your computer.

You don't need to remember the paths for ready-made and customized templates. As you have learned, ready-made templates are accessed by clicking the Spreadsheet Solutions tab in the Templates dialog box. Customized templates are accessed by clicking the General tab; however, if you save customized templates to a location other than the default folder, they will not appear on the General tab.

Opening and Modifying a Customized Template

When you want to open and use a customized template, simply display the Templates dialog box, click the General tab, and double-click the name of the template you want to use. If you've locked the customized content and you want to change the content or replace additional placeholders, you must first unlock the template to turn off worksheet protection. You then can make changes just as you did when you originally customized the template.

Open and modify a template

In this exercise, you open the customized invoice template that you created in the previous exercise, insert a logo, and add a phone number to the company information.

1 **On the File menu, click New, and in the Templates section of the New Workbook task pane, click On My Computer.**

2 **Click the General tab, if necessary.**

The template you customized in the previous exercise appears on the General tab of the Templates dialog box.

FIGURE 9-3

New template appears in the Templates dialog box

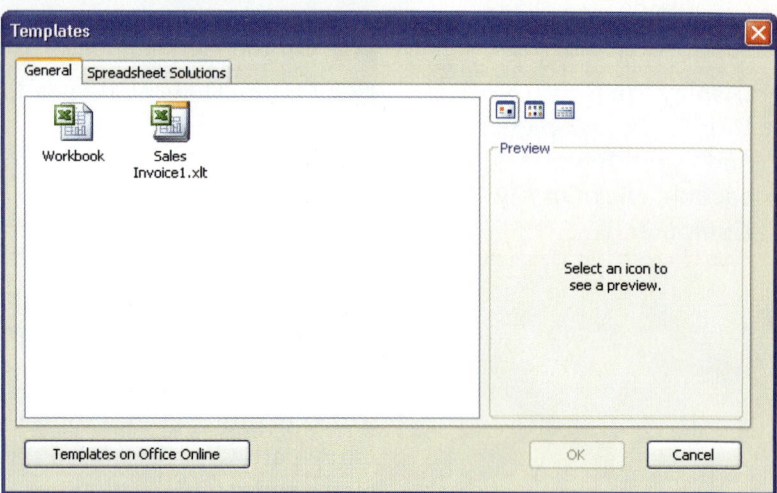

3 **Double-click the Sales Invoice1 icon (or the name that was assigned to the template).**

The template opens as a worksheet named Sales Invoice11.

4 **On the Tools menu, point to Protection, and click Unprotect Sheet.**

The worksheet is unprotected, and you can now make additional changes and customizations.

5 **Click in the cell that contains the company name and address, point to Picture on the Insert menu, and click From File.**

Excel displays the Insert Picture dialog box.

6 **Click the Look In down arrow, navigate to the Lesson09 folder in the Excel Expert Practice folder, click AW Logo.tif, and click Insert.**

The logo is inserted in the worksheet.

7 **Resize the logo so that it fits next to the company information.**

FIGURE 9-4

Inserting a logo

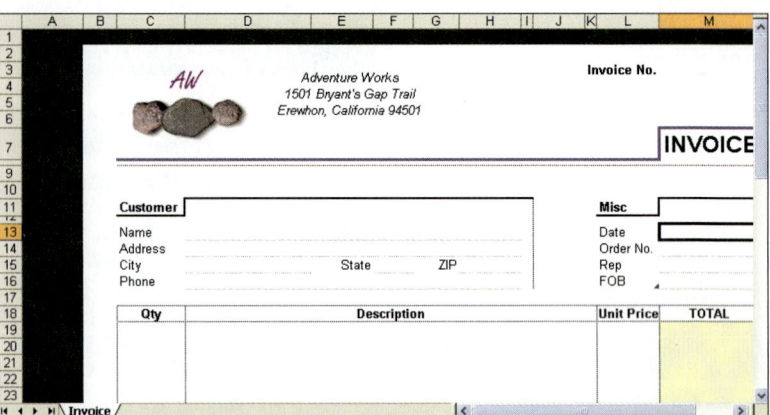

8 Click the cell that contains the company information, and in the Formula bar, click after the ZIP Code.

9 Press Alt+Enter, type 800-555-1212, and press Enter.

The phone number is added to the company information and inserted in the cell.

10 On the Tools menu, point to Protection, and click Protect Sheet.

The Protect Sheet dialog box opens.

11 Click OK.

12 On the File menu, click Save As, click the Save As Type down arrow, and select Template (*.xlt).

13 Select Sales Invoice1 from the list of files (or the name that was assigned to the template when you first customized it).

Because you are modifying an existing template, you should save it with the previously used name.

14 Click Save.

Excel saves the template and displays an alert box notifying you that the template already exists.

15 Click Yes.

The modified template is now saved.

◆ Close the template.

QUICK REFERENCE ▼

Modify a template

1 On the File menu, click New.

2 On the New Workbook task pane, in the Templates section, click On My Computer.

3 Select the tab that contains the template you want to use.

4 Double-click the template you want to edit.

5 Change the desired settings and content in the template.

6 Save the template.

TIP

Excel provides dozens of additional templates that are available through the Templates On Office Online link in the New Workbook task pane.

QUICK CHECK

Q. What is the file extension for an Excel template?

A: **The file extension is** *xlt*.

CHECK THIS OUT ▼

Setting a Print Area

Any settings that you establish in a template become part of the template when you save it. You can define settings for formats, formulas, margins, and header and footer content. In addition, you can establish a **print area** to simplify proper printing for users of the template. To establish a print area for a template, display the template. Select the range of cells that you want to include in the print area. On the File menu, point to Print Area, and click Set Print Area. A dashed line appears around the print area. To save the print area as part of the template, click the Save button.

Creating a Template from an Existing Workbook

Creating a Template from an Existing Worksheet

THE BOTTOM LINE

Creating a template for a type of worksheet you use frequently increases your efficiency and productivity.

Although the templates that come with Excel are useful for creating common worksheets, you may need a wider variety of templates to accommodate your needs or the needs of your company or organization. Instead of creating a new worksheet each time, you can start with a template you design from an existing workbook. This saves you time and provides consistency in the appearance and functionality of worksheets. For example, your company might use the same color and font for worksheet titles and headings so that all of the worksheets your company produces look consistent and professional. Standard functionality can make worksheets easy to use. For example, if all of the budget worksheets for your company work the same way, updating them will be easy for all departments across the company.

Creating a template is just like creating a worksheet. Open a blank workbook, and enter the content that will be part of the structure of all workbooks based on the template; that is, row and column headings, titles, and other instructional or identifying text. If applicable, enter numeric data and formulas and any graphics or design features that are appropriate.

You've probably already created a worksheet for a particular purpose, deciding that you want to use this worksheet as a template. In this case, creating the template is a simple matter of saving the existing workbook as a template. For example, you've developed a personal budget worksheet, and you want to create a budget every month. The title, the line items, and the formulas to calculate income and expenses will remain basically the same from month to month. So you can create a template from the existing budget worksheet, open it at the beginning of each month, and simply type in the new income and expense figures. The formatting is already done, and the calculations are automatically performed.

IMPORTANT

Before you save an existing workbook as a template, be sure to delete existing values that are unique to that particular workbook. If you don't delete them, they'll appear in the template every time a user opens it.

◆ **Open 2005 Timesheet from the Excel Expert Practice/Lesson09 folder.**

Create a template

In this exercise, you create a template for part-time employees at Adventure Works to use in entering their work times for each pay period. You then type data into the template to test it and save the file as a workbook.

1 **Click cell I5, and type** Enter the ending date here.

The placeholder text is entered.

2 **Click cell B6, and type** Type your name here.

The placeholder text is entered.

3 **Select the range A10:P11, and press Delete.**

The values in the selected range are deleted, and the template is now complete.

FIGURE 9-5

Creating a template

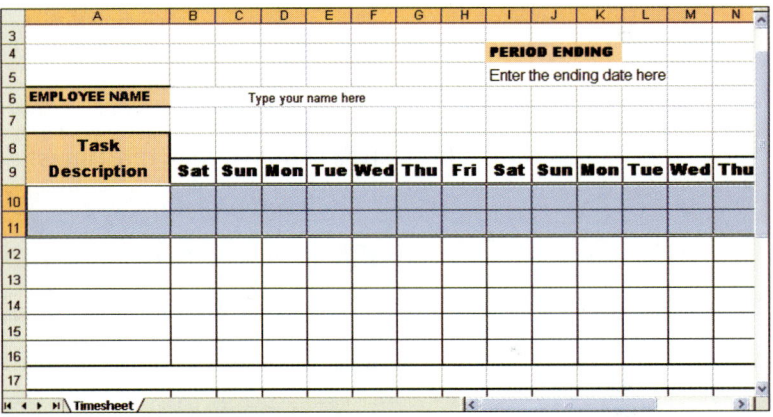

4 **On the File menu, click Save As, click the Save As Type down arrow, and click Template on the list.**

5 **In the File Name box, select the current file name, type** Timesheet Template, **and click Save.**

The template is saved, and it will be represented by an icon in the General tab of the Templates dialog box.

TIP

You can use cell protection to lock labels on your template if you don't want users to be able to change the labels. First, select all of the cells into which you *do* want users to be able to enter data. On the Format menu, click Cells, and click the Protection tab. Clear the Locked check box, and click OK. On the Tools menu, point to Protection, and click Protect Sheet. For more information on applying worksheet protection, see the "Protecting Worksheets and Workbooks" section in Lesson 7, "Sharing Workbooks."

---

6 **Close the template.**

You now can base a new worksheet on the template you created.

7 On the File menu, click New, and in the Templates section of the New Workbook task pane, click On My Computer.

The Timesheet Template appears in the Templates dialog box.

FIGURE 9-6

New template appears in the Templates dialog box

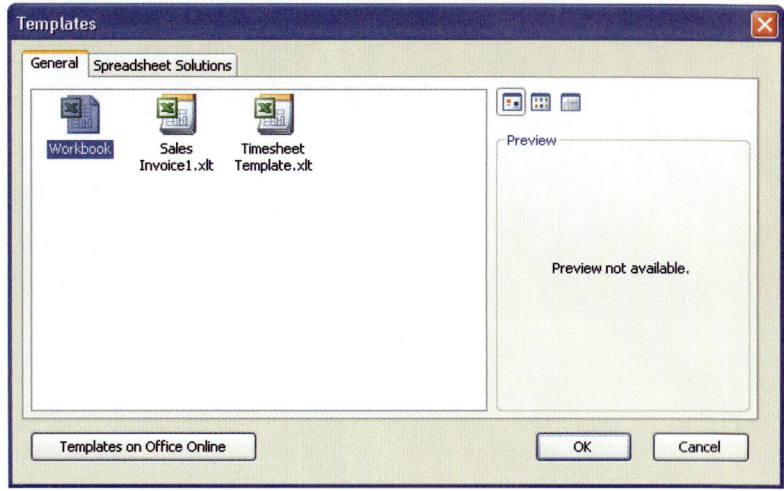

8 Double-click the Timesheet Template icon.

The template opens.

9 Click cell I5, type 1/31/05, and press Enter.

The ending date for the current time period is entered.

10 Click cell B6, type your name, and press Enter.

Your name is entered.

11 Click cell A10, type Housekeeping, and press Tab three times.

The task is entered into cell A10, and cell D10 is the active cell.

12 In cell D10, type 8, and press Tab three times.

Cell G10 is the active cell.

13 In cell G10, type 5.5, and press Enter.

Cell A11 is the active cell.

14 Scroll to the right until you can see cell Q10.

The total hours worked is calculated (13.5), and it appears in cell Q10.

15 On the File menu, click Save As.

The Save As dialog box appears.

TIP

In the Save As dialog box, notice that the File Name box displays the current name of the file but assigns the extension .xls to the file. When you change a template and then save it, Excel saves it as a workbook to prevent you from overwriting the template.

16 Click the Save In down arrow, navigate to the Lesson09 folder in the Excel Expert Practice folder, type January 31 Hours in the File Name box, and click Save.

The workbook is saved with the name you specified.

◆ Close the workbook. If you are continuing to other lessons, leave Excel open. If you are not continuing to other lessons, save and close all open workbooks. Click the Close button in the top right corner of the Excel window.

QUICK REFERENCE ▼

Create a template from an existing workbook

1 On the Standard toolbar, click the New button to open a new, blank workbook.

2 Format the worksheet's cells for the text and numeric content you anticipate entering in worksheets based on this template. Add formulas or graphics or make any other changes that are needed.

3 On the File menu, click Save As.

4 Click the Save As Type down arrow, and click Template.

5 Type a name for the new template in the File Name box.

6 Click the Save button.

Key Points

✔ *Templates serve as the framework for workbooks that you use over and over again. They are useful for standardizing the appearance and functionality of workbooks.*

✔ *Excel's built-in templates and the customized templates that you save are stored in different locations. You don't need to know in which folder they're stored. You can access the templates that come with Excel from the Spreadsheet Solutions tab of the Templates dialog box. You can access customized templates or templates that you create from the General tab of the Templates dialog box.*

✔ *You can customize a standard template so that it suits your needs. Simply open the template; make your changes; and in the Save As dialog box, choose Template from the Save As Type list box.*

✔ *Creating a template for a type of worksheet you use frequently increases your efficiency and productivity.*

✔ *You can create a template from an existing workbook. Simply delete the data that will not be standard in the workbook, and then save the workbook as a template.*

Quick Quiz

True/False

T   F   1. You can customize a standard template that is provided with Excel.

T   F   2. You cannot modify the formulas that are in a standard template.

T   F   3. A placeholder in a template is typically where you enter data that's unique to the workbook that's based on the template.

T   F   4. All templates must be saved to the Templates folder.

T   F   5. In a time card template, all data that's unique to the user, such as name and hours worked, should *not* be entered as standard information in the template.

T   F   6. Once you save a template, you cannot change its file name.

Multiple Choice

1. What is the extension on a template file name?
   a. tem
   b. temp
   c. xls
   d. xlt

2. Which of the following would *not* be a standard item in a template?
   a. individual user's name
   b. logo
   c. column labels
   d. formulas

3. Which tab in the Templates dialog box displays icons for customized templates?
   a. General
   b. Spreadsheet Solutions
   c. Preview
   d. Custom

4. Which of the following would you set to control the range in a template that a user can print?
   a. placeholder
   b. print area
   c. ScreenTip
   d. sheet structure

Short Answer

1. What are the basic steps for creating a template from an existing workbook?

2. What are the procedures for inserting a logo in a template?

3. If you save and protect a template after you've customized it, how do you make additional customization changes later?

4. After you customize and save a ready-made template or create a template from an existing workbook, how do you open the template the next time you need it?

5. How would you set a print area for a template?

On Your Own

Exercise 1

Open the Expense Statement template that comes with Excel. Customize it so that your name and Social Security number (SSN) appear at the top of the template. For the department, enter Housekeeping; the employee number is **1365**; the position is Asst. Housekeeper; and the manager is Lisa Jacobson. At the bottom of the Expense Statement template, delete the *Insert Fine Print Here* text. Save and lock the template, naming the template My Expense Statement. Close the template.

◆ **Open Purchase Order 185 from the Excel Expert Practice/Lesson09 folder.**

Exercise 2

Delete the entries for the current purchase order (but not the title, labels, or address). Make cell C12 the active cell, and save the workbook as a template using the name Purchase Order Template.xlt. Close and reopen the template.

◆ **Close the template.**

Exercise 3

Open the Loan Amortization template from the Spreadsheet Solutions templates available with Excel. Use this worksheet to determine what your monthly payment would be for a house loan of $200,000. Assume the loan is a 30-year loan at 6 percent interest. Payments are made monthly and begin the first of next month. How many actual payments would you make if you paid an extra $500 each month? Save your workbook as My House Loan.

IMPORTANT

In the One Step Further section below, you must have Internet access in order to complete Exercise 1.

One Step Further

Exercise 1

Click the Templates On Office Online link in the Templates section of the New Workbook task pane. Scroll in the Web page that appears, and select Personal Finance from the Finance and Accounting category. Choose the Personal Budget template, and click Download Now. Fill in the fields of the worksheet, and compare your income to your expenses. Save the workbook as **My Budget**.

Exercise 2

Open the Personal Budget template that you downloaded in Exercise 1. Change the formatting and any other template information you desire. Set a print area for the worksheet. Save and close the template.

Using Macros

After completing this lesson, you will be able to:

✔ *Plan and record a macro.*
✔ *Assign a macro to a toolbar button.*
✔ *Run a macro.*
✔ *Edit a macro using the Visual Basic Editor.*

KEY TERMS

- global macro
- local macro
- macro
- record
- Visual Basic for Applications (VBA)
- Visual Basic Editor

A **macro** is a set of instructions that can be carried out using a single command. A macro is valuable when you perform the same set of steps repeatedly, either in the same workbook or in different workbooks. When you create a macro, you **record** a set of actions that you perform on a workbook or worksheet. After you've created the macro, you can run it anytime you need to perform these same steps again. Instead of *you* performing the steps, however, the macro performs them for you—much faster than you could perform the steps on your own. Macros automate such repetitious tasks as entering headings, formatting data, setting up a page layout, and printing a document. They also simplify the complex calculations that are often performed in a workbook.

There are two types of macros: local and global. A **local macro** is created and stored in a specific workbook and can be used only in that workbook. A **global macro** is stored in the Personal Macro Workbook and can be used with any workbook file.

When you create a macro, follow these general steps:

- Plan what you want the macro to do.
- Decide whether you need a local macro or a global macro.
- Name the macro.
- Record the macro.
- Run the macro to test it.

After you've tested the macro, you can edit it if you discover problems or decide to change the macro slightly.

IMPORTANT

Before you can use the practice files in this lesson, you must install them from the book's companion CD to their default location. For additional information on how to find and open files used in this book, see the "Using the CD-ROM" section at the beginning of this book.

Planning and Recording a Macro

Creating and Modifying Macros

THE BOTTOM LINE

Macros carry out individual commands, keystrokes, and selections in sequence, saving you the time of manually performing the same task. That's why you must carefully plan the exact actions you want the macro to execute.

Planning is the most important step in creating a macro, especially when the macro is complex. If you don't plan ahead, you might find yourself rerecording the macro several times because you missed a step or because steps are not in the correct order.

Planning begins by determining what you want the macro to do. For example, at Adventure Works, the accountant creates a budget for each department and stores each budget in a separate worksheet. At the start of a new year, she must copy each departmental budget into a new worksheet, change the year labels, copy the ending totals from the previous year, paste them into the previous year column in the new worksheet, and clear the remaining values in the worksheet.

With nearly ten departments at the resort, this is a time-consuming process—one that the accountant dreads performing at the start of a new year. She wants to simplify this yearly task by creating a macro that will automate the process for each departmental budget. She uses the Salaries and General Administration (SG&A) budget as the basis for creating the macro, which she will store in the Personal Macro Workbook. This budget worksheet is shown in the following illustration.

FIGURE 10-1

Budget worksheet

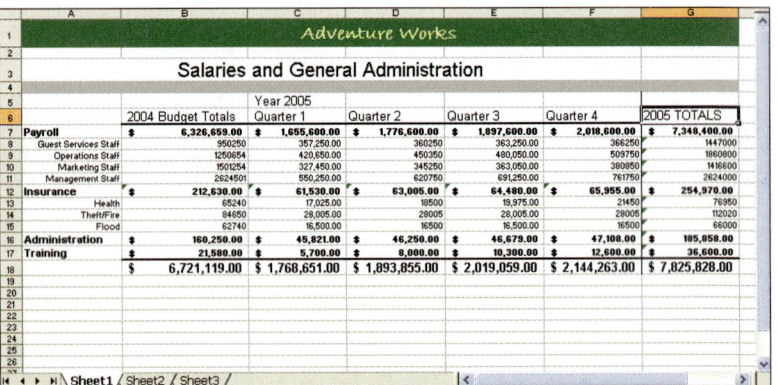

The accountant begins by opening and reviewing the SG&A workbook, looking for cells and ranges that need to be changed or cleared in preparation for the new year. She then jots down the following macro steps:

1. Select the entire worksheet.
2. Copy the worksheet.
3. Insert a new worksheet.
4. Paste the copied worksheet to the new worksheet.
5. Replace all occurrences of the year 2004 with the year 2005.
6. Replace all occurrences of the year 2005 with the year 2006.
7. Copy the range G7:G18 (yearly totals).
8. Paste the values into the range B7:B18. (The current values become the starting values for the new year.)
9. Delete the values in the range C7:G18.

After you write down the steps you want your macro to perform, you should perform a dry run—that is, you should perform the steps without actually recording the macro. By doing so, you can see if your steps achieve the desired result. It's not unusual to discover that some steps are out of order or don't do what you want. For example, the accountant performed a dry run of the macro steps for the SG&A budget and discovered an error. Steps 5 and 6 were out of order. When she replaced all occurrences of *2004* with *2005* and then replaced all occurrences of *2005* with *2006*, all of the year labels in the worksheet became *2006*—not what she wanted. She reversed the order of steps 5 and 6, performed another dry run, and achieved the desired result—creating a departmental budget template for the new year. She was then ready to record the macro.

◆ **To complete the procedures in this lesson, you must use the files SG&A Budget and Figures in the Lesson10 folder in the Excel Expert Practice folder located on your hard disk.**

◆ **Open SG&A Budget from the Excel Expert Practice/Lesson10 folder.**

Record a macro

In this exercise, you record a macro that creates a budget template for the next year.

1 **On the Tools menu, point to Macro, and click Record New Macro.**

The Record Macro dialog box appears.

FIGURE 10-2

Record Macro dialog box

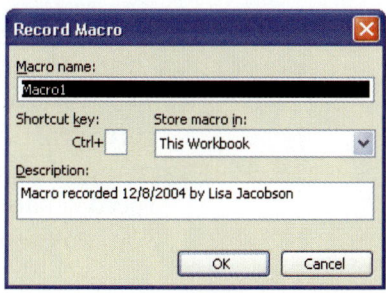

2 In the Macro Name box, type **NewBudget**.

IMPORTANT

A macro name cannot contain any spaces.

3 Click the Store Macro In down arrow, and click Personal Macro Workbook, if necessary.

The macro will be available to other worksheets and workbooks that you create or open on your computer.

4 Click OK.

The Macro toolbar appears, and the message *Recording* appears on the status bar at the bottom left corner of your worksheet.

FIGURE 10-3

Macro toolbar

TIP

The Macro toolbar contains two buttons: Record and Relative Reference. Once you start recording a macro, the Record button changes to the Stop Recording button. When you click the Stop Recording button, macro recording ends. The Relative Reference button is useful when you create a formula for a cell or range of cells in the workbook in which you are recording the macro, but in which you want the formula to calculate a different range of cells when you run the macro.

5 Click the Select All button in the top left corner of the worksheet (between the column A and row 1 selectors).

6 On the Edit menu, click Copy.

The contents of the worksheet are copied to the Windows Clipboard.

7 On the Insert menu, click Worksheet.

A worksheet is inserted in the workbook, and cell A1 in the new worksheet is selected.

TROUBLESHOOTING

Take your time as you record macro steps to make sure you record correctly. The speed at which you record a macro has no relationship to the speed at which the macro runs. The macro will run at the full speed capability of your computer's processor, regardless of how long you took to record the macro.

8 **On the Edit menu, click Paste.**

The contents of the SG&A Budget worksheet are pasted to the new worksheet.

9 **On the Edit menu, click Replace.**

The Find And Replace dialog box appears.

FIGURE 10-4

Find And Replace dialog box

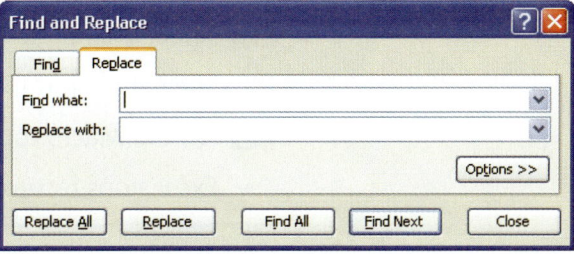

10 **Type 2005 in the Find What box, press Tab, type 2006 in the Replace With box, and click Replace All.**

Excel finds all occurrences of *2005* and replaces them with *2006*. A message box appears indicating that two occurrences were found and replaced.

11 **Click OK to close the message box.**

12 **Click in the Find What text box, type 2004, press Tab, type 2005 in the Replace With text box, and click Replace All.**

Excel finds all occurrences of *2004* and replaces them with *2005*. A message box appears indicating that only one occurrence was found and replaced.

13 **Click OK to close the message box, and then click Close to close the Find And Replace dialog box.**

14 **Select the range G7:G18, and on the Edit menu, click Copy.**

15 **Select the range B7:B18, and on the Edit menu, click Paste Special.**

The Paste Special dialog box appears.

FIGURE 10-5

Paste Special dialog box

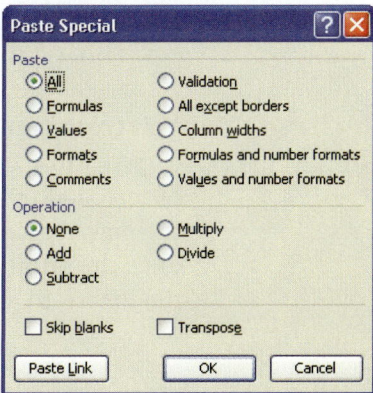

16 **In the Paste section of the Paste Special dialog box, click the Values option, and click OK.**

The values from G7:G18 are pasted to B7:B18.

17 **Select the range C7:G18, and press Delete.**

The values and formulas are removed from the selected range.

18 **On the Macro toolbar, click the Stop Recording button.**

Excel stops recording the macro.

◆ **Save the workbook, and leave it open for the next exercise.**

QUICK REFERENCE ▼

Record a macro

1 On the Tools menu, point to Macro, and click Record New Macro.

2 In the Macro Name box, type a name for the macro.

3 Assign a keyboard shortcut to the macro if desired.

4 Type a description of the macro if desired, and click OK.

5 Perform the operations that you want to include in the macro.

6 Click the Stop Recording button on the Macro toolbar.

Assigning a Macro to a Toolbar Button

THE BOTTOM LINE

When a macro is assigned to a toolbar button, it can easily be applied with the click of the mouse. This is ideal for users who might not be familiar with Excel menu commands.

You create a macro to save time and reduce the steps you must complete to perform a task. After you've created a macro, you can run it from the Macro dialog box—the same dialog box that you used to name and start the macro recording in the previous exercise. However, you also can reduce the number of steps required to execute the macro itself by assigning the macro to a toolbar button.

Assign a macro to a toolbar button

In this exercise, you create a toolbar button for the NewBudget macro, name the button, change the button image, and assign the NewBudget macro to the toolbar button.

1 **Click cell G18, and on the Tools menu, click Customize.**

The Customize dialog box opens.

2 **Click the Commands tab, if necessary.**

FIGURE 10-6

Customize dialog box

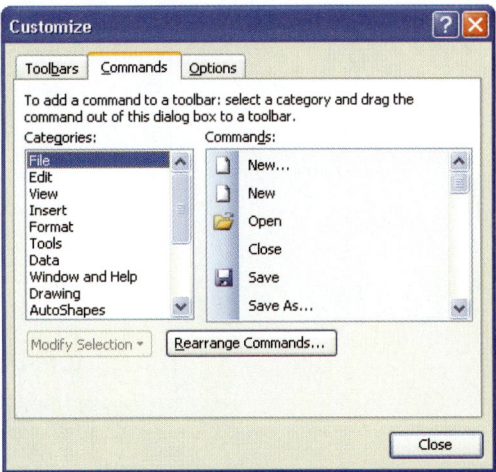

3 **On the Categories list, scroll down, and click Macros.**

> **TIP**
>
> The Commands list contains two entries: Custom Menu Item and Custom Button. Use Custom Menu Item to add a macro to a menu; use Custom Button to add a macro to a toolbar.

4 **From the Commands list, drag Custom Button to the Standard toolbar, and position the button to the right of the Sort Descending button.**

A black I-beam appears at the location where the button will be inserted on the toolbar.

FIGURE 10-7

Dragging a macro button to the toolbar

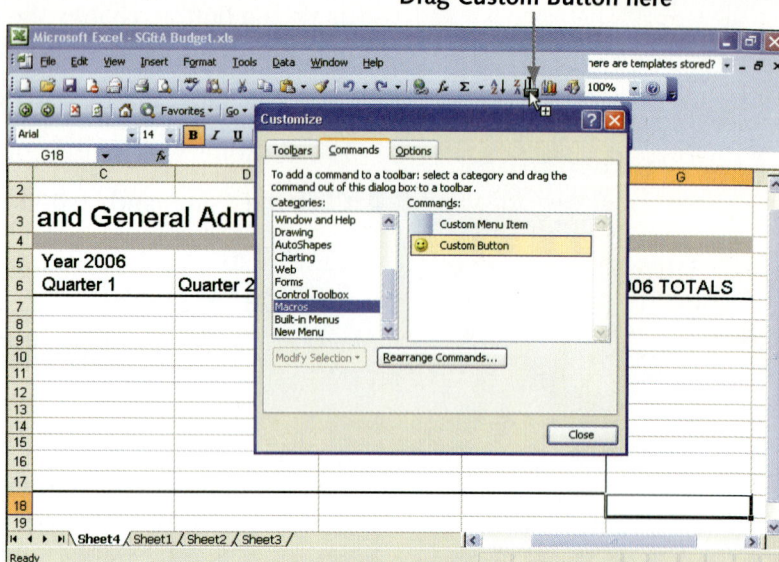

Drag Custom Button here

5 Release the mouse button if you haven't already done so.

The Custom Button appears on the Standard toolbar.

TIP

You also can use this menu to change the button image.

6 On the Standard toolbar, right-click the Custom Button.

Excel displays a shortcut menu that you can use to name, edit, and assign a task to the button.

FIGURE 10-8

Naming a toolbar button

7 **Select the text in the Name box, and type New Budget.**

The button is named. When the Excel window is active, the ScreenTip *New Budget* appears when you position the mouse pointer on the button.

8 **Point to Change Button Image.**

A menu of available button images appears.

FIGURE 10-9

Button images

Video Recorder →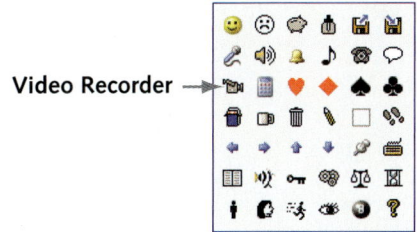

9 **In the menu of buttons, click the video recorder (first item in the third row).**

The button image changes from the happy face to the video recorder, and the menu no longer appears.

10 **On the Standard toolbar, right-click the video recorder button.**

The shortcut menu reappears.

TROUBLESHOOTING

The NewBudget macro begins with the expression PERSONAL.XLS! to indicate that the macro is stored in the Personal Macro workbook. If you had stored the macro in the current workbook, you would not see this expression as part of the macro name.

11 **At the bottom of the menu, click Assign Macro.**

The Assign Macro dialog box appears.

FIGURE 10-10

Assign Macro dialog box

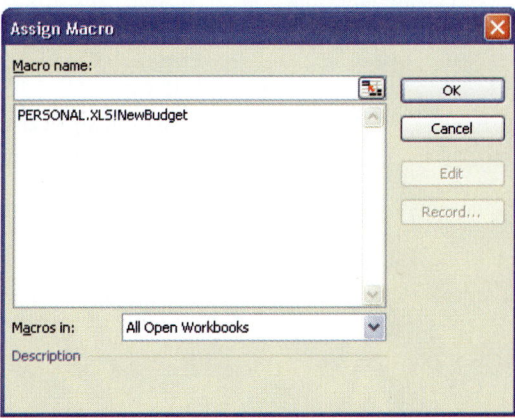

12 **Click PERSONAL.XLS!NewBudget, and click OK.**

The NewBudget macro is assigned to the toolbar button. When you click the toolbar button, the macro runs.

13 **In the Customize dialog box, click Close.**

The Customize dialog box closes, and you can now click the button to run the macro.

◆ **Save the workbook, and leave it open for the next exercise.**

QUICK REFERENCE ▼

Add a button to a toolbar, and assign a macro to it

1 On the Tools menu, click Customize.

2 Click the Commands tab, if necessary.

3 On the Categories list, click Macros.

4 From the Commands list, drag the Custom Button to the desired location on the toolbar.

5 On the toolbar, right-click the new button.

6 Click Assign Macro on the shortcut menu.

7 In the Assign Macro dialog box, click the name of the macro that you want to assign to the toolbar button, and click OK.

Using Macros

Introducing Macros

THE BOTTOM LINE

Once you've created a macro, you can apply it using a number of simple methods. You also can modify a macro using the Visual Basic Editor, which saves you the time of rerecording it.

Once you've created a macro, you can apply, or run, it using one of four methods:

- On the Tools menu, point to Macro, and click Macros. In the Macro dialog box, select the macro you want to apply, and click the Run button.
- If you assigned the macro to a toolbar button, click the toolbar button.
- If you assigned the macro to a keyboard shortcut, press the assigned shortcut key.
- If you assigned the macro to a menu item, open the menu, and click the command.

If you run a macro and discover that the macro doesn't do exactly what you want, you can rerecord it. However, if a macro contains several steps, this process can be time-consuming and prone to errors.

When you create a macro, Excel converts your commands, keystrokes, and selections into instructions in a programming language called Microsoft **Visual Basic for Applications (VBA).** All Microsoft Office applications use VBA as the macro language. If you need to make modifications to a macro, you can use the **Visual Basic Editor,** which is a window that displays the VBA code for the macro.

For example, you might need to edit a macro so that a range of cells specified is larger or smaller to accommodate a different workbook in which the macro will be run. Instead of rerecording the whole macro, you simply open the Visual Basic Editor and change the ranges that are specified.

Consider another example: For the current year, the accountant at Adventure Works can use the NewBudget macro to create templates for each departmental budget worksheet. However, for the next year, she'll need to make some minor changes to the macro. Instead of replacing *2005* with *2006* and *2004* with *2005*, she will want to replace *2006* with *2007* and *2005* with *2006*. These changes are easy to make in the Visual Basic Editor.

To start the Visual Basic Editor, point to Macro on the Tools menu, and click Macros. In the Macro dialog box, click the name of the macro that you want to change, and then click the Edit button. When you display a macro in the Visual Basic Editor, you'll see several programming language commands that may be unfamiliar to you. You don't need to know Visual Basic in order to edit a macro. If you know the steps that you used to record a macro, you can use the Visual Basic Editor to identify clues that will help you understand which commands perform which steps in the macro. You can then modify a Visual Basic program command by changing one word or a few words within the command.

For example, suppose you see this command in the Visual Basic Editor:

```
Selection.Replace What:="2005", Replacement:="2006",
LookAt:=xlPart, SearchOrder:=xlByColumns, MatchCase:=True
```

You don't need to understand this VBA command in order to change the way the replacement is made. Simply change *2005* to *2006* and *2006* to *2007*.

Run and edit a macro

In this exercise, you run the NewBudget macro using the toolbar button you created, and you edit the macro to change the years to accommodate a new budget year.

1 **Click the Sheet1 tab, and click any cell in the worksheet.**

The selection highlighting is removed from the worksheet.

2 **On the Standard toolbar, position the pointer on the New Budget macro button, but don't click the button yet.**

The ScreenTip *New Budget* appears.

3 **Click the New Budget macro button.**

The macro runs. The result is a new worksheet that contains a departmental budget for the new year.

4 **Click any cell in the worksheet.**

FIGURE 10-11

Running the macro

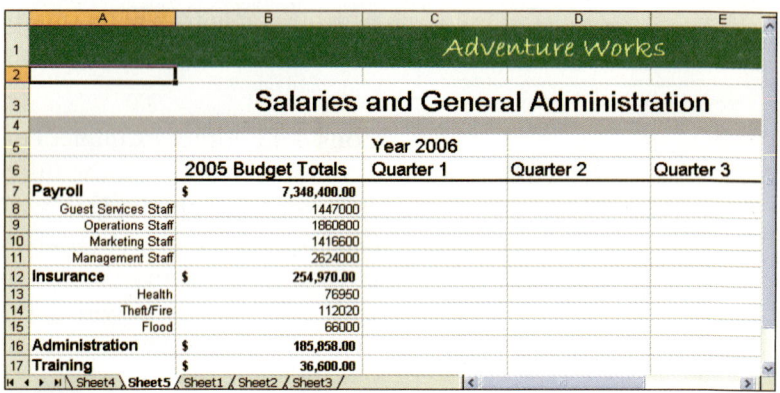

5 **On the Window menu, click Unhide.**

The Unhide dialog box appears. You must unhide the Personal Macro Workbook before you can edit any macros stored within it.

FIGURE 10-12

Unhide dialog box

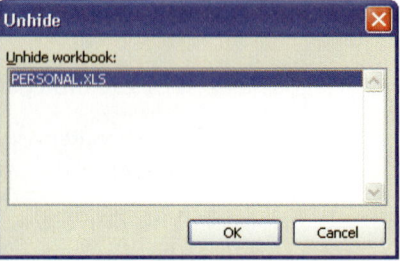

TIP

Depending on your settings, your dialog box may display the file extension.

6 Click PERSONAL if it isn't already selected, and click OK.

The Personal Macro Workbook is unhidden and can now be edited.

7 On the Tools menu, point to Macro, and click Macros to display the Macro dialog box.

8 If necessary, click NewBudget, and click Edit.

The macro code appears in the right pane of the Visual Basic Editor.

FIGURE 10-13

Visual Basic Editor window

Click the Close buttons on these three panes   Code window

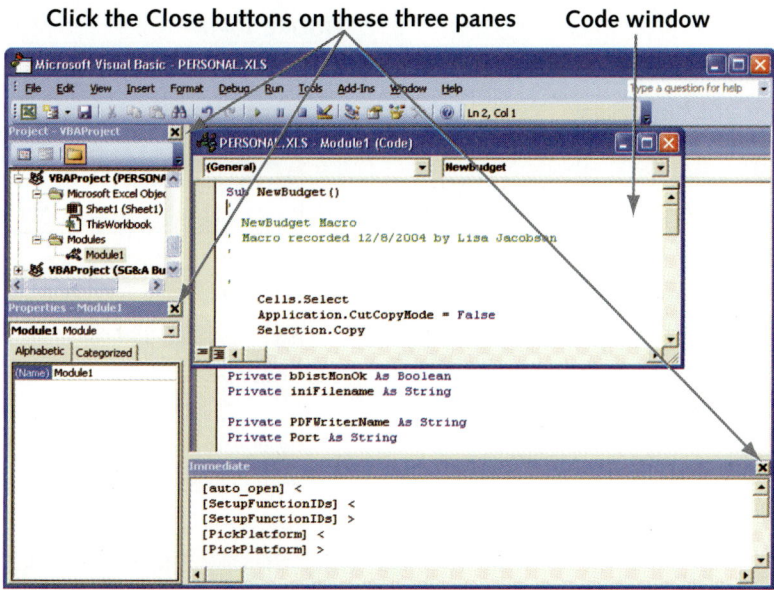

9 If necessary, click the Close buttons for the Project and Properties panes on the left side of the window and the Immediate pane below the Code pane.

The panes close, and you can see more of the Visual Basic code in the window.

10 Enlarge the Code window by dragging the sizing handle in the lower right corner; then locate the following lines of code:

Selection.Replace What:="2005", Replacement:="2006",
LookAt:=xlPart, _SearchOrder:=xlByRows, MatchCase:=False

11 Double-click 2005, and type 2006; then double-click 2006 (the one following Replacement=), and type 2007.

The selected years, *2005* and *2006*, are replaced with *2006* and *2007*.

12 Two lines down, replace 2004 with 2005, and replace 2005 (the one following Replacement=) with 2006.

All of the year replacements have now been made.

 13 On the Visual Basic Editor Standard toolbar, click the Save button.

Your changes are saved in the Personal.xls workbook.

14 On the File menu, click Close And Return To Microsoft Excel.

The Visual Basic Editor closes.

 15 If necessary, display the SG&A Budget workbook, and on the Standard toolbar, click the New Budget macro button.

The macro runs and creates a new worksheet with the year labels for the next year. Because no values existed in column G of the worksheet that was active when you ran the macro, no values are pasted into column B.

FIGURE 10-14

Running the edited macro

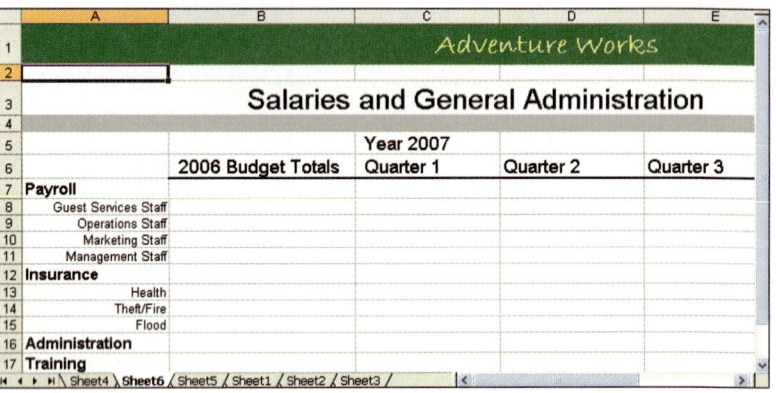

TIP

To delete a macro, on the Tools menu, point to Macro, and click Macros. Click the macro name, and click the Delete button.

◆ **If you are continuing to other lessons:**

1. **On the Tools menu, click Customize to display the Customize dialog box.**

2. **On the Standard toolbar, drag the New Budget macro button to the worksheet, and release the mouse button to remove the button from the toolbar.**

3. **Close the Customize dialog box.**

4. **On the Tools menu, point to Macro, and click Macros.**

5. **If necessary, click the PERSONAL.XLS!NewBudget macro, and click Delete.**

6. **Click Yes to confirm the deletion.**

7. **Close all open workbooks without saving changes.**

◆ **If you are not continuing to other lessons:**

1. On the Tools menu, click Customize to display the Customize dialog box.

2. On the Standard toolbar, drag the New Budget macro button to the worksheet, and release the mouse button to remove the button from the toolbar.

3. Close the Customize dialog box.

4. On the Tools menu, point to Macro, and click Macros.

5. If necessary, click the PERSONAL.XLS!NewBudget macro, and click Delete.

6. Click Yes to confirm the deletion.

7. Close all open workbooks without saving changes.

8. Click the Close button in the top right corner of the Excel window.

QUICK REFERENCE ▼

Run a macro using the Macro command

1 On the Tools menu, point to Macro, and click Macros.

2 Select or type the macro name in the Macro Name box.

3 Click the Run button.

Delete a macro

1 On the Tools menu, point to Macro, and click Macros.

2 Select or type the macro name in the Macro Name box.

3 Click the Delete button.

Unhide the Personal Macro Workbook

1 On the Windows menu, click Unhide.

2 Click PERSONAL.XLS, and click OK.

Edit a macro using the Visual Basic Editor

1 On the Tools menu, point to Macro, and click Macros.

2 Click the name of the macro, and click Edit.

3 Make any desired changes to the Visual Basic code.

4 On the Standard toolbar, click the Save button.

5 On the File menu, click Close And Return To Microsoft Excel.

QUICK CHECK

Q. How do you run a macro if you choose *not* to assign the macro to a toolbar button, a menu item, or a keyboard shortcut?

A: You run the macro by opening the Tools menu, pointing to Macro, and clicking Macros. In the Macro dialog box, you select the macro and click Run.

Key Points

✔ *Macros carry out individual commands, keystrokes, and selections in sequence, saving you the time of manually performing the same task.*

✔ *Planning is an important step in creating a macro. If you don't carefully plan the macro, you might find yourself rerecording it several times because you missed a step or because steps are not in the correct order.*

✔ *When a macro is assigned to a toolbar button, the macro can easily be applied with the click of the mouse. This is ideal for users who might not be familiar with Excel menu commands.*

✔ *You can run a macro from the Macro dialog box. You also can assign the macro to a toolbar button, to a menu item, or to a keyboard shortcut, which allows you to run it by clicking the button, selecting the menu command, or pressing the keyboard shortcut.*

✔ *You can make modifications to a macro in the Visual Basic Editor, which is a window that displays the VBA code for the macro.*

Quick Quiz

True/False

T F 1. A local macro can be used only in the workbook in which it is created.

T F 2. A global macro can be used in any workbook file.

T F 3. A macro name cannot contain any spaces.

T F 4. You can record menu commands, but not keystrokes, in a macro.

T F 5. A toolbar button must have the exact same name as the macro assigned to it.

T F 6. The easiest way to make minor changes to a macro is to rerecord it.

T F 7. You can assign a keyboard shortcut to a macro, which allows you to run the macro by pressing the keystroke combination.

Multiple Choice

1. Which type of macro is stored in the Personal Macro Workbook?
   a. local
   b. global
   c. personal
   d. editor

2. Which of the following is an acceptable macro name?
   a. MyMacro
   b. My Macro
   c. my macro
   d. All of the above

3. Which programming language is used for macros?
   a. Visual Basic Editor
   b. Visual Basic for Applications
   c. Microsoft Word
   d. Personal Macro Application

Short Answer

1. What step must you perform before you can edit a macro stored in the Personal Macro Workbook?

2. If you want to use a macro in more than one workbook, in what file should you save it?

3. If you record a macro using the same name as an existing macro, what happens?

4. How do you add a button to a toolbar and then assign a macro to the button?

5. In what program do you edit a macro?

6. What is the programming language in which macros are created?

> **IMPORTANT**
>
> In the following exercises, you must first complete On Your Own Exercise 1 in order to complete the remaining exercises.

On Your Own

◆ **Open Figures from the Excel Expert Practice/Lesson10 folder.**

Exercise 1

Create a macro named **TotalSum** that sums all of the figures in cells C5:C9 and places the result in cell D11 (and not in any other cell). Store the macro in the current workbook. Assign a keyboard shortcut of Ctrl+T to the macro.

Exercise 2

Add a button for the TotalSum macro (created in Exercise 1) to the Standard toolbar. Edit the macro so that the total appears in cell C12.

Exercise 3

Add a menu item for the TotalSum macro (created in Exercise 1) to the Tools menu.

One Step Further

Exercise 1

In the Figures workbook, open the Macro dialog box, and select the TotalSum macro. Click the Step Into button, and observe what happens. Step through the entire macro; then close the Visual Basic Editor.

Exercise 2

Delete the macro you created in On Your Own Exercise 1. Remove the macro button from the Standard toolbar, and remove the macro item from the Tools menu.

◆ **Close Figures without saving changes.**

Customizing the Excel Environment

After completing this lesson, you will be able to:

✔ *Move toolbars and toolbar buttons.*
✔ *Modify button images.*
✔ *Create a custom toolbar.*
✔ *Test a custom toolbar.*
✔ *Save custom views of a workbook.*
✔ *Modify the working folder.*
✔ *Customize Excel to help you work more efficiently.*

KEY TERMS

- docked toolbar
- floating toolbar
- move handle
- working folder

Excel is designed so that you can customize your environment to suit your specific needs. It's not essential that you do so; many people prefer the default settings. However, if you don't like some of the default settings, you can change them so that the Excel environment is set up to best suit your working style.

For example, you might find that you like to have the buttons you use most often located on different toolbars or in different locations on a toolbar. When you start Excel, you might want a particular file to open at the same time, or when you open a file, you might want a worksheet to be displayed in a particular way. You also might want to save most of your Excel files in a folder other than the default folder, My Documents. All of these customization options are easy to set in Excel.

In this lesson, you'll learn how to customize the Excel environment, including moving and modifying the Formatting and Standard toolbars and changing several default options.

IMPORTANT

Before you can use the practice files in this lesson, you must install them from the book's companion CD to their default location. For additional information on how to find and open files used in this book, see the "Using the CD-ROM" section at the beginning of this book.

Moving Toolbars and Toolbar Buttons

THE BOTTOM LINE

You can easily modify the setup of toolbars and toolbar buttons in the Excel window to optimize their functionality and the way in which you interact with them.

There are hundreds of commands in Excel, but only some of them appear as buttons on toolbars. You can modify the toolbars to include different buttons and to remove buttons that you seldom use. In addition, you can change the way toolbars and menus are displayed.

Some toolbars appear when you perform tasks that relate to them. For example, the Chart toolbar displays when you create or select a chart. When you want to display a toolbar, you can point to Toolbars on the View menu and click the name of the toolbar you want to display.

Toolbars can be either floating or docked. A **floating toolbar** appears within the Excel window. You can drag the title bar of a floating toolbar to move it to a different location or to dock it. A **docked toolbar** is anchored to a side of the Excel window. By default, the Standard and Formatting toolbars are docked, and most other toolbars float. You can move or resize a docked toolbar within its row, and you can drag it into the Excel window when you want to use it as a floating toolbar.

To facilitate the exercises in this course, your instructor has adjusted your Standard and Formatting toolbars so that each toolbar appears docked on a separate row near the top of the Excel window. If you install and start Excel at your home or office, however, these toolbars will appear on the same row below the menu bar, as shown in Figure 11-1.

FIGURE 11-1

Default setup of toolbars

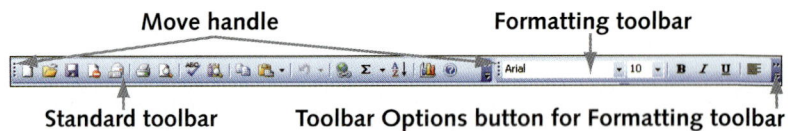

If you want the Standard and Formatting toolbars to appear on two rows, you can change the setting for these toolbars in the Customize dialog box. You also can drag the **move handle,** the vertical dotted bar that appears at the left edge of a toolbar when it is docked, to reposition either of the toolbars.

The screen width of most monitors doesn't allow for all of a toolbar's buttons to appear at one time. With the toolbars sharing a row, you must click the Toolbar Options button to see the rest of the buttons on each toolbar. The additional buttons appear on a menu, such as the one shown in Figure 11-2 for the buttons on the Formatting toolbar.

FIGURE 11-2

Additional buttons

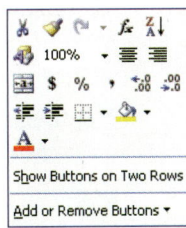

The menu commands and toolbar buttons you use are monitored by Excel, and the ones you use most often are displayed automatically. If you want to see all of the commands on a menu whenever you open it, you can turn off the personalized menus feature. On the Tools menu, click Customize. On the Options tab of the Customize dialog box, click the Always Show Full Menus option.

As you've observed in previous lessons, only a few of Excel's toolbars appear by default. To see the list of additional toolbars that are available, on the View menu, point to Toolbars. On the list, a check mark appears next to toolbars that are displayed. You can click a toolbar name to display or hide that toolbar.

You can add toolbar buttons, and you can remove others that you don't often use. If you remove a toolbar button and later decide you want to use it, you can easily add it back to the toolbar.

> **TIP**
>
> To reset a toolbar to its original state, on the Tools menu, click Customize. On the Toolbars tab of the Customize dialog box, click the name of the toolbar you want to reset. Click Reset, and then click Close.

◆ **To complete the procedures in this lesson, you must use the files SG&A Budget, Quarterly Quota, AW Personnel, and AW Marketing in the Lesson11 folder in the Excel Expert Practice folder located on your hard disk.**

◆ **Start Excel.**

Customize toolbars

In this exercise, you turn on the setting that displays the Standard and Formatting toolbars on one row, you move and float the Formatting toolbar, and you display the Drawing toolbar. You also add a button to the Standard toolbar, move that button to a different location, and delete it.

1 A new blank workbook should be open. Close the task pane, if necessary.

2 On the Tools menu, click Customize, and then click the Options tab, if necessary.

TROUBLESHOOTING

If no workbooks are open, the Standard and Formatting toolbars appear grayed out, and you are not able to reposition them.

3 Deselect the Show Standard And Formatting Toolbars On Two Rows check box, if necessary.

4 Click Close.

The Standard and Formatting toolbars appear on one row in the Excel window.

5 Drag the move handle on the Formatting toolbar down so that the toolbar floats anywhere in the Excel window, as shown in Figure 11-3.

FIGURE 11-3

Floating the Formatting toolbar

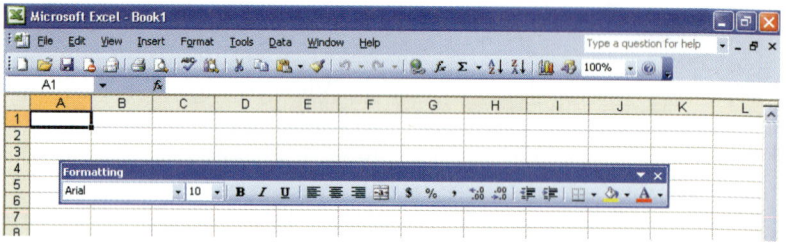

6 Drag the title bar of the Formatting toolbar up and to the left so that it's docked under the Standard toolbar, as shown in the following illustration.

FIGURE 11-4

Docking a toolbar

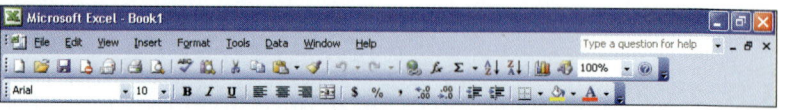

7 On the View menu, point to Toolbars, and click Drawing.

The Drawing toolbar appears and might be docked or floating, depending on where it was when the toolbar was opened and used previously on your computer.

TIP

To hide any floating toolbar, click the Close button at the right end of the toolbar's title bar. To hide a docked toolbar, on the View menu, point to Toolbars, and click the name of the toolbar that you want to hide.

8 At the right end of the Standard toolbar, click the Toolbar Options button, point to Add Or Remove Buttons, and point to Standard.

A menu of available Standard toolbar buttons appears.

FIGURE 11-5

Toolbar Options menu

Click to bring more buttons into view

For information on changing the name of a button, assigning a macro to a button, or changing the image for a button, see the "Assigning a Macro to a Toolbar Button" section in Lesson 10, "Using Macros."

9 On the menu of toolbar buttons, click PivotTable And PivotChart Report. You may need to point to the arrow at the bottom of the menu to bring this button option into view.

The PivotTable And PivotChart Report button appears at the end of the Standard toolbar.

10 Click anywhere outside the menu of toolbar buttons.

The menu closes.

11 Hold down the Alt key, and drag the PivotTable And PivotChart Report button to the left. When a black I-beam appears to the right of the Sort Descending button, release the mouse button.

The button is moved to the specified location on the Standard toolbar.

FIGURE 11-6

Moving a button

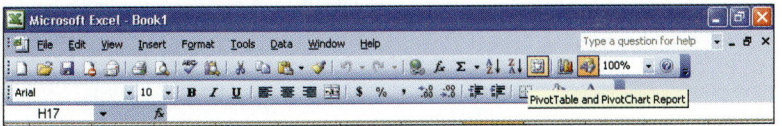

12 On the Standard toolbar, click the Toolbar Options button, point to Add Or Remove Buttons, and point to Standard.

The menu of available Standard toolbar buttons appears.

13 On the menu of toolbar buttons, click PivotTable And PivotChart Report, and click anywhere outside the menu.

The menu closes, and the PivotTable And PivotChart Report button no longer appears on the Standard toolbar.

◆ Leave the blank workbook open for the next exercise.

QUICK REFERENCE ▼

Display the Standard and Formatting toolbars on separate rows

1 On the Tools menu, click Customize.

2 Click the Options tab.

3 Select the Show Standard And Formatting Toolbars On Two Rows check box.

4 Click OK.

Move a button to a different location on a toolbar

1 Display the toolbar from which you're moving the button and the toolbar to which you want to move the button.

2 Hold down the Alt key, and drag the button to its new location.

Add and remove a toolbar button

1 Display the toolbar that contains the button you want to add or remove.

2 Click the Toolbar Options button, point to Add Or Remove Buttons, point to Standard, and click the button to select it. If it is already selected, click the button to remove it.

TIP

You also can use the Customize dialog box to add buttons from other command categories. On the Tools menu, click Customize (or right-click any toolbar, and click Customize), and click the Commands tab. In the Categories list, click the desired category to display a list of buttons for that category on the right side of the dialog box. Drag the button that you want to add onto a toolbar at the desired location. You can delete any button later by displaying the Customize dialog box and then dragging the button from the toolbar into the Excel window.

Creating a Custom Toolbar

THE BOTTOM LINE

If your work in Excel requires the use of certain commands that are not typically available as buttons on Excel's toolbars, you can create your own toolbar with these buttons. A custom toolbar can streamline the way you execute certain actions and enhance productivity.

Adding and removing buttons on the Standard and Formatting toolbars is an effective way to customize the toolbars for the way you work. However, you might want more flexibility in deciding which buttons appear at any given time. For this reason, you can create your own toolbars, which you display or hide as needed. There are three basic reasons why you might want to create a toolbar:

- You are performing a related set of commands for a current project, but these commands aren't available on any of the available toolbars— only from the menus. For example, if you are tracking changes as you collaborate on a workbook with others, you must use the Tools menu to access commands related to that feature. No toolbar exists that contains these commands. However, you can create a toolbar that contains buttons for turning on change tracking, turning off change tracking, accepting a change, rejecting a change, and inserting a comment. (The Insert Comment button is available on the Reviewing toolbar, but none of the other tracking commands are.) When you're working in other workbooks, you can hide your custom toolbar. When you return to the shared workbook, you can display the custom toolbar again.

TIP

You can include the same commands or buttons on more than one toolbar. This option is especially handy when you want to include frequently used buttons on a short custom toolbar rather than trying to locate them on the longer Standard and Formatting toolbars.

- You use several commands on a regular basis, but these commands are scattered across several existing toolbars. To use the commands, you often display a toolbar, select the desired command, hide the toolbar, display a different toolbar, select the desired command, hide the toolbar, and so on. A better approach is to add these frequently used commands to one custom toolbar.
- You routinely perform tasks that have no corresponding button on any toolbar or can be accessed only from menus. For example, suppose you frequently select a print area prior to printing, you frequently want to paste only the formatting from one worksheet into a new worksheet, and you frequently experiment with colors on the Font Color palette to find the most desirable color for headings and labels. You can create a custom toolbar that allows you to perform each of those tasks with the click of a button. The Set Print Area command is available only from the File menu, but you can add a button that sets selected cells as the print area. To paste formatting, you must use the

Paste Special dialog box, but you also can add a button that performs this task automatically. No menu command lets you quickly cycle through different text colors, but Excel has a little-known Cycle Font Color button that you can use to quickly cycle through the 40 basic colors available on the Font Color palette.

Create a custom toolbar

In this exercise, you create a custom toolbar for the accountant at Adventure Works. You name the toolbar *My Formats*, and then you add the appropriate buttons to the custom toolbar.

1 **A blank workbook should be open. On the Tools menu, click Customize, and click the Toolbars tab, if necessary.**

The Toolbars tab is displayed in the Customize dialog box.

TIP

You do not need to display a workbook to create a custom toolbar, but the buttons on the toolbar aren't active unless a workbook is open.

FIGURE 11-7

Toolbars tab in the Customize dialog box

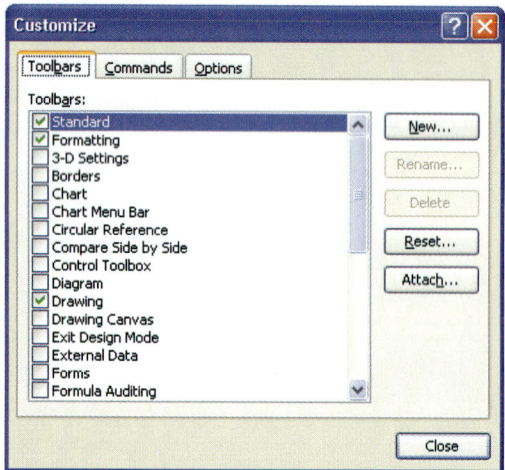

2 **Click the New button.**

Excel displays the New Toolbar dialog box, which you use to name your custom toolbar.

FIGURE 11-8

New Toolbar dialog box

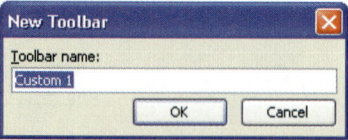

3 Type **My Formats**, and click OK.

Excel displays the My Formats toolbar as a floating toolbar. The toolbar appears as only a small gray rectangle because no buttons have yet been added to the toolbar.

FIGURE 11-9

My Formats toolbar

4 In the Customize dialog box, click the Commands tab.

A list of command categories appears on the left side of the dialog box.

FIGURE 11-10

Commands tab in the Customize dialog box

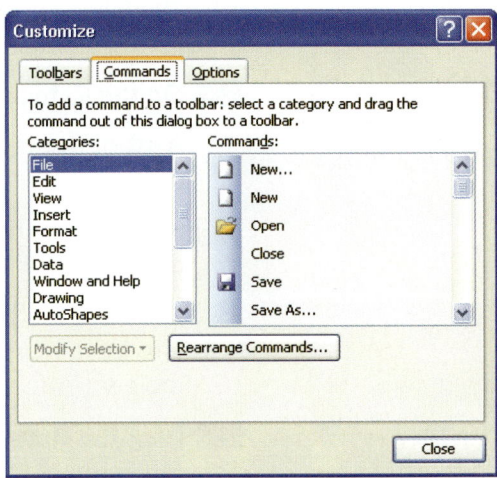

5 On the Categories list, click Format.

A list of formatting commands appears on the right side of the dialog box.

6 Scroll down the list of commands to the Cycle Font Color command, and then drag it from the Commands list onto the My Formats toolbar.

The Cycle Font Color command appears as a button on the My Formats toolbar.

FIGURE 11-11

Adding a command to the toolbar

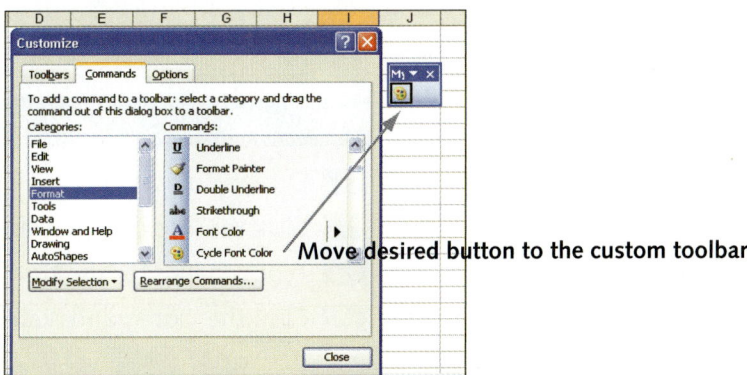

Move desired button to the custom toolbar

7 On the Categories list on the left side of the dialog box, click **File**.

A list of commands from the File menu appears on the right side of the dialog box.

8 Scroll down the list of commands to the Set Print Area command, and drag it from the Commands list onto the My Formats toolbar, to the right of the Cycle Font Color button.

The Set Print Area command appears as a button on the My Formats toolbar.

9 On the Categories list, click **Edit**.

A list of editing commands appears on the right side of the dialog box.

10 Scroll down the list of commands to the Paste Formatting command, and drag it from the Commands list onto the My Formats toolbar, to the right of the Set Print Area button.

The Paste Formatting command appears as a button on the My Formats toolbar.

11 On the Categories list, click **Format**.

A list of formatting commands appears on the right side of the dialog box.

12 Scroll down the list of commands to the Merge Cells command, and drag it from the Commands list onto the My Formats toolbar, to the right of the Paste Formatting button.

The Merge Cells command appears as a button on the My Formats toolbar.

13 Drag the Unmerge Cells command from the Commands list onto the My Formats toolbar, to the right of the Merge Cells button.

Your custom toolbar is now complete and should look like that shown in Figure 11-12.

FIGURE 11-12

Completed My Formats toolbar

14 Close the Customize dialog box.

QUICK REFERENCE ▼

Create a toolbar

1 On the Tools menu, click Customize.

2 Click the Toolbars tab, and click the New button.

3 Type a name for the new toolbar, and click OK.

4 Click the Commands tab.

5 Select the categories that contain the buttons and commands you want to add to your toolbar, and drag the buttons and commands from the Commands list to your toolbar.

Add a button or menu command to a toolbar

1 Display the toolbar to which you want to add the button or menu command.

2 On the Tools menu, click Customize.

3 Click the Commands tab.

4 Select a command category from the Categories list, and then find the desired button or command on the Commands list.

5 Drag the button or command from the Commands list to the toolbar.

6 Close the Customize dialog box.

Testing a Custom Toolbar

After you've created a custom toolbar, you should test each button to make sure it does what you expect it to. If a particular button doesn't do what you want, you can easily remove it from your custom toolbar. You also can experiment by adding buttons from other categories to see how they work. If you find that some of these buttons are useful but unrelated to the other tasks on your custom toolbar, you can remove them, create another custom toolbar, and add the buttons to the new toolbar.

Each custom toolbar can be displayed at any time by pointing to Toolbars on the View menu and then clicking the name of the toolbar. If you don't need a particular custom toolbar to perform your current tasks, click the Close button on the toolbar's title bar to hide it. You also can dock a custom toolbar to any side of the Excel window.

◆ Open SG&A Budget from the Excel Expert Practice/Lesson11 folder.

Test a custom toolbar

In this exercise, you test each button on your My Formats custom toolbar.

1 Click cell C5, and then select the contents of the Formula bar.

2 On the My Formats toolbar, click the Cycle Font Color button five times.

Excel displays the contents of cell C5 in a different color each time you click the button.

3 Select the range A6:B17.

4 On the My Formats toolbar, click the Set Print Area button.

The selected cells become the print range.

5 On the Standard toolbar, click the Print button.

The selected print range is printed.

QUICK CHECK

Q. If a custom toolbar is not displayed, how do you display it?

A: On the View menu, you point to Toolbars and then click the custom toolbar to display it.

◆ **Close the SG&A Budget workbook without saving changes. Open Quarterly Quota from the Excel Expert Practice/Lesson 11 folder.**

6 **Select the range C6:F12, and press Ctrl+C.**

The selected range is copied to the Windows Clipboard.

ANOTHER METHOD

- On the Edit menu, click Copy.
- Click the Copy button on the Standard toolbar.

7 **Click the Sheet2 tab, and click cell C4, if necessary.**

8 **On the My Formats toolbar, click the Paste Formatting button.**

The formatting from the copied cells is pasted to the range in Sheet2, but values are not pasted.

9 **Type 32500, and press Enter.**

The value is formatted in currency format with no decimal places—the same formatting that was defined for cells C6:F12 of Sheet1.

10 **Click cell B1, and on the My Formats toolbar, click the Unmerge Cells button.**

The cells for the worksheet heading are unmerged.

11 **On the My Formats toolbar, click the Merge Cells button.**

The cells for the worksheet heading are merged again into one cell.

◆ **Close the workbook without saving changes.**

Saving Custom Views of a Workbook

THE BOTTOM LINE

You can save your preferred view of a workbook so that you do not need to modify the view manually each time you want to use the workbook.

If you often display a workbook in a certain way—for example, with certain columns hidden or certain toolbars displayed—you can save these display settings for later use by creating a custom view of the workbook. This is especially helpful if you frequently use large workbooks or shared workbooks.

A custom view saves all of your preferred view settings—including which rows and columns are hidden and your AutoFilter settings. You also can save your preferred print settings in a custom view. For example, you frequently open an employee workbook to review employee salaries or seniority; you also use this workbook periodically to print an employee directory listing. However, you don't want the employee numbers or salaries to appear in the printed directory. For the first view, you might turn on AutoFilter and then save the worksheet as a custom view. For the second view, you might hide the salary column (to make sure you don't accidentally print it), select all data except for the employee numbers, and set the print area to match your selection. You then would have two custom views for the same worksheet, which you can switch between at any time.

TIP

You also can create a workspace to save the layout of a group of workbooks so that you can reopen them to look exactly the way they looked when you saved them. For more information on creating a workspace, see Lesson 1, "Working with Workbooks."

◆ **Open AW Personnel from the Excel Expert Practice/Lesson11 folder.**

Create a custom view

In this exercise, you configure the AW Personnel workbook to display the employee list in AutoFilter mode with the Salary column hidden. You also set a print area and save these display settings as a custom view.

IMPORTANT

Make sure you use the shortcut menu in step 1. The Hide command on the Window menu hides the entire worksheet.

1 **Right-click column F (the salary column), and click Hide on the shortcut menu.**

Column F is hidden.

2 **Click any filled cell in the worksheet.**

3 **On the Data menu, point to Filter, and click AutoFilter.**

AutoFilter arrows appear next to all of the displayed column headings.

4 **Select the range B4:G12. On the File menu, point to Print Area, and click Set Print Area.**

A dashed border appears around the selected range.

ANOTHER METHOD

You also can use the Set Print Area button on your My Formats toolbar to set the print area.

FIGURE 11-13

Setting the print area

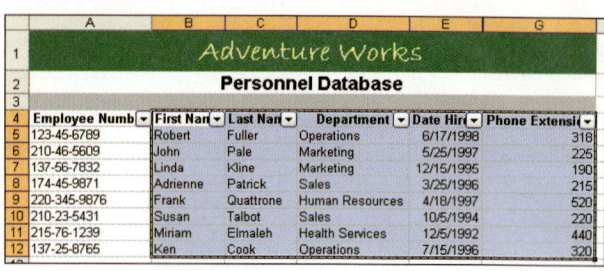

5 **On the View menu, click Custom Views.**

The Custom Views dialog box appears. The Views box is empty because you haven't saved any custom views yet.

FIGURE 11-14

Custom Views dialog box

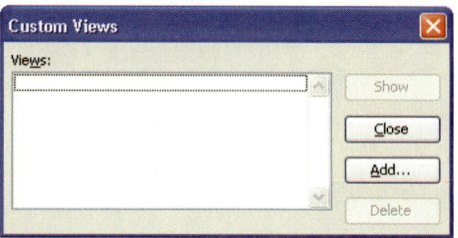

6 **In the Custom Views dialog box, click the Add button.**

The Add View dialog box appears.

7 **In the Name box, type Search Employee List.**

8 **Make sure both check boxes in the Add View dialog box are selected.**

FIGURE 11-15

Add View dialog box

Print settings, hidden rows, columns, and filter settings will be saved in the custom view.

9 **Click OK.**

Now that you've saved your custom view, you return the worksheet to its normal view.

10 **Select columns E and G. Right-click anywhere in the selected range, and click Unhide on the shortcut menu.**

Column F, the salary column, is visible again.

11 **On the Data menu, point to Filter, and click AutoFilter.**

The AutoFilter arrows next to the column headings are removed.

12 **To try out your Search Employee List view, on the View menu, click Custom Views.**

The Custom Views dialog box appears, with Search Employee List in the Views box.

FIGURE 11-16

Custom Views dialog box

13 **If necessary, click Search Employee List in the Views box, and click Show.**

The custom view is displayed. Column F is hidden, AutoFilter is on, and the print range is set.

◆ **Close the workbook without saving changes.**

QUICK REFERENCE ▼

Create a custom view

1 Configure your worksheet the way you want it for your custom view.

2 On the View menu, click Custom Views.

3 In the Custom Views dialog box, click the Add button.

4 In the Name box, type a name for the view.

5 Select or clear the check boxes depending on whether you want the custom view to include print settings, hidden rows, columns, and filter settings.

6 Click OK.

Display a custom view

1 On the View menu, click Custom Views.

2 In the Custom Views dialog box, click the view you want to display.

3 Click the Show button.

Modifying the Working Folder

Modifying Workbook Settings

THE BOTTOM LINE

If you frequently store your Excel workbooks in a folder other than the default folder, you can minimize the time it takes to save and open a file by changing the working folder to this more frequently used location.

By default, the files you create in Excel are saved in the My Documents folder, which is called the **working folder.** Unless you change the working folder, Excel displays the contents of this folder whenever you open or save a workbook. However, if you save a file in a different folder, that folder becomes the working folder until you save a workbook in a different folder or exit Excel. Whenever you start Excel, the My Documents folder is the default location for opening and saving files. You can change the working folder, though, to a folder you use more often. You can save your files in whichever folder you like, but your specified working folder location will be restored whenever you start Excel.

Files in the C:\Program Files\Microsoft Office\Office\XLStart folder are opened every time you start Excel. If you have a workbook you use every time you start Excel, you might want to store it in this folder. If you use different workbooks at different times of the year, you can create alternate startup folders, with conditions that open all of the workbooks in a folder depending on the current date. For example, in January, you might want Excel to open every file in a folder called Year End; in April, you might want Excel to open all workbooks in the Quarter 1 folder.

You specify the working folder location and alternate startup folders on the General tab of the Options dialog box.

FIGURE 11-17

General tab in the Options dialog box

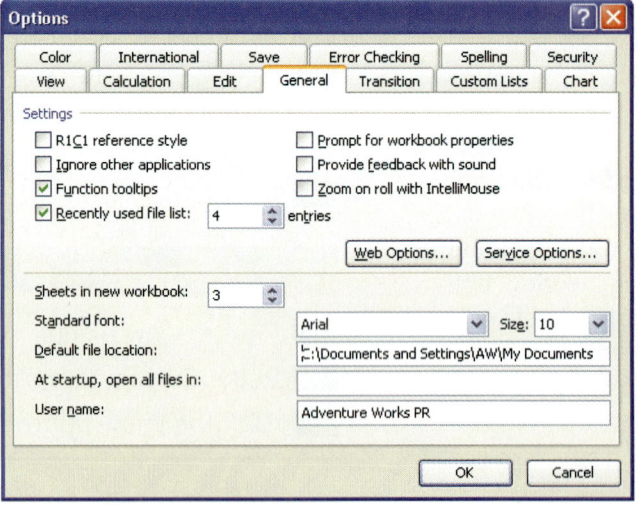

◆ **Open a new blank workbook.**

Change the working folder

In this exercise, you change the working folder to the Excel Expert Practice folder on your hard disk.

1 Click Options on the Tools menu, and click the General tab, if necessary.

IMPORTANT

Your hard disk may have a letter other than C. If this is the case, replace the letter C with the appropriate letter for your hard disk.

2 Note the location given in the Default File Location text box, select the contents of the text box, type C:\Excel Expert Practice, and click OK.

The default file location is changed to your Excel Expert Practice folder. Excel will display this folder each time you open or save a workbook.

IMPORTANT

If your default file location is something other than C:/My Documents, you should write the location information down for future reference.

3 Close and restart Excel.

 4 Click the Open button on the Standard toolbar.

The Open dialog box displays the contents of your Excel Expert Practice folder.

ANOTHER METHOD

- On the File menu, click Open.
- Press Ctrl+O.

5 In the Open dialog box, click Cancel.

6 Click Options on the Tools menu, and click the General tab, if necessary.

7 Select the contents of the Default File Location box, type C:\My Documents (or the path that you wrote down earlier or that your instructor specifies), and click OK.

The working folder is changed to the My Documents folder. When you exit and restart Excel, the My Documents folder will be the default location for opening and saving files.

◆ Leave the blank workbook open for the next exercise.

QUICK REFERENCE ▼

Change the default file location

1 On the Tools menu, click Options.

2 Click the General tab.

3 In the Default File Location box, type the path (including drive letter) where you want Excel files to be saved by default.

4 Click OK.

Customizing Other Excel Options

Modifying Workbook Settings

THE BOTTOM LINE

You can modify many of the settings that affect the look and feel of Excel so that you can work more efficiently and maximize the functionality of the program.

You can customize many Excel settings to match your preferences. The Options dialog box, as you might have noticed, has 13 tabs, which contain settings that determine how Excel looks and works. Some of the settings pertain to the active worksheet only. Other settings alter how the current workbook and all future workbooks appear and function. The following table describes the options on each tab of the Options dialog box.

Tab	Description
General	These options allow you to make basic changes to the way Excel displays information. For instance, if you change the cell reference style to R1C1, Excel will use numbers to identify columns as well as rows. If you use the A1 style (the default), Excel will reference columns by letter and rows by number. You also can specify how many file names appear in the recently used file list at the bottom of the File menu, the default number of sheets in new workbooks, the location where files will be saved by default, and your user name.
View	This option allows you to specify whether the Formula bar and status bar appear in the Excel window. You also can choose whether Excel displays a separate button on the Windows taskbar for each open workbook or just one button for the Excel program. You can specify the way comments in cells and embedded objects appear in worksheets, and you can customize the appearance of the Excel window in many other ways. The options in the Show, Comments, and Objects sections of the tab apply to the active workbook and all future workbooks. The options in the Window Options section apply only to the active workbook.

Calculation	The options on this tab control how and when Excel calculates formulas. You can choose to have formulas calculate automatically (the default) or only when the F9 key is pressed. Also, in the Workbook Options section of the tab, you can change how links and remote formula references are handled.
Edit	These options control how worksheet content is moved, copied, and pasted. This tab also allows you to disable the AutoComplete and Custom Lists features and to change the default number of decimal places for Number and Currency formatted cells. (The installed default is two decimal places, but the display of decimal places is turned off.)
Transition	This tab provides options for users of Lotus 1-2-3 and for those who need to share worksheets with people who use other spreadsheet and database software. You can choose the default file format for saved Excel worksheets, and you can choose whether help for Lotus 1-2-3 users appears.
Custom Lists	This tab allows you to define the sequence and content of lists that Excel uses when you drag the Fill handle for items that you want to list sequentially. By default, Excel includes lists for days of the week and months of the year.
Chart	This tab lets you set the defaults for chart options. The settings control how zero values appear and whether to display Chart Tips—the ScreenTips that identify parts of a chart when you point to them. You also can turn off the options to show names and values in a chart.
Color	This tab allows you to change the available colors for cell borders and fills. You can add colors to the palette that appears when you click the Fill Color or Line Color tools. You also can copy color options from another workbook to the active one by selecting an option on the Copy Colors From list.
International	This tab allows you to change the default decimal separators, to change the standard paper size, and to change the default direction of the worksheets, as well as how the insertion point moves through the worksheet.
Save	This tab provides options for setting how frequently an AutoRecovery save is performed and where these files are stored. You also can disable AutoRecovery.
Error Checking	This tab allows you to enable and disable error checking as well as to set the rules that will be evaluated when the error checking is performed.
Spelling	This tab lets you specify which dictionary will be used. (This dictionary is common to all of the Office applications.) You also can set which spelling rules will be applied and access the AutoCorrect options.
Security	This tab enables you to set the passwords to open as well as modify workbooks. You can choose the encryption type that will be used and set digital signatures. Additionally, you can choose privacy options and set the security levels for macros.

Change default settings

In this exercise, you change the number of new sheets in a workbook, change the color of gridlines in a worksheet, and create and use custom lists (names, dates, numbers) that can be inserted in adjoining cells by using the Fill handle.

TIP

For this exercise, assume that you typically work with only one worksheet per workbook and that when you want to work with more than one worksheet, you prefer to use the Insert Sheet menu command. You change the default number of worksheets to one so that you don't need to delete the unused worksheets from most of your workbooks. Unless you change this option again, all workbooks will contain only one worksheet when you create them.

1 On the Tools menu, click Options. Click the General tab if it's not already displayed.

2 In the Sheets In New Workbook box, select the 3, and type 1.

3 Click the View tab.

4 On the Gridlines color box at the bottom of the tab, click the down arrow to open the color palette.

FIGURE 11-18

Changing the default color of gridlines

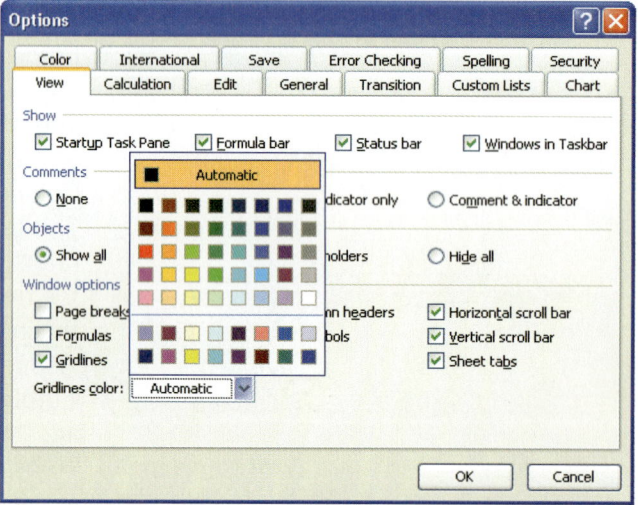

5 Select a different color from the palette, and click OK.

The gridlines on your worksheet change to the color you selected. All workbooks you create will have gridlines of this color unless you change this option.

6 To create the pattern for a new list, type the following entries in cells A1:A5:

Room 101
Room 102
Room 103
Room 104
Room 105

7 Select the range A1:A5.

8 On the Tools menu, click Options, and click the Custom Lists tab.

9 Under Custom Lists, click NEW LIST.

The range A1:A5 appears in the Import List From Cells box.

10 Click the Import button.

Your list has been added, and you can use it whenever you need to enter a sequence of room numbers.

FIGURE 11-19

Creating a custom list

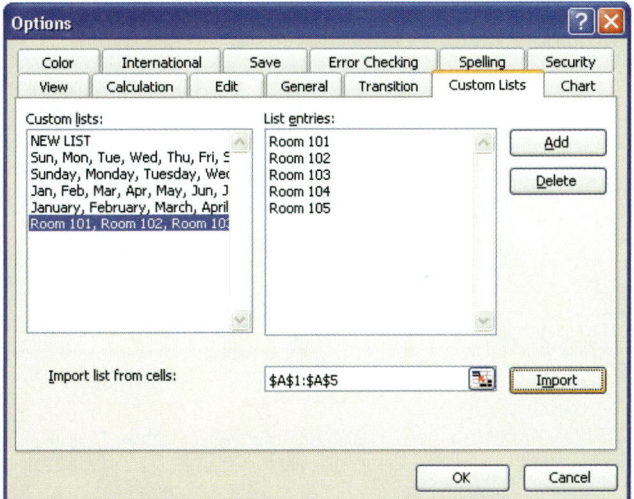

11 Click OK.

12 To test your new list, click cell D1, type Room 201, click the Fill handle, and drag down to cell D5.

Excel uses the custom list to fill the cells with entries Room 201 through Room 205.

FIGURE 11-20

Using the custom list

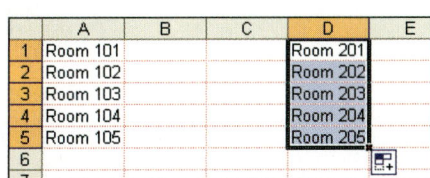

◆ If you are continuing to other lessons:

1. On the Tools menu, click Options, and click the General tab.
2. Double-click in the Sheets In New Workbook box, and type 3.
3. Click the Custom Lists tab. On the left side of the dialog box, click "Room 101, Room 102," and so on. Click the Delete button.
4. Click OK to close the alert box.
5. Click the View tab, and change the Gridlines Color to Automatic.
6. Click OK to close the Options dialog box.
7. On the Tools menu, click Customize, and click the Toolbars tab.
8. In the Toolbars list box, click My Formats, and click Delete. Click OK in the alert box.
9. Click Close.
10. Close all open workbooks without saving changes.

◆ If you are not continuing to other lessons:

1. On the Tools menu, click Options, and click the General tab.
2. Double-click in the Sheets In New Workbook box, and type 3.
3. Click the Custom Lists tab. On the left side of the dialog box, click "Room 101, Room 102," and so on. Click the Delete button.
4. Click OK to close the alert box.
5. Click the View tab, and change the Gridlines Color to Automatic.
6. Click OK to close the Options dialog box.
7. On the Tools menu, click Customize, and click the Toolbars tab.
8. In the Toolbars list box, click My Formats, and click Delete. Click OK in the alert box.
9. Click Close.
10. Close all open workbooks without saving changes.
11. Click the Close button in the top right corner of the Excel window.

QUICK CHECK

Q. Which tab in the Options dialog box lets you set how frequently an AutoRecovery save is performed?

A: The Save tab contains this option.

Key Points

✔ *You can easily modify the setup of toolbars and toolbar buttons in the Excel window to optimize their functionality and the way in which you interact with them.*

✔ *If your work in Excel requires the use of certain commands that are not typically available as buttons on Excel's toolbars, you can create your own toolbar with these buttons. A custom toolbar can streamline the way you execute certain actions and enhance productivity.*

✔ *You can save your preferred view of a workbook so that you do not need to modify the view manually each time you want to use the workbook.*

✔ *If you frequently store your Excel workbooks in a folder other than the default folder, you can minimize the time it takes to save and open a file by changing the working folder to this more frequently used location.*

✔ *You can modify many of the settings that affect the look and feel of Excel so that you can work more efficiently and maximize the functionality of the program.*

Quick Quiz

True/False

T F 1. A floating toolbar must be positioned at the top or bottom of the Excel window.

T F 2. By default, the Standard and Formatting toolbars appear on the same row below the menu bar.

T F 3. You can reposition the Formatting toolbar, but not the Standard toolbar.

T F 4. Once you add a button to a toolbar, it cannot be removed.

T F 5. You cannot include a button on more than one toolbar.

T F 6. Custom views are ideal for large or shared workbooks.

Multiple Choice

1. When a toolbar is anchored to a side of the Excel window, it is said to be
   a. floating.
   b. static.
   c. docked.
   d. locked.

2. By default, Excel displays the contents of which folder when you open or save a workbook?
   a. Default
   b. Startup
   c. My Computer
   d. My Documents

3. Which button on a toolbar do you click to display a menu of buttons that can be added to the toolbar?
   a. Toolbar Options
   b. More Buttons
   c. Buttons
   d. Add To Toolbar

4. Which tab in the Options dialog box contains settings for controlling how worksheet content is moved, copied, and pasted?
   a. View
   b. Edit
   c. Spelling
   d. Error Checking

Short Answer

1. How do you place the Standard toolbar and Formatting toolbar on separate rows?

2. How do you move a button from one location to another on a toolbar, either on the same or a different toolbar?

3. Which tab in the Options dialog box would you click to change the default file location?

4. Which tab in the Options dialog box would you click to hide gridlines?

5. What is the working directory for saving documents in Excel (assuming a standard installation)?

6. What menu contains the feature to create a custom view?

7. Why would you want to use the Custom Lists option in the Options dialog box?

IMPORTANT

In the On Your Own exercises, you must complete Exercise 1 in order to complete Exercise 2. And you must complete Exercise 3 before you complete Exercise 4.

On Your Own

◆ **Open AW Marketing from the Excel Expert Practice/Lesson11 folder.**

Exercise 1

Add the AutoFilter command to the Standard toolbar, placing it to the right of the Format Painter button. Create a custom view of the Marketing Programs worksheet named **2004 Costs Query.** The view should turn on AutoFilter and hide columns F, G, H, and I.

◆ **Save the workbook, and leave it open for the next exercise.**

Exercise 2

Using the AW Marketing workbook you edited in Exercise 1, turn off AutoFilter, and redisplay the hidden columns. Display the 2004 Costs Query view. Save the AW Marketing workbook as **Marketing Backup.**

◆ **Close Marketing Backup.**

One Step Further

◆ **Open a new blank workbook.**

Exercise 1

Create a new toolbar named **My Pictures.** Add buttons to this toolbar that will enable you to insert a picture from a file, to insert a piece of clip art, and to insert AutoShapes.

Exercise 2

On the My Pictures toolbar, edit the image that appears on the button to insert a picture from a file so that the background color is aqua and the sun is bright yellow. Change the image on the button to insert a piece of clip art to the smiley face. Change the image for the AutoShapes button to the pencil, and set it to the Default Style (so that the text does not appear on the button).

Exercise 3

Remove the AutoFilter button that you added to the Standard toolbar in the On Your Own Exercise 1. Delete the My Pictures custom toolbar you created and modified in Exercises 1 and 2.

Glossary

A

absolute reference A reference in a formula to a cell in a specific location.

arguments The values that a function uses to perform operations or calculations.

B

browser A program that lets users view Web documents.

C

change tracking The ability to mark and keep track of changes that have been made to a workbook, especially for a workbook that is shared and modified by multiple users. You can selectively accept or reject changes that have been made in a tracked workbook.

conditional formats Rules you create to determine how data appears, depending on the value of the cell.

constraints In Solver, restrictions that limit the range of values that can be placed in cells in order to create a desired solution.

criteria range Range in a worksheet that includes list headers and the criteria that you want to match.

D

data analysis Any steps that you take to reveal meaning behind data stored in worksheets, including creating charts, PivotTables, and "What if?" scenarios.

data entry list A set of values that can be entered into a cell by selecting one of the valid entries from a list that appears.

data form A window that displays the fields of a record on a list that can be used for entering or updating data.

dependent workbook A workbook that contains a formula that refers to data in another workbook.

dependents Formulas that are dependent on the content or value of a particular cell.

docked toolbar A toolbar that appears at the top or bottom or along a side of the Excel window.

E

error code A brief message that appears in a worksheet cell, describing a problem with a formula or a function.

export To save an Excel worksheet or workbook in another data format.

Extensible Markup Language (XML) A content marking system that lets you store data about the contents of a document in that document.

external reference A formula in one workbook that refers to a cell in a different workbook.

F

field A column of data on an Excel list.

filter A feature that lets you easily hide list data that doesn't match criteria you specify.

floating toolbar A toolbar that appears within the Excel window.

Formula Auditing toolbar A toolbar that includes buttons that allow a user to trace errors and formula precedents and dependents.

G

global macro A macro that is stored in the Personal Macro Workbook and is available to all other workbooks that you open or create.

Goal Seek An Excel feature that allows you to specify the result of a formula and which cell value must change in order to achieve the desired result.

grouping Organizing data so that it can be viewed as a collapsible and expandable outline.

H

headers The labels that appear at the top of columns or the left of rows. Headers designate the kind of information that you will find in a particular column or row.

Hypertext Markup Language (HTML) The language that defines how text and multimedia appear on the Web.

I

import To add data created by a program other than Excel to an Excel worksheet.

import filter A component used to open files that were created in other programs so that they can be viewed in Excel.

input message A message that appears when a user selects a cell, usually indicating the specific type of data that must appear in the cell.

interactive Web format A format in which you can save a worksheet or PivotTable that allows the data to be displayed and modified in Internet Explorer.

L

list An organized collection of data in fields and records.

local macro A macro that is stored in the current workbook and is available only from within that workbook.

locked Cells that can't be changed when password protection is applied to a worksheet.

lookup functions Functions used to look up information stored in a table in an Excel worksheet. You can look up information by rows (HLOOKUP) or by columns (VLOOKUP).

M

macro A set of instructions that can be performed in sequence by clicking a macro name in the Macros dialog box, pressing a keyboard shortcut, or clicking a toolbar button or menu command.

move handle The vertical bar that appears at the left edge of a toolbar when it is docked.

O

object Any picture or file created in another program. Objects can be stored as a single unit in a worksheet.

P

page fields In a PivotTable or PivotTable list, fields that display only summary information for a specific field, filtering out all other data.

password An authentication entry required to open a workbook or to protect a workbook, worksheet, or range of cells from being changed.

PivotTable A tabular presentation of data that allows you to control the way the data appears and which portions of the data appear.

PivotTable list A PivotTable that has been saved as a Web page so that it can be viewed (and modified if it was saved in interactive Web format) in Internet Explorer.

placeholder A temporary label included in a template that specifies what kind of information (graphics, text, numbers, etc.) you can enter at that location.

precedents Cells that are referenced in a particular formula.

print area An area or range of cells that will be printed. In an Excel template, you can select a print area and then save the template so that each time a user prints, only the selected print area prints.

Properties The dialog box, accessible from the File menu, that provides summarized information about a workbook. The properties can be customized as much as desired. You can add properties to further explain the content of a workbook or to facilitate searching for a workbook based on a particular property.

R

record A row of data in an Excel list.

record To issue commands, select cells, and make cell changes in order to create and store a macro.

relative reference A cell reference in a formula that is relative to the cell that contains the formula.

round-trip The process of saving an Excel worksheet as a Web page, saving the Web page to a Web site, viewing the page in a Web browser, saving the page as a file on your hard disk, and then opening the new file in Excel.

S

scenarios Multiple "What if?" calculations for the same cells or range of cells that can be saved separately from the data in a worksheet.

shared workbook A workbook in which multiple users can simultaneously make changes.

Smart Tags A technology that recognizes values in a spreadsheet and finds related information on the Web.

Solver An add-in program for Excel that allows you to perform data analysis on multiple cells by restricting, or constraining, the range of values that can appear in cells.

source workbook A workbook that contains information that a formula in another workbook references.

T

tab-delimited Text that is prepared using tabs to separate data.

table In an Excel worksheet, a range of cells that can be used by a lookup function.

tags Marks used to indicate display properties or to communicate data about the contents of a document.

template A workbook that contains text and formatting that can be reused to create other workbooks. In Excel, you can use the ready-made templates or you can create your templates based on existing workbooks.

three-dimensional formula A formula that refers to data in other worksheets and workbooks.

U

unlock To allow certain cells to be changed when a worksheet is protected by a user on another computer that is networked to the one that stores the workbook, or by a user that has a different logon ID than the one used when the workbook was created.

V

Visual Basic Editor The tool that you can use to edit the Visual Basic code for a macro.

Visual Basic for Applications (VBA) The programming language used to create macros in Microsoft Office. VBA is based on Microsoft Visual Basic.

W

working folder The location where Excel looks by default when you specify that you want to open or save a file. If you save a workbook to a different location, that location becomes the working folder until you restart Excel.

workspace A file that saves customized settings about a group of workbooks. When opened, a workspace places the workbooks in the same positions that they were in when the workspace was saved.

Index

A

System Requirements

Important

This course assumes that Excel 2003 has already been installed on the PC you are using. Microsoft Office Professional Edition 2003—180-Day Trial, which includes Excel, is on the second CD-ROM included with this book. Microsoft Product Support does not support these trial editions.

For information on how to install the trial edition, see "Installing or Uninstalling Microsoft Office Professional Edition 2003—180-Day Trial" in the "Using the CD-ROMs" section at the front of this book.

Your computer system must meet the following minimum requirements for you to install the practice files from the CD-ROM included with this book and to run Microsoft Excel 2003.

- A personal computer running Microsoft Excel 2003 on a Pentium 233-megahertz (MHz) or higher processor.
- Microsoft Windows® 2000 with Service Pack 3 (SP3), Windows XP, or later.
- 128 MB of RAM or greater.
- At least 2 MB of available disk space (after installing Excel 2003 or Microsoft Office).
- A CD-ROM or DVD drive.
- A monitor with Super VGA (800 X 600) or higher resolution with 256 colors.
- A Microsoft mouse, a Microsoft IntelliMouse, or other compatible pointing device.